DEFEATED

DEFEATED

Losing Presidential Candidates in American History

MARTIN GITLIN

BLOOMSBURY ACADEMIC
NEW YORK · LONDON · OXFORD · NEW DELHI · SYDNEY

BLOOMSBURY ACADEMIC

Bloomsbury Publishing Inc, 1359 Broadway, New York, NY 10018, USA
Bloomsbury Publishing Plc, 50 Bedford Square, London, WC1B 3DP, UK
Bloomsbury Publishing Ireland, 29 Earlsfort Terrace, Dublin 2, D02 AY28, Ireland

BLOOMSBURY, BLOOMSBURY ACADEMIC and the Diana logo are trademarks of
Bloomsbury Publishing Plc

First published in the United States of America 2025

Copyright © Martin Gitlin, 2026

Cover images: Courtesy of Library of Congress (McClellan pin) and Harvard Kennedy School
Library (All other pins), © istock/LeMusique (flag)

All rights reserved. No part of this publication may be: i) reproduced or transmitted in
any form, electronic or mechanical, including photocopying, recording or by means of
any information storage or retrieval system without prior permission in writing from the
publishers; or ii) used or reproduced in any way for the training, development or operation
of artificial intelligence (AI) technologies, including generative AI technologies. The rights
holders expressly reserve this publication from the text and data mining exception as per
Article 4(3) of the Digital Single Market Directive (EU) 2019/790.

Bloomsbury Publishing Inc does not have any control over, or responsibility for, any third-
party websites referred to or in this book. All internet addresses given in this book were
correct at the time of going to press. The author and publisher regret any inconvenience
caused if addresses have changed or sites have ceased to exist, but can accept no
responsibility for any such changes.

Library of Congress Cataloging-in-Publication Data
Names: Gitlin, Marty author
Title: Defeated : losing presidential candidates in American history / by Martin Gitlin.
Description: New York, NY : Bloomsbury Academic (US), [2026] |
Includes bibliographical references and index. | Audience: Ages 12-18
Identifiers: LCCN 2025018017 (print) | LCCN 2025018018 (ebook) | ISBN 9781538192955
cloth | ISBN 9781538192962 epub | ISBN 9798881862589 adobe pdf
Subjects: LCSH: Presidential candidates–United States–History–Juvenile
literature | Presidents–United States–Election–Juvenile literature | United States–Politics
and government–Juvenile literature | United States–History–Juvenile literature
Classification: LCC JK524 .G58 2026 (print) | LCC JK524 (ebook)
LC record available at https://lccn.loc.gov/2025018017
LC ebook record available at https://lccn.loc.gov/2025018018

ISBN: HB: 978-1-5381-9295-5
ePDF: 979-8-8818-6258-9
eBook: 978-1-5381-9296-2

Typeset by Deanta Global Publishing Services, Chennai, India
Printed and bound in the United States of America

For product safety related questions contact productsafety@bloomsbury.com.

To find out more about our authors and books visit www.bloomsbury.com and
sign up for our newsletters.

CONTENTS

Introduction 1
1 Thomas Jefferson 2
2 John Adams 7
3 Charles Pinckney 11
4 DeWitt Clinton 17
5 Rufus King 21
6 The Two-Party System 25
7 Andrew Jackson 27
8 Henry Clay 32
9 William Crawford 36
10 John Quincy Adams 39
11 William Henry Harrison 45
12 Martin Van Buren 51
13 Lewis Cass 58
14 Winfield Scott 62
15 John C. Fremont 67
16 John C. Breckinridge 72
17 George B. McClellan 77
18 Horatio Seymour 83
19 Horace Greeley 88
20 Samuel J. Tilden 93
21 Winfield Scott Hancock 99
22 James G. Blaine 104
23 Grover Cleveland 109
24 Benjamin Harrison 114
25 William Jennings Bryan 119
26 Alton B. Parker 127
27 Theodore Roosevelt 132

28 Charles Evans Hughes 139
29 James M. Cox 143
30 John W. Davis 148
31 Al Smith 153
32 Herbert Hoover 158
33 Alf Landon 164
34 Wendell Willkie 169
35 Thomas E. Dewey 174
36 Adlai Stevenson 180
37 Richard Nixon 187
38 Barry Goldwater 192
39 Hubert Humphrey 196
40 George McGovern 200
41 Gerald Ford 204
42 Jimmy Carter 208
43 Walter Mondale 212
44 Michael Dukakis 216
45 George H. Bush 220
46 Bob Dole 224
47 Al Gore 228
48 John Kerry 232
49 John McCain 235
50 Mitt Romney 240
51 Hillary Clinton 244
52 Donald Trump 248
53 Kamala Harris 252

Notes 255

About the Author 265

Introduction

Every presidential election cycle figuratively follows the same path as a human's existence. It begins with a birth. It ends with a death. Each spotlights a radically different life based on candidate personalities, issues of the day, viewpoints, and unpredictable events that often cause seismic shifts in momentum and conclusion.

The elementary result? A winner and loser. But the consequences extend far beyond. It has been claimed that the president holds the most important job in the world. That is no exaggeration. History screams that often the winner has been the right person for the job. But it also states emphatically that sometimes the person who lost might have performed better.

This book focuses on the losing presidential candidates. But it features far more. It answers many questions. What were the issues of the day? How did the hopefuls differ on those issues? Why did the losers lose? Were their campaigns ineffective, or were their viewpoints simply too unpopular? Did global or national events during the election cycle negatively impact their chances of winning? How did debates (including Lincoln-Douglas, then from Kennedy-Nixon forward) impact the elections? Did third-party candidates play a role in outcomes? How did ad campaigns negatively or positively sway voters? Did political and background differences between vice-presidential hopefuls play a role?

From first loser Thomas Jefferson to Kamala Harris, this book takes readers on a journey through American history. It is a reflection of that history. Many losers were not losers at all. They were simply defeated by more popular candidates. Others were rejected by voters who perceived them as unacceptable based on the political, social, and economic climates of the day.

Whether the results were landslides or nailbiters, some losing candidates were incumbents, others won the presidency later through persistence, and still others faded into obscurity. But each have stories that need to be told about the many reasons they lost. And that is what this book is all about.

1

Thomas Jefferson

Party: Democrat-Republican
Birth state: Virginia Colony
Represented: Virginia
Year of defeat: 1796
Winner: John Adams (Federalist)
Other notable candidates: Thomas Pinckney (Federalist), Aaron Burr (Antifederalist), Samuel Adams (Democrat-Republican)

Thomas Jefferson. Courtesy of the Library of Congress, Popular Graphic Arts Collection, LC-DIG-pga-12975

All About Jefferson

One of the greatest statesmen in American history, Jefferson was born in Albemarle County, Virginia, on April 13, 1743, to wealthy parents of strong social standing. His father owned a 5,000-acre farm. Jefferson studied law at The College of William and Mary before marrying Martha and moving to their mountaintop home in Monticello.

A tall and awkward young man, Jefferson displayed greater eloquence as a writer than as a speaker. He drafted the Declaration of Independence as a member of the Virginia House of Burgesses and Continental Congress. A decade later, a year after succeeding Benjamin Franklin as minister to France, he penned a bill that established religious freedom in his home state. His ties to the nation that had helped the patriots fight off the British in the Revolutionary War motivated his support of the French Revolution.

Jefferson served as Secretary of State under first president George Washington before resigning in 1793 after expressing his support of the French Revolution, which led to a conflict with Hamilton. Three years later, in 1796, Jefferson ran for the presidency.

Issues of the Day

The Federalists, whose views were expressed by Secretary of the Treasury Alexander Hamilton and others, pushed for a national bank and a strong central government that would assume the burden of Revolutionary War debts carried by the states. That party also yearned to limit voting rights to property-owning men and sought to strengthen ties with Great Britain, a major trading partner. Democrat-Republicans advocated for limited federal and strong state governments, envisioning a nation of small farmers and artisans with the power to vote. They pushed back against a 1795 treaty between the United States and Great Britain that aided New England but refused to compensate southern states for slaves stolen by the British during the war. This thorny issue inspired the Democrat-Republicans to draw closer to France, which had backed the patriots against England during the revolution.

The 1796 Campaign

Two George Washington terms had passed before 1796 marked the first year with a presidential campaign. At this time, the Constitution included no stipulations about term limits. The nation awaited word from Washington about seeking another four years in office until he declined on September 17, 1796, and offered a farewell address to the American people in a speech crafted by Hamilton and future president James Madison. And Washington knew it. He understood the ramifications.

"They serve to organize faction, to give it an artificial and extraordinary force; to put, in the place of the delegated will of the nation the will of a party, often a small but artful and enterprising minority of the community," he said in his farewell address. "They are likely, in the course of time and things, to become potent engines, by which cunning, ambitious, and unprincipled men will be enabled to subvert the power of the people and to usurp for themselves the reins of government, destroying afterward the very engines which have lifted them to unjust dominion."[1]

Twelve candidates ran for president. Running mates had yet to exist. Those with the highest popular vote and electors—who cast second ballots—earned the presidency. The second-place finisher was automatically named vice-president. But each party named an intended VP—Thomas Pinckney for the Federalists and Aaron Burr for the Democrat-Republicans.

The battle began. And so did the mudslinging between the supporters of Vice-President Adams and Secretary of State Jefferson, whose party was better known simply as the Republican. The nastiness peaked in October when a mysterious writer named Phocion authored an article that appeared in the *Gazette of the United States*, a Federalist-leaning newspaper. The piece charged Jefferson with having an affair with one of his female slaves and cowardly fleeing from British troops during the Revolutionary War. It also heaped praise upon Adams and asserted that Jefferson intended to free all the slaves if he was elected.

Jefferson fought back. He claimed that Adams yearned to be king and start a family succession to the throne with son John Quincy Adams as his immediate replacement. Then, Jefferson got personal. He offered that the elder Adams was fat and nicknamed him "His Rotundity."

Fighting wasn't limited to the main combatants and their minions. In-party squabbles raged. Hamilton served as Adams' running mate but proved quite the backstabber. He secretly worked to push Thomas Pinckney of South Carolina into the White House by convincing southern Federalists to withhold their votes for

Adams. The strategy might have worked given the election system of the day in which each elector cast two votes and the top two candidates became president and vice-president. Six states featured popular elections but 11 others allowed state legislatures to select the electors. Hamilton sought to make Pinckney the president and Adams vice-president if several Federalists kept Adams off their ballots completely.

It didn't work. His plot was exposed in New England, which housed many more Adams supporters who refused to vote for Pinckney. Adams defeated Jefferson by three electoral votes to become second president of the United States. The results were a contentious relationship between the head of state and his VP and a bitter feud between Adams and Hamilton.

After the Loss

After serving as Vice President for four years under Adams, Jefferson ousted his 1796 foe from office in 1800. The two had suffered through an untenable relationship given their philosophically opposed political differences.

His notable first term in the new White House (in which Adams was the first presidential resident) was marked by the slashing of the military budget, elimination of tax on whiskey, reduction of the national debt, and a successful attack against Barbary pirates who had harassed American commerce in the Mediterranean. Jefferson also spearheaded the effort to acquire the Louisiana Territory from Napoleon and the French in 1803.

After easily defeating Federalist Charles Pinckney in 1804, he worked to prevent American involvement in the Napoleonic wars despite French and British harassment of US merchants in Europe. His attempt at an embargo of American shipping proved unpopular and unsuccessful.

Jefferson left office for a quiet life in Monticello. One French nobleman offered that Jefferson's home was on a mountaintop so he could ponder the universe from up high. Jefferson died appropriately on July 4, 1826.

Coming From Jefferson

What a stupendous, what an incomprehensible machine is man! Who can endure toil, famine, stripes, imprisonment & death itself in vindication of his own liberty, and the next moment ... inflict on his fellow men a bondage, one hour of which is fraught with more misery than ages of that which he rose in rebellion to oppose.[2]

Did You Know?

Thomas Jefferson was a prolific writer and reader. He owned thousands of books and read everything he could get his hands on, even books written in Latin. He sold 10,000 of his works to the Library of Congress. Jefferson was also an avid star gazer. He often stood on his porch to examine the stars, planets and comets.

2

John Adams

Party: Federalist
Birth state: Massachusetts
Represented: Massachusetts
Year of defeat: 1800
Winner: Thomas Jefferson (Democrat-Republican)
Other notable candidates: Charles Pinckney (Federalist), Aaron Burr (Democrat-Republican)

John Adams. Courtesy of the Library of Congress, Popular Graphic Arts Collection, LC-DIG-pga-12974

All About Adams

Adams was born in the Massachusetts Bay Colony in 1735 and studied law at Harvard before becoming fueled by the revolutionary spirit and gaining a reputation as one of the most fervent patriots among those yearning to forge a new nation.

Many historians consider Adams more a philosopher than politician, which perhaps explains his lack of fervor as a national political leader. But he understood the motivations of his time, particularly in the contentious relations between the colonies and Mother England, offering that a nation and its people forge new paths by battling adversity.

Adams toiled as a diplomat in France and Holland during the Revolutionary War and helped negotiate the peace agreement that ended it, thereby creating the United States of America. He later served as minister to the Court of St. James before his election as vice-president during the two George Washington administrations.

That did not satisfy Adams. He considered the role insignificant and meaningless for a man of such intellectual stature and energy. He yearned for a greater role in impacting American domestic and foreign policy.

Adams got his chance after defeating Jefferson in the 1796 election for president. Soon thereafter, he forged American involvement in the war between Britian and France, whose ruling group turned back a US envoy and suspended commercial relations between the two countries. Adams sought a diplomatic solution in 1798, sending three diplomats to France. But French foreign minister Charles-Maurice de Talleyrand refused to negotiate unless the United States paid him. Adams refused to be bribed, inspiring support from the Senate and the American people for himself and the Federalist Party.

One result was the passage of the Alien and Sedition Acts to motivate foreign agents to leave the country. Adams did not declare war on France, but increased hostilities led to attacks on American ships. The French continued to yearn for peace, and finally achieved it through negotiations.

Some Federalists expressed anger over what they deemed to be yielding to French interests. The party was divided while the Republicans united. The result was an Adams defeat to Jefferson in the 1800 election. But not before Adams became the first president to inhabit the White House on November 1, 1800.

Issues of the Day

Though the attacks on American commercial shipping by the French inspired criticism of Adams from both inside and outside the Federalist Party, the bitter 1800 campaign was less about policy and more about backstabbing and trading personal attacks tossed about in newspaper ads, though neither candidate hurled insults directly. Adams backers branded Jefferson an atheist and downright dangerous. Jefferson partisans went so far as to claim Adams to be a hermaphrodite with both male and female reproductive organs. One Massachusetts publication even labeled Adams as "bald, blind, crippled and toothless."[1] Adams felt uncomfortable with the rancor. He privately yearned to retire but his political toughness re-emerged, inspired by those whose policies and morality he strongly opposed.

The 1800 Campaign

The frayed Federalists desperately sought inner-party peace as Adams and Jefferson battled for a second time for the presidency. In an attempt to attract southern votes the Federalists chose Charles Pinckney of South Carolina to serve as the running mate.

The electoral college as constituted at the time resulted in each delegate casting two votes, which meant that despite working with a rival party, Jefferson could conceivably again be selected as vice-president under Adams. That seemed untenable given the contentious nature of the campaign on both sides. The two sides traded attacks in newspapers. Rival factions in Georgia, New York, and Virginia changed voting district regulations to reach a majority despite balloting having already begun. Some state legislatures switched from direct popular voting for electors to legislative selection in an attempt to provide an advantage for the candidate favored by that legislature.

Fellow Federalist Alexander Hamilton, who disagreed with the sitting president on policy, worked feverishly from the start to derail the Adams campaign. He attempted to advance the nomination of Secretary of State Charles Pickering instead. Adams summarily fired Pickering upon hearing of the plot. Soon thereafter, Hamilton penned a scathing attack against Adams' record that delighted Jefferson and the Republicans. And though Jefferson was also criticized among those in his own party for alleged cowardice during the Revolutionary War and for his supposed atheism, the campaign on their side proved far more harmonious.

The shenanigans worked against Adams even in Federalist strongholds. He even worried that he would receive fewer votes than Pinckney. That concern was not unfounded. Adams landed just one more electoral vote than Pinckney. But fears of defeat were more reasonable. Both Jefferson and Aaron Burr defeated

Adams, sending the latter out of the White House. The two Republicans finished in a flat-footed tie, which led to more bickering before votes in the House and by Federalist legislatures gave Jefferson the presidency.

After the Loss

Soon thereafter, Adams retired to his farm in Quincy, Massachusetts. He spent some of his time writing letters to Jefferson. His last words, uttered appropriately on Independence Day in 1826, were "Thomas Jefferson survives." Amazingly, however, Jefferson had passed away a few hours earlier. Adams had lived long enough to experience the victory of son John Quincy Adams in the 1824 presidential election.

Coming From Adams

The prospect now before us in America ought . . . to engage the attention of every man of learning to matters of power and right, that we may be neither led nor driven blindfolded to irretrievable destruction.[2]

Did You Know?

Though Adams was a fervent patriot before and during the Revolutionary War, he promoted British traditions of royalty upon his ascension to the highest office in the land. He believed the president should be given a grand title. Adams offered that first president George Washington should be referred to as "His Majesty the President" or "His Highness, the President of the United States." But Americans yearned to rid themselves of any forms of a monarchy. The idea did not catch on.[3]

3

Charles Pinckney

Party: Federalist
Birth state: Province of South Carolina
Represented: South Carolina
Years of defeat: 1804 and 1808
Winners: 1804: Thomas Jefferson (Democrat-Republican); 1808: James Monroe (Democrat-Republican)

Captain Charles Pinckney. Courtesy of the Library of Congress, Popular Graphic Arts Collection, LC-DIG-pga-13168

All About Pinckney

Pinckney was born the fourth son of eight children to wealthy plantation owners in Charleston, South Carolina, on October 26, 1757. His family owned several properties, including a country estate and summer home. The boy received an education at elite schools, where he excelled in such subjects as government, philosophy and history, while becoming proficient in various languages such as Latin, Greek, French, Spanish, and Italian.

Under his father's tutoring, he studied law at Charleston, earning admission to the bar at the tender age of 16 before opening a private practice. His work and relationship with his father presented him with opportunities to fulfill a childhood dream and meet many of the notable politicians of the era, including founding father and jurist John Rutledge. Pinckney had yearned for a career in public service as a youth and it would soon be realized. His personal life appeared to be solidified years later with a marriage to Polly Laurens in 1788 and later the birth of three children. But his wife died in 1794.

By that time, Pinckney had been elected to the South Carolina House of Representatives and had served as captain in the Charleston Regiment during the Revolutionary War. He fought during the siege of Savannah. After the siege of Charleston, he was arrested by the British and imprisoned until 1781.

Pinckney returned to politics following his release and was voted into the South Carolina Congress in 1784, after which, he twice gained an appointment to the Congress of Confederation. He gained notoriety in 1786 and 1787 by railing against the body as ineffective and by penning pamphlets titled, "The Three Letters to the Public," in which he argued in favor of a permanent flow of revenue for the federal government.

He was rising fast. At age 29, he became the youngest of four South Carolina delegates to the Constitutional Convention. His energy and eloquence in promoting a powerful central government and expressing his ideas made a significant impact on the framing of the Constitution, though in more modern times, his advocacy for policies that benefitted only white men are certainly frowned upon. His suggestion that no test of religion be required for presidential candidates was among those adopted.

Pinckney claimed to have authored the only plan for the document that was divided into articles and clauses. The subject of that heatedly debated assertion became known as the "Pinckney Draught." Many historians believe his contention to be exaggerated. but also agree that it contributed strongly to the adoption of the United States Constitution.

His philosophies and policies eventually evolved. He gave birth to the South Carolina Democratic Party in 1795 and subsequently managed Jefferson's victorious presidential campaign. He later earned ministerial positions in both France and Spain. Pinckney played a significant role in negotiating the treaty with France that completed the Louisiana Purchase and doubled the size of the United

States. Pinckney also impacted his home state by convincing the South Carolina legislature to push such changes as free public education for children.

Issues of the Day

Pinckney simply could not compete in 1804 against the highly popular Jefferson, who had gained favor among the American people with his expansionist policies culminating in the 1803 Louisiana Purchase and limited government spending. Personal attacks against Jefferson alleging that he fathered children with slave Sally Hemings also failed to gain traction. By 1808, the issues had changed but the popularity of Jefferson and his promotion of James Madison as the Democrat-Republican candidate doomed Pinckney again. Pinckney failed to take advantage of the unpopular Embargo Act that hurt some Americans economically.

The 1804 Campaign

Pinckney had no chance against Jefferson, particularly after Federalist spearhead Alexander Hamilton succumbed to the wounds suffered in his duel with Aaron Burr, which was motivated by a longstanding feud between his party and the Democratic-Republicans. The seeds of the showdown were planted in 1791 when Burr won a US Senate seat from Hamilton's father-in-law and Federalist supporter Philip Schuyler. Hamilton then drew the ire of Burr in 1800 by maneuvering the House of Representatives to favor Jefferson over him in his bid for the presidency. Also, simply, Hamilton hated Burr and considered him more self-serving than loyal to the new nation.

Hamilton ruined Burr's political career. He forced Jefferson to drop Burr from the ticket as the 1804 election drew near. Burr was relegated to run for the governorship of New York. That did not satisfy Hamilton, who campaigned feverishly against him and caused him to lose to Democrat-Republican Morgan Lewis.

The murder of Hamilton, however, likely did not cause Pinckney's defeat. The biggest factor was Jefferson's popularity. He was considered by most Americans the leader of all people, as he famously stated in his 1801 inaugural address when he insisted:

> We are all Republicans – we are all Federalists. If there be any among us who would wish to dissolve this Union or to change its republican form, let them stand undisturbed as monuments of the safety with which error of opinion may be tolerated where reason is left free to combat it.[1]

Jefferson let his actions speak louder than his words by following through with a moderate agenda that limited partisanship. The highly popular Louisiana Purchase that reduced French influence in the New World sealed the fate for Pinckney, who had little support aside from some New England Federalists. The result was a landslide. Jefferson captured the electoral college victories in every state except Connecticut and Delaware.

The 1808 Campaign

The road to the White House got no easier for Pinckney four years later despite the political retirement of Jefferson. The third president threw all his weight behind fellow Democrat-Republican James Madison. Most popular among that party's planks was the rights of individuals and states over the powers of the federal government. That platform was particularly popular in Southern states.

Meanwhile, the Federalists flailed away in vain trying to connect with the majority of Americans. Voters felt negatively familiar with Pinckney and returning running mate Rufus King after they had lost badly to Jefferson in 1804. It remains the first time in US history when a major party renominated the same losing candidates from the previous election.

Pinckney attempted to ride to victory the unpopularity of the controversial Embargo Act of 1807, which had been implemented by the Jefferson administration. It had been a response to the Napoleonic Wars in Europe and led to British interference with American merchant ships and even the coercion of US sailors to join the British Navy. The embargo caused more economic distress among

Americans than the British or French. It severely limited exports and income for farmers. It increased hostilities between the United States and Britain, helping push the two nations to the War of 1812.

That was Jefferson's problem. But he was no longer running for the presidency. The Embargo Act did little to boost Pinckney's candidacy despite the consistent attempts to brand Jefferson as a tyrant for enforcing it. And some even favored the action. They believed it protected American business and offered that it served to prevent military action, though the Embargo Act was repealed in 1809 and the British and Americans launched the War of 1812 three years later.

The problem for Pinckney was that despite the widespread criticism of the Embargo Act, Jefferson remained greatly popular and his endorsement of Madison carried much weight. Pinckney managed to increase his support from four years earlier, taking more New England states. But Madison more than doubled Pinckney in the overall vote count and carried 12 of the 17 states.

After the Losses

Though Pinkney lost his 1804 White House bid he continued to serve. He returned to Charleston in 1806 as part of the South Carolina General Assembly and was elected to his fourth and final term as governor. Pinckney continued to work in the political machinery of that state until 1813, supporting universal white male suffrage and the elimination of primogeniture, a feudal law that provided an entire inheritance to the first-born child.

Pinckney retired from politics at age 56 in 1814 but remained active supporting Democratic-Republican Party leaders and their policies. He backed James Monroe in his successful presidential bid in 1816. Fearing a Charleston District seat victory for the Federalists in 1818, he threw his hat back into the ring and won, serving in that office from 1819 to 1823.

By that time, he had expressed strong opposition to the abolitionist movement. All the Northern states had banned slavery by 1804, then the Missouri Compromise, 16 years later, sought to maintain a balance between free and slave states. Pinckney vehemently opposed the proposal based on Congressional interference regarding importation of slaves at Southern ports. But he also feared prophetically that slavery could force the union into a civil war.

Pinckney permanently retired in 1821. He spent his remaining years writing of his travels and political life before dying in his beloved Charleston on October 29, 1824.

Coming From Pinckney

We have been taught here to believe that fill power of right belongs to the people; that it flows immediately from them and is delegated to their officers for the public good; that our rulers are the servants of the people, amenable to their will, and created for their use. How different are the governments of Europe! There the people are the servants and subjects of their rulers; there merit and talents have little or no influence; but all the honors and offices of government are swallowed up by birth, by fortune, or by rank.[2]

Did You Know?

Pinckney's mother was Eliza Lucas. She gained prominence in her own right. Lucas helped spearhead efforts to make indigo a strong cash crop in South Carolina. This promoted indigo cultivation.

4

DeWitt Clinton

Party: Democrat-Republican, Federalist
Birth state: New York
Represented: New York
Year of Defeat: 1812
Running mate: James Ingersoll
Winner: James Madison (Democrat-Republican)
Other notable candidate: Rufus King (Federalist)

DeWitt Clinton. Courtesy of the Library of Congress, Popular Graphic Arts Collection, LC-DIG-pga-13281

All About Clinton

Clinton was the son of a farmer, surveyor and Revolutionary War general. He received an education worthy of the prominent family in which he was raised. Clinton attended the Kingston Academy in New York before enrolling in Columbia and embracing a philosophical approach to leadership marked by a hatred for the abuse of power and the importance of education. Upon graduation, he attended law school, where he worked with uncle and New York governor George Clinton, who appointed him private secretary in 1787.

The young Clinton at the time was an Antifederalist. He railed against a strong national government as written in the Constitution, asserting his belief that it would enable an aristocracy to rise more easily to power and humble the ordinary people that he believed was the backbone of society. He shared his uncle's hostility toward pro-British Federalists as a dangerous elite powered by the banking industry.

Clinton practiced law only briefly, opting instead by the mid-1790s to delve into land speculation. He managed more than 600,000 acres in four states, then soon married heiress and Quaker Maria Franklin, who brought sizable wealth and landholdings to the family and bore 10 children before dying in 1818.

A drive toward a political career motivated Clinton to run for the New York State Assembly. He lost twice, then won in 1797 and advanced to the state senate, where he served until 1802 before being appointed mayor of New York City a year later. He spearheaded passage of the 12th Amendment to the US Constitution, which fended off attempts by Aaron Burr to exploit the system in an attempt to win the presidency in 1800. Clinton even fought a duel against Burr supporter John Swartwout and refused to kill him after putting two bullets in his leg.

Issues of the Day

Clinton attempted to become the first presidential candidate to unseat an incumbent in wartime. The War of 1812 had begun in June, and he sought to paint himself as a critic of the Madison approach to a second battle against the British in 35 years. Clinton took an anti-war stance among New Englanders, as well as Pennsylvania and his home state of New York, but was ineffective in his efforts.

The 1812 Campaign

History claims that though Clinton was technically a Jeffersonian Republican, he ran as a candidate for the faltering Federalists. Though that party nominally supported Rufus King for the presidency, its members greatly backed Clinton as King barely created a ripple during the campaign. The Federalists believed Clinton could attract votes among antiwar Democrat-Republicans.

Clinton, however, remained in spirit tied to the same party as his opponent Madison. He campaigned with little vigor, though it should be cited that it was considered bad form at that time to campaign strongly and openly. Voters preferred that viewpoints be expressed in newspaper articles and other printed material. Therefore, surrogates were more responsible than the candidates themselves for conveying candidate platforms to the people.

Those working for Clinton failed to state a convincing argument against the War of 1812, which was easily the most controversial issue of the day. A statement from his proxies proved too mild. And rather than taking a strong stance against American involvement in the hostilities, it instead claimed that Madison was running the war incompetently.

Clinton might have won had he run a more robust and skilled campaign. He won every northeastern state aside from Vermont and even took New Jersey and the largest prize—29 electoral votes from New York. But Madison swept the South, where the war was more popular, as well as Pennsylvania and Ohio. Clinton would have won had he secured Pennsylvania and perhaps he would have had he ran with more passion. Only he knew if he truly had the stomach for it.

After the Loss

After losing the presidency to Madison in 1812, Clinton won four terms as a governor. His defeat to Madison proved to be a hiccup in a political career otherwise marked by achievement.

Clinton supported legislation that aided merchants and immigrants. And in his unending drive to educate and enlighten the masses, he supported the Free School Society, the New York Academy of the Fine Arts, and the New York Historical Society.

Most notably, however, Clinton pushed for the construction of the Erie Canal to run between Lake Erie and the Hudson River. He created a commission to explore routes. When federal funds were denied, he argued to the state legislature that such an undertaking would stimulate business. He overcame severe criticism of the potential project to gain widespread support as mayor, then pushed it through as governor. He finally celebrated the opening of the Erie Canal by pouring the waters of Lake Erie into the New York Harbor on November 4, 1825.

Clinton failed to make inroads on a second presidential bid in 1824 so he threw his support towards Andrew Jackson, whom he considered similar philosophically and politically in his opposition to what they perceived as a meddlesome central government. The defeat of Jackson, who won the popular and electoral vote but not a majority, inspired Clinton to consider another run at the White House in 1828. But failing health resulted in a heart attack that cost him his life that year.

Coming From Clinton

The best way to predict the future is to create it.[1]

Did You Know?

Clinton refused to throw his support to the Federalists after the election despite their support in 1812. He remained affiliated with the Democrat-Republicans when he returned to New York politics following his defeat.

5

Rufus King

Party: Federalist
Birth state: Province of Massachusetts Bay
Represented: Massachusetts
Year of defeat: 1816
Running mate: John E. Howard
Winner: James Monroe (Democrat-Republican)

Rufus King. Courtesy of the Library of Congress, Popular Graphic Arts Collection, LC-DIG-ppmsca-31799

All About King

King was a comparatively old presidential candidate for his time at age 61 in 1816. He had been born the son of a wealthy merchant and farmer father in Scarborough, Massachusetts, which later became part of Maine. His dad held fervent loyalist views and even defended the hated Stamp Act, which led to the ransacking of their home by revolutionary group The Sons of Liberty in 1766. The incident taught Rufus a life lesson about the value of law and order.

The untimely death of his father forced Rufus into a position of family responsibility financially and as a protector of his mother and siblings. But rather than viewing those burdens negatively, he used them to create new opportunities. He thrived academically in boarding school then at Harvard College, from which he graduated in 1777 with the Revolutionary War raging.

King was exposed at Harvard to the ideologies of the insurrectionists who sought to end British rule. His viewpoints changed dramatically from those of his father to the ones that fueled the patriots. He studied law and the principles of the American revolutionaries to forge the path for a political career.

That began upon his election to the Massachusetts state legislature in 1783. He embraced a centrist philosophy of both a strong central government and individual freedom. A year later, he was voted into the Continental Congress as a delegate, which expanded his influence from the state to national level. His greatest impact in that role was felt in 1787, when he teamed with James Madison to launch an initiative that favored greater federal control and less state autonomy. King's articulate promotion of his views as debates raged over the creation of the Constitution earned him a reputation as both pragmatic and passionate.

Among his motivations was the addition of a Bill of Rights to strengthen personal liberties and federal power while weakening the threat of despotic rule. His contributions to the authoring of the Constitution cemented his legacy as one of the nation's founding fathers. But his influence expanded to an international level. He was appointed US ambassador to Great Britain in 1796 and maintained that responsibility under presidents Adams and Jefferson. His negotiation skills helped America weather the storm during the tense political relationships between the two countries before the War of 1812. Included were agreements involving naval impressment and commercial restrictions. His diplomacy planted the seeds for the Monroe Doctrine, which asserted a policy against future European colonization of US territory.

His ascension in American politics continued, leading to an unsuccessful run for president in 1816.

Issues of the Day

The War of 1812 remained a consequential debate topic during the 1816 election despite the fact that hostilities had ended a year earlier. A second American victory over the British in 40 years, and its achievement under a Democrat-Republican administration continued to increase the popularity of that party and shrink that of the Federalists.

King attempted to lambast his opponent for the trade embargoes against France and England established by Monroe predecessor James Madison. That criticism played well with delegates in New England, who felt the most significant negative effect of that policy. Federalists also tried to embrace states' rights and a perceived overextension of federal government power to win voters, but the party had little to fall back on in its platform after the Treaty of Ghent officially ended the war and the two sides renegotiated a new trade agreement.

The 1816 Campaign

The Federalist Party had yet to reach its death bed in 1816 but it was certainly on its last legs. It primarily consisted of New England delegates, but the country was growing westward and the Federalists simply could not keep up. They did not even officially pair King with a running mate.

The successful outcome of the War of 1812 and the fragmentation of the Federalists as they gave a half-hearted attempt to back King made the election of Monroe a foregone conclusion. His popularity and that of his party, limited to a few New England states, resulted in victories only in Delaware, Massachusetts, and Connecticut. Monroe won an incredible 73 percent of the popular vote. King managed a mere 16,983 votes nationwide.

After the Loss

In subsequent years, King increased his involvement in the growing debate surrounding slavery. As a civil libertarian, he railed in vain against Missouri's inclusion as a slave state—the Missouri Compromise produced the opposite result. And throughout his waning years in the political arena, he continued to support diplomacy over conflict in both foreign and domestic policy. He played a significant role connecting Federalist values with an anti-slavery philosophy. His views were embraced for years to follow by abolitionists.

King died at age 72 on April 29, 1827. He was just two years removed from his career as a New York senator.

Coming From King

In the end, it's not the years in your life that count, it's the life in your years.

Did You Know?

King graduated first in his class from Harvard in 1777.

6

The Two-Party System

Year of Defeat: 1820
Winner: James Monroe (Democrat-Republican)

What Happened?

The demise of the Federalist Party left Monroe basically unopposed in 1820. The Federalist Party gained nearly 20,000 votes on election day but hadn't nominated a candidate. DeWitt Clinton of New York had not campaigned but managed to secure nearly 2,000 votes nationwide. The result was that Monroe attracted almost 80,000 votes and swept the electoral college aside from one for John Quincy Adams cast by a dissatisfied elector from New Hampshire.

That does not mean there were not controversial issues for voters to ponder in 1820 or that Monroe was uniformly popular. A financial panic in 1819 had followed what became known as the Era of Good Feelings following the War of 1812. The economic disaster was characterized by mounting unemployment, failing banks, foreclosed mortgages, and a severe downturn in agricultural prices that destroyed farmers. Property value plunged in heavily populated states such as New York and Pennsylvania. Thousands were sent do debtors prison. Urban poverty became a first-time problem in the United States. Government agencies began opening up soup kitchens to feed the hungry.

The alarm among Americans inspired political theorist and eventual vice-president John C. Calhoun to assess the crisis. "There has been within these two years an immense revolution of fortunes in every part of the Union; enormous number of persons utterly ruined, multitudes in deep distress."[1]

Foreign competition played a role in the Panic of 1819. The reactions varied during an era of sectionalism in the country. Northern manufacturers demanded increased protection from foreign imports but many in the south believed that high tariffs that raised the costs of imported goods and reduced their flow had caused the problem. Many also blamed the nation's banks and called for less federal and state government control.

The financial woes had arrived quite late during the first Monroe term as president while the collapse of the Federalist Party and temporary loss of the two-party system could not be fixed in time to raise a viable candidate to run against him. Monroe enjoyed several years of peaceful power. His renomination by the Democrat-Republicans and that of vice-president Daniel Tompkins was so certain and assumed that the party never bothered to formalize it. Meanwhile, the Federalists, who had been stung by the lopsided defeat of Rufus King in 1816, declined to endorse anyone.

7

Andrew Jackson

Party: Democrat-Republican
Birth state: Waxhaw Settlement (between North Carolina and South Carolina)
Represented: Tennessee
Year of defeat: 1824
Winner: John Quincy Adams (Democrat-Republican)
Other notable candidates: William Crawford, Henry Clay

Andrew Jackson. Courtesy of the Library of Congress, Popular Graphic Arts Collection, LC-DIG-pga-10989/

All About Jackson

Jackson was born the son of Scotch-Irish immigrants on March 15, 1767, near Lancaster, South Carolina. His father died a mere three weeks after his birth, leaving his mother Elizabeth to raise Andrew and his two brothers. The family settled near the North Carolina border, where they shared a community with other Scotch-Irish settlers. Despite his tender age of 13, Andrew joined his older brothers in battling the British toward the end of the Revolutionary War as the fight raged in the Carolinas. He was left as the only son after both older brothers were killed.

Jackson moved to North Carolina to study law. He eventually joined the massive migration westward, which brought new opportunities. Jackson landed work as a district attorney in Tennessee and practiced law throughout that state before settling in Nashville. He threw himself into the political ring around the turn of the nineteenth century and was elected General of the Tennessee Militia in 1802. President Madison took notice of his work and commissioned him Major General of the US Volunteers. Jackson spearheaded a military campaign that subdued the Creek Nation, which was giving aid to the British during the War of 1812. Jackson is viewed as taking an antagonistic approach to relations with Native Americans during the early years of the Indian Wars. He imposed treaties upon various tribes to secure millions of acres of land for white settlers and later agreed to wage war against the Seminoles. Jackson also planned an invasion of Spanish Florida that resulted in the ceding of that territory to the United States in 1819.

He was not deterred politically following his defeat in the House as he sought the presidency in 1824.

The Electoral Mess

The dissolving of the Federalists left the Democrat-Republican as the only viable party in America. Aside from a lack of clear distinction between the candidates, all might have run smoothly. But the electoral college, which has remained a point of controversy for centuries, robbed the American people of their initial choice for president in 1824 and handed the decision to the House.

Andrew Jackson won both the popular vote and the electoral delegate count. But he did not take the majority, greatly because the party had nominated three other candidates besides him, namely, John Quincy Adams, William Crawford, and Henry Clay. That made securing more than 50 percent of the votes or delegates nearly impossible and by law prevented Jackson from assuming the presidency.

Issues of the Day

The four Democrat-Republicans shared many views, which made distinguishing each candidate particularly difficult for voters. Clay and Adams both supported protective tariffs for American manufacturers and federal government aid for such infrastructure improvements as railroads and canals. Both also backed the continuation of a national bank.

One debate among the candidates centered on what became known as the "American System" economic philosophy that sought to unite the country. Its intent was to force the United States to grow its self-reliance and become less dependent on Great Britain. The argument was that the growing number of Western states needed to link themselves economically to both the North and South.

Clay coined the term "American System" during a speech he gave during the 1824 campaign. His idea was that particular areas of the country would produce commodities that they would share with the rest of the nation. The American System was divided into three sections. One was transportation. The plan was to provide federal support for roads, canals, and bridges that would link regions of the country and increase accessibility. The second was revenue. That idea was to raise money by selling public land, imposing tariffs, and protecting American products from imported ones. The third was the federal bank and developing a strong national currency that assisted interstate trade and helped stabilize the Bank of America.

The American System was one issue that polarized the four candidates despite their link to the same party. While Clay and Adams expressed support, Jackson was mildly against it, and Crawford was strongly opposed.

The 1824 Campaign

Candidates fell by the wayside well before the election. Clay voiced his support for Adams despite the House delegation of his home state of Kentucky been instructed by the legislature to cast its ballots for him. Meanwhile, Crawford was struggling with his health and his temper, which alienated many in the Congress. The result was Adams and Jackson rising to the top.

As the nineteenth century rolled on, some politicians continued to embrace the old strategy of allowing their supporters to campaign on their behalf. While Jackson embarked on this path, Adams peppered Congressmen with his desire to retain the presidency. This act caused suspicion. A rumor spread that Clay had stepped down under the assumption based on a deal with Adams that he would be named Secretary of State, which he could then be used as a catapult to the White House.

The electoral rules worked in their favor. The Constitution holds than each state has one vote no matter how many delegates are represented when the House chooses the president. So when no candidate attracted half the electoral college votes, and despite Jackson winning the popular vote, he proved to be doomed by the House. Adams won 13 of the 24 state delegates. Jackson carried seven and Crawford four.

Jackson angrily asked how he could receive more popular and electoral votes and be denied the presidency. He asserted that the election was rigged—which became a familiar refrain from a candidate nearly two hundred years later, when Donald Trump made the same claim. He claimed a sneaky deal between Adams and Clay had doomed his chances. Jackson had no recourse, but he did plot revenge. His supporters in Congress and elsewhere clenched their teeth and fought vehemently against every Adams policy throughout his next term. Jackson stated that his campaign promises had been the will of the people and even nicknamed Clay "the Judas of the West."[1]

After the Loss

Jackson ran for president again in 1828. He fought a bitter campaign against incumbent John Quincy Adams and survived to win, though his wife Rachel did not. She died of a heart attack that December. He believed the contentious fight for the White House contributed to her death, and he forever blamed his political enemies. He was especially vengeful against Clay, whose backdoor deal with Adams had cost Jackson the White House the first time around.

Jackson shared the views of most southerners about slavery, though he was not outwardly supportive of ending slavery. He did own slaves, however, and even employed them at the White House. He railed against the disunity on the issue, criticizing both pro-slavery fanatics and abolitionists. But his backing of the "Gag Rule" that would suppress abolitionist writings proved his support for slavery. His outlook was tied to his philosophy on individual rights, though they certainly did not respect those held in bondage.

The same was true about his views about the growing friction between white settlers and the Native Americans. He continued to force unfair treaties upon the Indian population that were eventually broken. Jackson even signed the Indian Removal Act of 1830, boasting wrongly that it would preserve their culture, prevent unwanted assimilation, and limit violence. But the result was massive death and destruction as the indigenous population was forced westward by the American military.

Jackson returned to Tennessee following his presidency. His remaining years were spent writing his memoirs and managing his plantation. He died on June 8, 1845, twenty years before the abolition of slavery.

Coming From Jackson

The mischief springs from the power which the monied interest derives from a paper currency which they are able to control, from the multitude of corporations with exclusive privileges which they have succeeded in obtaining . . . and unless you become more watchful in your states and check this spirit of monopoly and thirst for exclusive privileges you will in the end find that the most important powers of government have been given or bartered away.[2]

Did You Know?

It is believed Jackson participated in many duels over his lifetime and that he even killed a man who had insulted him in a newspaper article. He survived them all and even made it through an assassination attempt in 1835, during his second time as president. House painter Richard Lawrence had pulled a pistol on him when he was leaving the US Capitol. The gun misfired, and so did the second one with which Lawrence tried to shoot Jackson—the first target of a presidential assassination attempt in American history.

8

Henry Clay

Party: Democrat-Republican
Birth state: Virginia
Home state: Kentucky
Years of defeat: 1824, 1832, 1844
Winners: John Quincy Adams (1824); Andrew Jackson (1832); James Polk (1844)
Other notable candidates: Andrew Jackson (1824); William Crawford (1824)

Henry Clay. Courtesy of the Library of Congress, Popular Graphic Arts Collection, LC-DIG-ppmsca-46437

All About Clay

Clay did not enjoy the fortune of growing up in wealth after his birth in Hanover County, Virginia, during the height of the Revolutionary War, on April 12, 1777. His family lived on a modest tobacco farm. His father, who also served as a Baptist minister, died when Henry was four years old. His mother remarried and, contradicting some later claims that Henry was raised in poverty, he enjoyed a decent education and rather comfortable upbringing.

Among his family connections was the notable Richmond, Virginia judge George Wythe, who paved the way for Clay professionally by giving him a job as clerk in the state chancery court, and then later placed him under the tutelage of state attorney general and former governor Robert Brooke. Clay proved himself adept and was admitted to the bar in 1797 before moving to Lexington, Kentucky and opening a law practice as a defense attorney there in 1797.

His stock continued to rise. Clay earned a reputation as an intimidating force in the courtroom. In 1821, he became the first attorney to file a "friend of the court" brief with the US Supreme Court and, it has been claimed, the first to successfully use a plea of temporary insanity to spare a client from a death sentence. Clay had become quite the innovator.

He emerged as a standout in the Lexington community. He helped promote civic improvements and support the nearby Transylvania University, where he taught law. But he also gained a reputation as a heavy drinker and gambler, which inspired his nickname "Prince Hal"—a reference to the alcoholic Shakespeare character Sir John Falstaff.

Clay married into a wealthy family, which allowed him to purchase a large farm outside Lexington, which he named Ashland for its many blue ash trees. He bred sheep, cattle, and race horses in a state known for horse racing. He even purchased a thoroughbred stallion for competition.

Like many of his contemporaries and those throughout American history, his law career proved to be a natural path to politics. His work in the courtroom made him an experienced and powerful speaker. He developed strong and sometimes unpopular viewpoints, including, from the 1970s onward, an abolitionist stance against slavery in Kentucky.

Clay was elected to the state House of Representatives in 1803 and remained in that post until 1806 before bouncing from a senator post back to the state House until 1811. He spearheaded an anti-British wing of the Congress known as the War Hawks before and during the War of 1812. He continued to serve in that capacity through 1825, during which time he answered higher aspirations by first seeking the presidency, then supposedly making a deal with incumbent John Quincy Adams and accepting the position of Secretary of State, which some believed would eventually lead him to the White House.

That dream remained unfulfilled. But his work as Secretary of State earned him a legacy and historical notoriety. He contributed greatly to economic development and pacifying tensions in foreign relations. But there were disappointments, such as his failure to settle a boundary dispute with Great Britain over the joint occupation of Oregon. But his push for US economic expansionism paved the way for future American diplomacy.

The presidency of bitter political rival Andrew Jackson motivated severe criticism by Clay, whom he considered power-hungry akin to royalty. Clay ran against Jackson in 1832, both as National Republican candidates, and sought to make the election a referendum on his opponent's job performance. But Jackson's virulent accusations regarding the deal Clay struck with John Quincy Adams in 1824, as well as his own popularity, continued to play well with voters. Jackson won in a landslide.

Clay helped give birth to the Whigs, a name borrowed from the British party opposed to the privileges of royalty. The American Whigs, who believed in a strong central government, ran presidential candidates in 1836 from four areas in the country. Clay was disappointed at not being one of them as William Henry Harrison and three others divided Whig support, leading to an easy victory for Democrat Martin Van Buren. Clay returned to the Senate but planned on a stronger push for the White House in 1840. Economic problems in the country had weakened Van Buren's popularity and strengthened that of the Whigs. Clay hoped to secure the nomination, but it went instead to Harrison. Clay swallowed his pride and campaigned for Harrison, who easily defeated Van Buren, then died a month after his inauguration.

Clay earned admiration for backing Harrison. But he forged a contentious relationship with Harrison replacement and fellow Whig John Tyler, with whom he disagreed on several issues, including slavery. Clay even helped establish the American Colonization Society, which promoted emancipation and the gradual return of freeborn blacks and slaves to the African nation of Liberia. But he also favored the annexation of Texas, which would become a slave state. He was called out for being hypocritical based on his antislavery stance and backing of annexing what would be a slave territory.

Persistence failed to pay off in 1844, when Clay earned the Whig nomination and campaigned against Democratic candidate James Polk. He performed better than he had in previous tries, losing closely in the popular vote but more decisively in the electoral college and taking just 11 of 26 states, including the entire Deep South.

Clay believed he was done with politics when he retired at age 67, but the Mexican-American War in which his son was killed inspired his return in 1848. He yearned for another Whig presidential nomination, but it was handed instead to war hero Zachary Taylor. By that time, he was dealing with tuberculosis. Yet Clay felt he had more to give. He returned to the Senate and created a bold plan to end slavery in regions where it already existed—this naturally proved quite unpopular among Southerners. Though it was not adopted, his plan led to the Compromise of 1850 that temporarily staved off civil war.

Clay finally succumbed to tuberculosis in June 1852. It is believed that millions of Americans viewed his funeral journey to Lexington by train and steamboat.

Coming From Clay

The majority should dismiss from their minds all vindictive feelings. . . . Nothing should be done from passion, nor in passion. . . . Repeal bad laws but preserve good ones even if they have been passed by the late dominant party.[1]

Did You Know?

Clay earned the complimentary nickname "The Great Compromiser" for his work as Secretary of State in subduing crises in various regions of the growing country.

9

William Crawford

Party: Democrat-Republican
Birth state: Virginia
Represented: Georgia
Year of Defeat: 1824
Winner: John Quincy Adams (Democrat-Republican)
Other notable candidates: Andrew Jackson, Henry Clay

A Foot Race: John Quincy Adams, William Crawford, Andrew Jackson, and Henry Clay. Courtesy of the Library of Congress, Cartoon Prints American Collection, LC-DIG-ds-05217

All About Crawford

Born on February 24, 1772, Crawford was the sixth of eleven children born to Fanny Harris and Joel Crawford. His American roots extended back from 1643 when great-grandfather John Earl of Crawford reached the shores of Virginia. William's family moved several times in that state before settling in Georgia in 1783. His early tasks including toiling on the family farm.

Crawford spent his early adult years as a teacher and farmer before enrolling at Moses Waddel's Carmel Academy in Appling, then Richmond Academy, in Augusta. He studied law privately, gained admission to the bar, and in 1799, launched his career as an attorney in Lexington, Georgia, where he married and purchased a Woodlawn estate, at which he became overseer. His landholdings grew into a sizeable plantation with 45 slaves.

The plain-talking Crawford gained influence in the state even before launching a political career. He came out against the Yazoo Act of 1795, which allowed land to be sold to companies at a low price. Bribery and fraud ran rampant as 35 million acres of Georgia frontier (now in Alabama and Mississippi) were driven into speculation. It led to the 1810 Fletcher v. Peck case in the Supreme Court, which ruled that the Yazoo Act had indeed been approved by those who expected payouts and accepted money illegally.

Crawford's strong views against the Yazoo Act drove him into politics. He was appointed in the year of its passage to co-author the *Digest of the Laws of the State of Georgia*, which was published in 1801. Two years later, he was elected to represent Oglethorpe County in the House of Representatives, where he aligned himself with state senator, former Georgia governor and Revolutionary War hero James Jackson, and his views against gross land speculation. Crawford and Jackson led a group of wealthy plantation owners who worked politically toward their own interests. They were opposed by the Clarkites, a faction led by Elijah Clarke and son John who supported small farmers and frontier settlers.

The rivalry exploded into violence in 1802, when Crawford killed Clark ally Peter Van Aken. A vengeful John Clark wounded Crawford in a duel four years later. Crawford later refused to again duel Clark, who instead ambushed Crawford ally Judge Charles Tait and whipped him with a riding crop.

The death of US Senator Abraham Baldwin in 1807 allowed Crawford to ascend in his career. He was appointed as the replacement. He was driven in Washington by his free-spirited personality and refusal to engage in partisan politics. That reputation as a man for the people of Georgia helped him get reelected in 1811. Among the policies he supported was the rechartering of the Bank of America as an economic stabilizer and an institution that restrained often reckless state banks. Crawford also supported trade embargoes against Great Britain and France during the James Madison administration. Though leery of British military strength as the War of 1812 approached, he backed a military buildup and solution. Appreciative of Crawford's support, Madison offered him the position of secretary of war. Crawford declined but soon accepted the job as minister to France.

Madison was persistent. He appointed Crawford secretary of war in 1815. Crawford felt obligated to accept despite his plan to retire from public life. He served in that capacity for less than a year, but during that short time, succeeded in making the department more efficient while preparing it for an era of peace.

So much for retirement. A stint as secretary of the treasury was followed by his nomination for president by the Republican congressional caucus. He lost a close balloting to eventual president James Monroe, who asked him to continue in his role with the treasury. Crawford achieved success by overseeing the building of a fort system along the Eastern Seaboard and construction of the Cumberland Road that extended from Virginia into the Midwest.

Soon, the demise of the Federalist Party altered national politics. Among the impacts were the policy divisions among Republicans, leading to the selection of four presidential candidates in 1824. One was Crawford, who had suffered a stroke the year before but accepted the nomination. His recovery put him behind the others as a campaigner. The result was a third-place finish behind Andrew Jackson and John Quincy Adams.

Crawford was done with politics. He had been anticipating retirement for several years and embraced it. He refused to serve as treasury secretary under Adams and returned to his beloved Georgia, where he was appointed judge of its Northern Circuit of its Superior Court. He was still serving as a judge when he died on September 15, 1834.

Coming From Crawford

It has become . . . extremely fashionable to eulogize this Constitution, whether the object of the eulogist is the extension or the contraction of the powers of government . . . whenever its eulogium is pronounced I feel an involuntary apprehension of mischief.[1]

Did You Know?

Many towns throughout the South and Midwest are named after Crawford, including two in Georgia, as well as others in Indiana, Illinois, Iowa, Missouri, Arkansas, and Wisconsin.

10

John Quincy Adams

Party: National Republican
Birth state: Massachusetts
Represented: Massachusetts
Year of defeat: 1828
Running mate: Richard Rush
Winner: Andrew Jackson (Democrat)

John Q. Adams. Courtesy of the Library of Congress, Popular Graphic Arts Collection, LC-DIG-pga-06824

All About Adams

Born on July 11, 1767, Adams was raised mostly by his mother Abigail, a math teacher—his father was a little too busy to spend much time with his son. The family of John Adams lived in what is now Quincy, Massachusetts, a few miles south of Boston. Dad doted upon his boy when he was around but his political activity often called him away. John was just six years old when his father began ramping up his involvement in forming a new nation, helping in leading the Continental Congress, drafting the Declaration of Independence, then serving in France and Holland during the Revolutionary War and eventually assisting the negotiation of a peace treaty with England.

It was a traumatic time for John Quincy, who feared for his father's life and the safety of his family if the British won the war. After all, the elder Adams had committed an act of treason against England on signing the Declaration of Independence—and treason was punishable by death. Despite his tender age, he felt a sense of responsibility as a protector of his family. As a boy, he watched the war launch in the Battle of Bunker Hill in 1775, as the first men were killed. He watched solemnly as soldiers passed through his town. Most boys learned of the fighting from afar. For John, the early years of the war were up-close and personal, with tragic implications for his family as well as his country.

Soon, a new adventure awaited. Adams traveled in 1778 to Paris, where his father had been sent as part of a special envoy. Yet to reach his teenage years, he nevertheless traveled to the Netherlands, England, Sweden, and Prussia with his father. He learned about world affairs and diplomacy, planting the seeds for his own political career. Adams was educated at the Passy Academy in Paris alongside the grandson of Benjamin Franklin, studying fencing, dance, music, and art. After three months back in America, he traveled with his father as the family relocated to Amsterdam.

These experiences made John quite mature and advanced for his age. He was merely 14 when asked by the US emissary to St. Petersburg to serve as his translator and personal secretary. He moved permanently back to the new nation in 1785 to attend Harvard, where he received his diploma in just two years. He had become an avid reader of ancient history and modern literature, as well as an admirer of Thomas Jefferson, a close friend of his father and the most noteworthy author of the Declaration of Independence.

Rough waters lay ahead. Deemed by potential clients as too young and inexperienced, Adams struggled in the early 1790s with his law practice, despite a perceived advantage of his father serving as vice president of the United States. He had just begun to gain success when President Washington, impressed with his fluency in French and Dutch, appointed him minister to the Netherlands. It was a good time for the young diplomat. He proved himself a natural, managing the repayment of Dutch loans made to America during the American Revolution and sent well-regarded official reports to Washington on the aftermath of the French Revolution. He remained in that post when his father assumed the presidency.

He carefully managed the repayment of Dutch loans made to America during the American Revolution and sent well-regarded official reports to Washington on the aftermath of the French Revolution.

His father soon appointed him US minister to Prussia, but his life changed when the elder Adams lost his 1800 reelection bid. He then began a career in local politics, winning a state senate seat before the Massachusetts legislature sent him to the US Senate in 1803. By that time, his Federalist viewpoints had changed to those held by the Democratic-Republicans and President Jefferson. Adams had even been one of just two Federalists in the senate to support the Louisiana Purchase and the 1807 embargo against foreign trade. Angry Massachusetts Federalists forced him to resign, leading to his official switch to the Democratic-Republican Party.

Adams was soon thrown into the international fray again after President Madison appointed him the first US Minister to Russia during the Napoleonic Wars. Adams, who had previously criticized that country, grew to respect Czar Alexander as the nation withstood the French invasion. Adams convinced the czar to permit commerce from American ships, while providing Madison with reports from Russia after Napoleon forces struck in 1812.

His stock continued to rise. Two years later Adams headed a delegation to negotiate a peace agreement with England to end the War of 1812. The treaty that was ratified in early 1815 was both a victory for Adams and the country. New president James Monroe elevated Adams to Secretary of State in 1817, a position he maintained for eight years. His diplomatic achievements included the framing of the Monroe Doctrine, which successfully warned European nations against meddling in internal American affairs and established a border with Canada extending from Minnesota to the Rockies. Adams also negotiated the transfer of Florida from Spain to the United States.

His presidency proved less beneficial to his legacy after the Federalist Party collapsed, and he became one of several Democratic-Republican Party candidates for the White House. His backroom dealings with Henry Clay that resulted in the House handing him the presidency despite a lopsided defeat to Andrew Jackson in the popular vote made Adams enemies, and he accomplished little over the next four years. He received little support for his grandiose plans, including the creation of the Department of the Interior and development of a system of roads and canals.

A vengeful Jackson defeated Adams for reelection in 1828, forcing him back to the Congress.

Issues of the Day

Clear distinctions between the two candidates and their parties, their contentious dislike for each other, simplified choices for the voters in 1828.

Formed from a coalition of politicians who opposed what became known as Jacksonian Democracy, the National Republicans embraced a nationalistic philosophy. Jackson backed limited government spending and meddling in the lives of Americans, as well as political favoritism. intrusion into the lives of Americans.

Among the policy disagreements between the National Republicans and Democrats revolved around the issue of tariffs, which are taxes on imported foreign goods and a significant source of government funding, as well as a protection for American manufactures against outside competition. Adams and his supporters favored tariffs, greatly because the region of the country they represented were strong manufacturing states that benefitted from such taxes. Jackson backers were split on tariffs but united against Adams.

A congressional vote to raise tariffs in 1828 highlighted the overall policy debates that year. The bill's passage had significant political impact. It upset voters, particularly in the South who yearned for lower tariffs, motivating them to vote for Jackson.

The 1828 Campaign

Fiery Andrew Jackson, whose violent temper led to frequent dueling and two bullets lodged in his body, carried an anti-tariff message in his campaign that attracted Southern voters. His viewpoints proved a clear contrast to those of Adams, a veteran diplomat who favored tariffs that were embraced by New Englanders.

Previously, each state had held specific laws determining voting eligibility, though all allowed just white male citizens with a certain level of wealth to cast ballots. Election rules had changed by 1828, as most of those rules had been eliminated, leading to a stricter two-party system that included the Democratic Party and the highest voter turnout in American history in 1828.

That campaign also led to greater divisiveness in American politics. The 1828 battle was certainly bitter as Jackson, still angry after charging Adams and Clay reaching a deal, leading to a House vote that denied the presidency four years earlier, pushed hard to win. His supporters established pro-Jackson newspapers while organizing rallies, parades, and other promotional events. Adams and his backers, meanwhile, got more personal, calling Jackson and his wife Rachel adulterers and blasting the Democratic candidate for dueling and gambling. Mudslinging ran rampant as the two fought for the sympathy of voters. Jackson's supporters accused Adams of corruption. They even claimed Adams offered an American girl to the Russian czar for sexual favors.

The result was the opposite of 1824. The unpopular Adams lost badly to Jackson, getting just 44 percent of the vote, carrying only New England, while his opponent dominated the South and Midwest. Jackson received 178 electoral college votes against just 83 for Adams.

After the Loss

After losing to Jackson in 1828, Adams served 17 years as a Massachusetts state representative. Adams became an increasingly vehement abolitionist. He opposed the annexation of Texas, which was destined to become a slave state. He collapsed in his House seat on February 21, 1848, and died two days later.

Coming From Adams

I am a warrior, so that my son may be a merchant, so that his son may be a poet.[1]

Did You Know?

Adams was involved in the legendary true story about *The Amistad*, a ship on which on July 1, 1839, abducted slaves staged a rebellion, killing the captain and crew, then attempted to direct it back to Africa before it was seized by US officials. Fights over property rights ensued, in which the slaves asserted their freedom. The case was appealed all the way to the Supreme Court, where Adams successfully argued on behalf of the slaves. The Court ruled overwhelmingly in their favor.

11

William Henry Harrison

Party: Whig
Birth state: Virginia
Represented: Ohio
Year of defeat: 1836
Running mate: Francis Granger
Winner: Martin Van Buren (Democrat)
Other notable candidate: Hugh L. White (Whig)

William Henry Harrison. Courtesy of the Library of Congress, Popular Graphic Arts Collection, LC-DIG-pga-10151

All About Harrison

Harrison was born into wealth and aristocracy as the youngest of seven children to a plantation owner on February 9, 1773. He sometimes referred to himself as a "child of the revolution" in reference to his birth just two years before the war against the British rule began.[1]

Among the connections of his father William, who served three terms as Virginia governor and was even a signer of the Declaration of Independence, was George Washington, who some historians believe his parents reminisced about often to their son. Their home rested a mere thirty miles from Yorktown, where the decisive battle of the Revolutionary War that doomed England to surrender.

William thrived despite his status as the youngest sibling during a period in which the eldest son gained control of the property. When their father died young, he left nearly his entire estate to his oldest male child. But William proved himself ambitious educationally after three years of home schooling. The boy spent three years at the prestigious Hampden-Sydney College in Virginia, then studied medicine under noted physician Bemjamin Rush in Philadelphia in his pursuit of becoming a doctor. But a lack of funds after his brother inherited all the family wealth forced William out of medical school and into the military.

He embraced that opportunity. Harrison had grown accustomed to learning about armed disputes in early American history, including the revolution against England and land disputes against the Spanish, French, and Native Americans. He used his family connections and talent to ascend to the officer's rank in an infantry division and even talked about eighty troublemakers off the streets of Philadelphia into enlisting.

Harrison was assigned to Fort Washington (near present-day Cincinnati), which protected white settlers against attacks by Native Americans, who were aided by the British as tensions that would lead to the War of 1812 escalated. Harrison earned commendation for his bravery and execution after a defeat of Indian forces at the 1794 Battle of Fallen Timbers that helped open the Northwest Territory for colonization. Harrison was given command of the fort two years later, then appointed Secretary of the Northwest Territory by President Adams in 1799, which allowed him to run for and win a spot as a Congressional delegate. He won over voters by reforming land-buying laws that allowed only large purchases. Struggling settlers were then able to purchase smaller plots of land on four-year installment plans.

Rise in the political ranks. Harrison was soon appointed governor of the Indiana Territory, which would eventually include sections of modern-day Indiana, Illinois, Michigan, Minnesota, and Wisconsin. He remained at that post for twelve years. His primary function was to claim as much territory as possible from Native Americans, who had no concept of land ownership. Harrison took advantage of this fact. He rammed through seven exploitive treaties from 1802 to

1805, including a merciless land grab of 51 million acres at one penny per acre in the last of those years.

One chief who saw through the rip-off was Tecumseh, who sought to organize tribes through negotiation with help from the British, who had yet to concede the idea of ruling America and began to build forts in the area. Some US politicians such as Henry Clay called for an all-out war against the Indian nation. Harrison reacted more peacefully, offering with approval from new president James Madison to buy nearly three million acres of Native American land for just under two cents an acre. The result was the Treaty of Fort Wayne.

Harrison had bypassed Tecumseh and other tribes hostile to the American government into the negotiations. Livid over the treaty, Tecumseh openly courted British military assistance and threatened war to retake Indian land. Harrison warned him of overwhelming army power. But Tecumseh remained undeterred. He and a group of warriors confronted Harrison outside his home on August 15, 1810, and warned that further land grabs would result in war. A battle threatened to break out at that moment but cooler heads prevailed.

In response to Indian raids, the following summer Harrison asked Madison to give him command of an armed force to strike against Tecumseh. The result was the legendary Battle of Tippecanoe that began with a surprise attack on the army camp, killing several officers and causing others to flee, and ended with a counterattack that routed the Native Americans. Public reaction to the battle was mixed—some railed against the loss of life while others commended Harrison for taking action against the Indian raids.

Praise for Harrison soon ended. Tippecanoe only served to strengthen warrior resolve. They increased the number and ferocity of raids against white settlers. The British supplied ammunition, leading to a declaration of war against them in 1812 with Harrison as commander of all forces in the Northwest as major general. He received orders to take a fortress in Detroit under British control and succeeded by September 1813. The Native Americans fought better and harder than the British. They initially fended off an assault by Harrison and his men but were eventually routed and Tecumseh was killed.

The War of 1812 had been unpopular among most Americans, but its victorious conclusion made Harrison a hero. But rather than furthering his military career, he toured New York, Philadelphia, and Washington, enjoying the adoration he received at each stop. He resigned from the army and retired into farming before pursuing a life in politics.

It was not an immediate success. He served in the House from 1816 to 1819, failed to land the secretary of war post he craved under President Monroe, then returned to Ohio, where he lost a bid for governor in 1820 and for a House seat in 1822. He finally won a senate seat two years later and earned an ambassadorship in 1828 to Colombia, which was in the midst of a revolution.

Harrison appeared destined for retirement upon his return from that South American nation, though he was sometimes mentioned as a potential gubernatorial or senatorial candidate by those who opposed Andrew Jackson's policies. He occasionally gave speeches on topics related to farming or politics before accepting work as Hamilton County clerk of courts in Ohio.

But Harrison was not done. He was nominated in 1836 as one of three major candidates by the new Whig Party, which had been founded rather hastily by anti-Jackson factions and held no convention nor platform to win. Harrison managed to attract many votes in the Midwest and West to finish second to winner in the electoral college to Jackson pick Martin Van Buren.

Issues of the Day

Several controversial decisions made by outgoing president Andrew Jackson heaped baggage on the shoulders of Van Buren, his personal replacement choice who was chosen unanimously as the standard bearer by the Democrats during its national convention in Baltimore.

Among them was his inaction to the Nullification Crisis in South Carolina during the early years of his term. That was the result of a battle between the federal government and the state, which declared the Tariffs of 1828 and 1832 unconstitutional and therefore null and void within its boundaries. South Carolina had merely echoed the objections of all mostly agrarian southern states to such tariffs they felt placed a harmful tax burden on them. Those representing these states believed Jackson, who dominated voting in that region, would act on their behalf but he did nothing. He also alienated those who favored nationalist economic policies by withdrawing government funds from the Bank of the United States in 1833.

The result was the rise of anti-Jackson factions that included the National Republican and Anti-Masonic Parties, which combined to form the Whigs.

The 1836 Campaign

The upstart Whigs attempted to overwhelm the electorate with a variety of candidates rather than one who could defeat Van Buren. So dedicated were the Whigs to that notion that they held no national convention. Candidates such as Harrison, Hugh Lawrence White, and Daniel Webster were placed at various state conventions and by legislatures to win statewide or regionally. Some contended that the strategy was to attract enough voters to prevent Van Buren from receiving an electoral college majority and thereby force the House to decide the winner, though the Whigs denied that was their scheme.

Either way it failed, as Van Buren garnered 51 percent of the total vote and 170 of the 294 electoral votes to reach the White House. Only Harrison proved popular in a large swath of America, and it has been offered that, had the Whigs placed only him in nomination, he might have defeated Van Buren.

After the Loss

Buoyed by his relative success, Harrison tried again in 1840 after defeating Henry Clay for the Whig nomination. The party was hopeful that his military heroism and reputation as a frontiersman would prove a winning formula and that vice-presidential nominee John Tyler would be popular in the South. A failing economy motivated Americans to vote for change. Harrison remained noncommittal on slavery. He opposed Congressional restrictions on slavery in new territories as a slave owner himself. He avoided condemning the practice, asserting that its legality should be left to individual states.

His policy strategies worked. Harrison easily defeated Van Buren in 1840 and gave folks a glimpse of the future by becoming the first president-elect to travel by railroad to Washington for his inauguration. He also tried to show his toughness by wearing neither gloves nor a coat despite freezing temperatures and cold drizzle while speaking for two hours.

Copies of his address were sped via railroad to Americans who could read it the same day. Harrison, who vowed to stay in office for just one term after turning the country around, could not remain in the White House more than a month. The cold he contracted during his inauguration speech resulted in pneumonia and he died exactly a month later, though some more superstitious folks blamed his passing on "Tecumseh's Curse." His death also killed the Whig Party.

Coming From Harrison

There is nothing more corrupting, nothing more destructive of the noblest and finest feelings of our nature, than the exercise of unlimited power.[2]

Did You Know?

Harrison wed Anna Tuthill Symmes in 1795 despite the objections of her father, who disapproved of his military career. Her family was wealthy and Anna was well-educated. She married him anyway and bore nine children, including John Scott, who would decades later father Benjamin Harrison, the 23rd president of the United States.

12

Martin Van Buren

Party: Democratic
Birth state: New York
Represented: New York
Year of defeat: 1840
Winner: William Henry Harrison (Whig)
Campaign slogan: "Tippecanoe and Tyler Too" (Harrison)

Martin Van Buren. Courtesy of the Library of Congress, C.M Bell Studio Collection, LC-DIG-bellcm-25573

All About Van Buren

Van Buren was born to parents of Dutch extraction on December 5, 1782, the first president who came into the world not under British rule. He was not raised in wealth unlike most of those who reached the White House in the first half-century of America's existence.

Parents Abraham and Maria lived in Kinderhook, New York, a town near Albany populated by others with Dutch backgrounds. The family struggled to make ends meet. Maria had been a widow with three children before marrying Abraham and bearing three more. Though they were not rich, they had enough money to purchase six slaves. Martin's father owned a tavern and inn often visited by government officials traveling between Albany and New York City. He even hosted political meetings there. Among the political luminaries who attended were Alexander Hamilton and Aaron Burr, whose presence gave young Aaron his first exposure to American politics. Abraham added income as a town clerk.

Unlike other youth of his generation whose family needed their teenage offspring to contribute financially, Martin continued his education until age fourteen. And though he did not attend college, he landed a job as a law clerk through his father's political connections. He served in that role for seven years, doing menial chores around the office and running errands by day before studying law at night. He then moved to New York City for a year and earned admission to the state bar at the age of 21, returning to Kinderhook in 1803, and opening a practice with half-brother James.

They were attorneys for the commoners. Their reputations and bank accounts were strengthened by clients such as tenants and renters who contested landlord claims to property in the Hudson Valley. Their backing of the common folk against the financial elite helped change the socio-economic fabric of the American society.

Van Buren soon turned his attention to politics. He bucked local trends by joining the Democratic-Republicans led by Thomas Jefferson and James Madison rather than the more popular Federalists. His affiliation resulted in hostility with many friends and colleagues, as well as soured relationships with Federalist judges and lawyers. But he remained loyal to his Jeffersonian political beliefs such as limited federal government, defense of individual liberties, and the protection of local and state choices in handling their own affairs.

Showing a keen political sense, Van Buren supported DeWitt Clinton over Burr as the two fought for statewide leadership in the Democratic-Republican Party. Clinton rewarded him with a county official post in 1808, a year after he had married lifelong friend Hamma Hoes and moved with her to Hudson, where he practiced law. Van Buren soon won a close race over a Federalist opponent to land a spot in the state senate. But it was not an ideal time to be a Democratic-Republican, whose party's conduct of the unpopular War of 1812 had lost them favor to the Federalists. But he remained loyal and soon Federalist approval, though still strong in New York, faded nationally.

Van Buren eventually served as a uniter amid harmful bickering among factions within his own party. He feared that infighting was natural but not when it became uncontrolled and particularly destructive. He yearned to foster productive and amiable relationships. So he helped form the Bucktails, so named for the distinguishing deer tails they wore on their hats. They embraced policies and goals such as the defeat of the Federalists and their beliefs in a strong central government. The Bucktails rallied around Jeffersonian ideas, contending that only the Democratic-Republicans could achieve their goals

By that time, Van Buren and the Bucktails had concluded that fellow party member DeWitt Clinton was bad for New York. He launched a campaign against Clinton that dominated state politics and earned him the reputation of being a crooked opportunist. Van Buren had won reelection to the state senate in 1816 and was named state attorney general but he could not bring down Clinton, who became governor a year later and set out to destroy the Bucktails. Van Buren was dismissed as attorney general in 1819.

He remained active, playing a critical role in the New York constitutional convention in 1821 to gain popularity among party members and earned that year an election to the United States Senate, quickly increasing influence in New York and nationally. He served on the finance committee and chaired the judiciary committee. He maintained his Jeffersonian allegiance to states' rights and limited government. He opposed federal spending at every turn, though for political reasons, refused to come out openly against all tariffs.

Despite his efforts as a unifier, party splits grew wider. Each Democratic-Republican felt a sense of loyalty and political need to please constituents and the country was growing in size and viewpoints. Van Buren supported William Crawford for president in 1824 because of shared political sentiments, but he lost badly to both Andrew Jackson and John Quincy Adams in a contentious battle that ended with the House voting for the latter to take the White House.

Van Buren opposed Adams in the belief he was essentially a Federalist despite his standing as a Democratic-Republican who favored big government. He toiled tirelessly and successfully toward the election of Jackson in 1828. His work helped inspire far more voters to stream to the polls and elect Jackson. The coalition planted the seeds for the modern Democratic Party.

That same year, Van Buren was elected governor of New York. But he only remained in that post until Jackson asked him to become secretary of state. He could not turn down a position of national importance that provided him an opportunity to succeed Jackson as president.

Controversies, both policy-driven and personal, during the two Jackson terms not only divided American public opinion but members of his own party, including Van Buren and vice-president John Calhoun. The latter disputes revolved around Peggy O'Neill, wife of Secretary of War John Eaton, who it was rumored had an affair with him while still married. She was snubbed by most in the party elite aside from Van Buren, who showed his independence and courage by inviting her to social functions.

Political issues that drove a wedge between Calhoun and Van Buren were far more significant. Calhoun backed an extreme states' rights position that Van Buren, despite his own dislike of a powerful national government, believed to be too extreme. The threat by South Carolina to defy the federal legislation on tariffs pushed conversation on states' rights with Calhoun backing the defiance and Van Buren fighting alongside Jackson to declare South Carolina's rebelliousness unconstitutional.

The in-fighting motivated Jackson to form what became known as the "Kitchen Cabinet" of advisers with Van Buren leading the way, who could best express his political beliefs. The Secretary of State drafted ideological texts that failed to soften tensions within the administration.

The result was a bold plan, the brainchild of Van Buren, who resigned from the cabinet along with Eaton, allowing the president to reorganize and appoint only allies. He then named Van Buren minister to England. Six months later, he lost a Senate confirmation to that post by one vote—that of his enemy Calhoun. So Jackson dumped Calhoun and named Van Buren his running mate for his 1832 election landslide.

His years as vice-president were highlighted by an epic clash with the Second Bank of the United States, whose immense power he believed benefited only the wealthiest Americans to the disadvantage of all others. The Bank War inspired an opposition party known as the Whigs that railed against "King Andrew" and called for a return to the ideals of the American Revolution. Meanwhile, more people began to understand and embrace Democratic principles as the party grew more unified. And when Jackson backed Van Buren as his successor in 1836, a contentious battle for power became unavoidable.

Enough Americans had gained respect for Van Buren's ability to get things done to nickname him "The Little Magician" (he was just 5-foot-6) and vote him into the White House. The economy had boomed under Jackson. But the financial panic of 1837 destroyed his favorability.

Many historians believe the new president was victimized by Jackson's destruction of the Second Bank of America that had a negative effect on other banks across the country and the economy itself after Van Buren began occupying the White House. He toiled tirelessly to end the crisis, fighting for an independent treasury system to handle government transaction and killing federal aid toward internal improvements. He also blocked the annexation of Texas to prevent another slave state from joining the union.

Nothing could save his presidency. Van Buren was defeated for reelection by the Whigs in 1840 and never recovered politically. He attempted to run again in 1848 on the fringe Free Soil Party ticket.

Inclined more and more to oppose the expansion of slavery, Van Buren blocked the annexation of Texas because it assuredly would add to slave territory—and it might bring war with Mexico. But his legacy also included participation in the shameful Trail of Tears, the forcible removal of Native Americans off their lands and into internment. He admitted that American policy toward the Indian began with the government as an aggressor but claimed that it eventually served as a protector.

Issues of the Day

The Whigs believed the military heroism of Harrison would win the day with voters, but they also felt they had an issue over the incumbent Van Buren and the Democrats. Among them was the severe economic downturn that became known as the Panic of 1837 that lingered into the campaign.

Harrison supporters pitched clean and honest government in claiming that Van Buren and predecessor Andrew Jackson had corruptly abused their power while destroying the economy with their anti-bank policies and short-term loans. Harrison portrayed himself as non-controversial on issues such as slavery after a long period out of the spotlight while Whig rival Henry Clay's ownership of slaves made him a tough sell to Northern voters.

The 1840 Campaign

Andrew Jackson was a populist president who had left office with a strong economy and had been glorified as a military hero. The opposite doomed Van Buren as he sought reelection in 1840. Whether or not it was the result of Jackson policies, the economy was struggling.

Instead, it was his opponent William Henry Harrison who was embraced for his heroism on the battlefields. The campaign featured a Whig push for mass political appeal, complete with slogans, parades, rallies, and campaign newspapers. Most notable was the first and perhaps most famous presidential campaign song, a ditty titled "Tippecanoe and Tyler Too" that praised Harrison's military achievements as well as his running mate. The Whigs also portrayed Van Buren as an Eastern snob.

The Democrats failed to push back effectively. They tried to paint Harrison as a nobody who belonged on a rocking chair in a log cabin, drinking a bottle of whiskey but that imagery backfired. Many Americans identified more with Harrison than Van Buren. The result was that Van Buren lost 19 of 26 states.

After the Loss

Defeated by the Whigs in 1840 for reelection, Van Buren was an unsuccessful candidate for President on the fringe Free Soil ticket in 1848, receiving just 10 percent of the vote. He never again ran for office, though he did speak his mind on political topics, including his growing ideological opposition to slavery and concern over the secession of Southern states as the Civil War approached. Van Buren lived to see its launch but not its conclusion. He died in 1862.

Coming From Harrison

All communities are apt to look to Government for too much. Even in our own country, where its powers and duties are so strictly limited, we are prone to do so, especially at periods of sudden embarrassment and distress. But this ought not to be. The framers of our excellent constitution, and the people who approved it with calm and sagacious deliberation, acted at the time on a sounder principle. They wisely judged that the less Government interferes with private pursuits, the better for the general prosperity.[1]

Did You Know?

Domestic affairs dominated the Van Buren presidency, but he did triumph in one foreign affair in 1839 when a border dispute arose between Maine and Canada along the Aroostook River. Maine officials received pushback when they tried to drive Canadians away, leading to both sides sending militia to the area. Van Buren dispatched General Winfield Scott to maintain peace. The result was a peaceful resolution.

13

Lewis Cass

General Lewis Cass. Courtesy of the Library of Congress, Popular Graphic Arts Collection, LC-DIG-pga-08943

Party: Democrat
Birth state: New Hampshire
Represented: Michigan
Year of defeat: 1848
Running mate: William Butler
Winner: Zachary Taylor
Campaign slogan: "For President of the People" (Taylor)
Other notable candidate: Martin Van Buren (Free Soil)

All About Cass

Born on October 9, 1782, in the farming community of Exeter, New Hampshire, Cass was the son of a Revolutionary War soldier. His father, whose ancestors were among the first settlers in that part of the country, joined the army the day after the Battle of Lexington and participated in such notable skirmishes such as Bunker Hill and Saratoga.

The family became one of many from New England to trek westward when Cass was 17. They moved to southeast Ohio, where he attended studied law under Jonathan Meigs, who was eventually elected the fourth governor of that state and eventually a US senator. Cass was admitted to the bar in 1802 and launched a successful practice.

Similar to many others lawyers in his generation and beyond, Cass quickly set his sights on a political career. He was elected to the Ohio Legislature in 1806, then appointed US Marshal by President Jefferson for that state a year later, before serving during the War of 1812 and governor of the Michigan Territory. He appeared satisfied in the role rather than working to further his career. Cass remained in that post for 18 years until the age of 49. But he gained national attention in 1831 when President Jackson appointed him Secretary of War, then the US Minister to France. He stayed there for six years.

By that time, he had weighed in further in internal affairs. Cass published an article for the *North American Review* in 1830 that asserted the inferiority of Native Americans and a perceived incapability of civilized behavior. He called for the removal of tribes from the eastern United States. President Jackson was impressed with its contents, and in appointing him Secretary of War, placed him in charge of implementing an Indian removal policy that Congress had passed a year earlier. Indians throughout the east and modern Midwest were forced to flee to present-day Kansas and Oklahoma.

Cass eventually thirsted for higher political aspirations. He failed in his bid to secure the Democratic presidential nomination in 1844, but did win election to serve Michigan as US senator in 1845. He defeated future president James Buchanan for the party nomination in 1848 and ran a respectable race against Taylor in defeat.

Issues of the Day

Slavery had taken center stage among political issues by 1848. The debates did not always revolve around the morality of owning human beings but the viability of opening options for new states and territories to incorporate the practice as the United States continued to expand westward.

The acquisition of vast land during the previous two years during the James Polk administration resulting from the Mexican-American War and a treaty with Great

Britain intensified arguments on both sides. The Wilmot Proviso, a congressional proposal to forbid slavery in any territory won from Mexico, added fuel to the fire.

Cass supported the notion that the residents of new territories should decide whether or not to become a free or slave state. That was not a popular position among many Democrats, so the party did not include it in its platform. The Whigs, who considered senators Henry Clay and Daniel Webster for its nomination before selecting Taylor, a hero in both the War of 1812 and Mexican-American War. Taylor, a slaveholder from Louisiana. The party also ignored the issue of slavery in its official platform to dodge the contentious issue.

That avoidance by both parties helped inspire the emergence of factions and alliances, such as antislavery Democrats and Whigs who formed the Free Soil Party. But nominee and former president Martin Van Buren failed to make inroads among voters.

The 1848 Campaign

The Polk promise to serve just one term resulted in a battle for the Democratic nomination at the national convention in Baltimore between Cass, Buchanan, and Supreme Court justice Levi Woodbury. But after a close vote on the first ballot Cass emerged as the winner.

Times were changing in American politics. Both the Democrats and Whigs established national committees to plan their campaigns. Voting by the general public had been adopted in every state but the always-rebellious South Carolina, which still chose its electors through its legislature. And 1848 became the first year in which every state ran its balloting on the same day, a move made by the federal government to discourage voter fraud.

The Whigs, who considered previously unsuccessful candidates Henry Clay and Daniel Webster, as well as general Winfield Scott, for its nomination, selected the war hero Taylor instead and paired him with New Yorker Millard Fillmore to give the ticket strong balance. Both parties avoided controversial issues during the campaign—the Whigs even more so than the Democrats. Cass supporters lambasted Taylor, even claiming falsely that he was illiterate. But even though both candidates proved popular in various parts of the country, victories in the most populous states of New York and Pennsylvania drove Taylor into the White House.

After the Loss

Cass returned to the Senate for eight more years, losing out to Franklin Pierce for the Democratic nomination in 1852 along the way.

The aging Cass was 75 when Buchanan appointed him Secretary of State in 1857. It was in that role he made his most significant impact on the country and the party, which was in desperate need of unification. But Cass also influenced foreign policy. He negotiated a treaty with Great Britain that limited the control of both countries in Latin America and ended the British practice of searching American vessels.

The election of Abraham Lincoln as president in 1860 and rise of the new Republican Party motivated Cass to criticize the outgoing Buchanan administration and tender his resignation that year. He complained that Buchanan had failed to mobilize the military to protect federal interests in the South and avoid widespread secession.

Cass retired to Detroit, where he died at age 83 on June 17, 1866.

Coming From Cass

The power of the government should be limited to prevent tyranny.[1]

Did You Know?

Though not a religious man, Cass understood the value of religion in maintaining order in the American society. His wife Elizabeth was a devout Presbyterian. Cass often transported her and his children in a cart to church every Sunday but rarely attended service. He would then return to pick them up. Elizabeth tried in vain to convince her husband to join the church.[2]

14

Winfield Scott

Party: Whig
Birth state: Virginia
Represented: New Jersey
Year of defeat: 1852
Running mate: William Alexander Graham
Winner: Franklin Pierce
Campaign slogan: "We Polked You in '44, We Shall Pierce You in '52" (Pierce)
Other notable candidate: John P. Hale (Free Soil)

Major General Winfield Scott. Courtesy of the Library of Congress, Popular Graphic Arts Collection, LC-DIG-pga-09393

All About Scott

Born into wealth on June 13, 1786, Scott spent his early years on the Laurel Hill plantation near Petersburg, Virginia. His father William had fought in the Revolutionary War before settling as a planter and officer in the county militia. But Winfield's childhood was far from easy. His father died when he was six years old and his mother, who did not remarry, passed away a decade later. And most of the family wealth went to older brother James, who inherited the plantation.

Winfield attended a boarding school before attending the College of William and Mary, then left to study law in the office of David Robinson. During that time, he witnessed the 1807 trial of Aaron Burr, who had been accused of treason for an alleged plot to seize territory in Louisiana and build his own empire. The experience had a profound effect on his life. He strongly disliked the tactics of prosecuting attorney General James Wilkinson for providing forged evidence and false testimony. Scott was then driven toward a military career.

His first action was indeed harrowing. He was captured by the British along the Niagara frontier during the War of 1812 but was released before earning praise and national attention for his efforts at the battles of Chippewa and Lundy's Lane. Cadet and future president Ulysses S. Grant acclaimed him as "the finest specimen of manhood my eyes had ever beheld."[1]

Scott was also nicknamed "Old Fuss and Feathers" as a general for his inclination toward military showiness and etiquette. He loved dressing in uniforms that displayed the glorification of his rank.

His legacy, however, proved not as glorious in modern times. He led a force of 7,000 men in 1838 that drove Cherokee Indians from their lands in Georgia in what became known shamefully as the Trail of Tears. An estimated 4,000 out of 15,000 Native Americans died in the operation despite their peaceful intentions and attempted adoption of white culture. Scott's men burned their homes and stole their possessions before sending them away on foot with little food and few provisions.

In the first half of the nineteenth century, at least in the hearts and minds of most Americans, that did more to further his career than hinder it. Scott became commanding general of the US Army in 1841. Soon he grew motivated by presidential aspirations. When the Mexican-American War broke out five years later, he stayed in Washington while General Zachary Taylor was dispatched to lead the troops. Scott felt a strong sense of jealousy. And when Taylor faltered in his mission at the Battle of Monterrey, he bolted to Mexico inspired with thoughts of heroism.

He succeeded beyond his wildest dreams. Scott began his drive in March 1847 and successfully attacked the port city of Veracruz. He then led his men without the benefit of supplies to the capture of Mexico City six months later. Yet Scott had not achieved his goal. It was Taylor who won the presidency in 1848. Motivated to follow him to the White House, Scott earned the Whig nomination in 1852 but lost badly to Pierce.

His failure to secure a nomination in 1848 was generated by President Polk, who had recalled and replaced him to avoid furthering the reputation of a Whig general, as well as feuds generated by ambitious officers. Charges filed against Scott for disciplining his subordinates were eventually dropped and Congress even presented him with a gold medal while making him a lieutenant general, the first person to earn that rank since George Washington.

Issues of the Day

The most contentious issue during the 1852 campaign revolved around the Compromise of 1850, which had been introduced by Henry Clay and passed by Congress to avert—only temporarily as events would occur—a civil war.

The Compromise was spurred by the admission of California as a free state the previous year. In order to please Southern slave states it included the Fugitive Slave Act, which mandated that those suspected of being fugitive slaves and even those helping them flee be arrested. But in placating abolitionists in Northern states it abolished slavery in Washington DC. The Compromise also forced Texas to give up on its northernmost claims and established a territorial government in Utah and New Mexico.

Few liked the Compromise. Most Americans perceived more bad than good. Both sides dug in their heels further as tensions grew. The Compromise did nothing to avert a civil war that was now less than a decade away.

The 1852 Campaign

Scott made the mistake of joining President Fillmore in expressing support of the widely unpopular Compromise of 1850 while Pierce, who had emerged from a large field that included such political luminaries as Lewis Cass, Stephen Douglas, and James Buchanan as the Democratic candidate, wisely avoided declaring a position publicly.

The Democrats stressed their traditional policy of limited government, which continued to sway voters. Both parties, however, were accused of anti-Catholic and abolitionist stands as the North and South grew more polarized. The result was the lowest voter turnout of any election from 1840 to 1860.

Another defeat served to doom the Whig Party, which failed despite great effort to appeal Scott to Catholic and immigrant voters. The result was a landslide. Voters from the deep south in particular embraced the states' rights promises of the Democrats and gave Pierce more than 60 percent of their votes. Pierce also dominated all other areas of the country as only Kentucky, Tennessee, Vermont and Massachusetts case more ballots for Scott.

The Whigs would never again run a presidential candidate. It officially died in 1854, giving way to temporarily to the Know-Nothing Party and the growing power of Lincoln and the Republican Party.

After the Loss

Scott was aging as the Civil War approached. President Lincoln replaced the 75-year-old with General George B. McClellan. But Scott's offered strategies helped the Union win. His ideas regarding the battle of Vicksburg and during the march through Georgia to the sea, including the notion of living off the land and cutting rebel supply lines, proved vital to the eventual triumph.

Scott lived long enough to experience that victory. He retired to write his memoirs and tour Europe before dying two weeks before his 80th birthday on May 29, 1866.

Coming From Scott

I give it as my fixed opinion that but for our graduated cadets the war between the United States and Mexico might, and probably would, have lasted some four or five years, with, in its first half, more defeats than victories falling to our share and a peace without the loss of a single battle or skirmish.[2]

Did You Know?

Scott's hatred for Commanding General of the Army James Wilkinson continued into his own military career. He openly criticized Wilkinson, resulting in a court martial for insubordination in 1810 and suspension of his commission for one year.

15

John C. Fremont

Party: Republican
Birth state: Georgia
Represented: California
Year of defeat: 1856
Running mate: William Dayton
Winner: James Buchanan
Campaign Slogan: "Free Soil, Free Labor, Free Speech, Free Men, Fremont" (Fremont)
Other notable candidate: Millard Fillmore (Know Nothing)

John C. Frémont. Courtesy of the Library of Congress, Popular Graphic Arts Collection, LC-DIG-pga-07354

All About Fremont

The son of a French immigrant in a scandalous relationship, John was born on January 21, 1813, in Savannah, Georgia. His dad had run away with the young wife of an elderly Revolutionary War hero to begin a relationship before returning to John's mother, though the couple never married.

His father died when John was 13. Soon after, the teenager gained employment as a clerk in a local law office. Impressed by his acumen, the lawyer helped pay for his education. He demonstrated a particular aptitude in math and astronomy, skills that would prove quite useful in his later years as he explored the wilderness.

Fremont launched his career teaching math to US Navy cadets before accepting a job working on a government surveying expedition. That position allowed him to meet Missouri senator Thomas Benton and his daughter Jessie, with whom he eloped, to the outrage of her father. But the senator grew to respect Fremont and even promoted his professional talents. The influential Benton, a believer in Manifest Destiny, the theory of the inevitability of white domination of the North American continent, was consumed by Western expansionism. He gave Fremont a leadership role of an 1842 exploration beyond the Mississippi river to the Rocky Mountains along with legendary guide Kit Carson and a group of French trappers. Fremont reached the mountains, climbed its highest peak, and placed on it an American flag.

That journey gained Fremont fame and respect. He authored a detailed report that featured geographical data taken from astronomical readings. It was published in March 1843 and became must reading for many throughout the country. Americans perceived Fremont a hero for planting their flag atop a mountain in the West, much of which Spain and Great Britain still claimed as their own territory. He eventually became known as the Old Pathfinder.

Fremont continued to explore. He led expeditions in 1843 and 1844 to plot a route across the Rocky Mountains to Oregon. After completing the assignment he kept moving southward, then west across the Sierra Nevada mountain range into California despite the tough and dangerous terrain. He eventually returned to St. Louis, where the expedition had begun, and to Washington to write another report. A book that included both reports was published and widely read. They helped inspire fascination with the wide open spaces and a general migration westward in the United States.

By that time, he had accepted a commission into the Army and soon got himself into trouble for his rebelliousness. He returned to Northern California and disobeyed Army orders by revolting against Spanish rule there. Fremont was arrested and found guilty. And though President Polk overturned the court martial he was forced to resign from the Army.

Fremont was vindicated in 1848 when California was granted American statehood. He was placed in charge of another expedition to find a route for the transcontinental railroad and eventually served a short term as a California senator. The new Republican Party provided him an opportunity to further his political career and earn its first presidential nomination.

Issues of the Day

The secession of a series of Southern states was not motivated until after Republican abolitionist Abraham Lincoln won the 1860 election but slavery had been the most contentious issue in America for decades and continued to be in 1856. The party of Lincoln had been born with no pretense about the issue from which so many previous presidential candidates refused to take a strong stand in an attempt to avoid turning off large numbers of voters, particularly in the South.

First Republican presidential candidate John Fremont did not shy away in 1856—and it cost him the election. Among the issues on which he campaigned was the repeal of the Kansas–Nebraska Act that many believed would reopen the practice of slavery in the North. But voters fearful of a civil war were simply not prepared for their government to call for the end of slavery nationwide.

The 1856 Campaign

The divide driven by free and slave states became starker than ever in 1856 as that expressly abolitionist Fremont did not stand a chance in the South and lost enough other states to fall in a landslide after one of the most bitter campaigns in American history.

Fremont campaigned unapologetically on "slave power" and the repeal of the Kansas-Nebraska Act that allowed people on those territories to vote whether or not they wanted slavery. The battle between both sides in Kansas grew so heated and physical that the territory was nicknamed "Bleeding Kansas."

Democratic supporters, who called the Republicans a party of disunity and even characterized Fremont as a drunken bastard, pushed a platform of conciliation and state-by-state determination on the issue, warning that any other tact could result in a civil war. That failure to take a moral stand turned off abolitionists throughout the country and many Northerners but not enough to cost Buchanan the election. The Republicans adopted a stand that denied the right of Congress to give legal existence of slavery in the territories. One Ohio representative even called for a slave insurrection.

The result was an election decided along strict regional lines. Fremont, who even failed to make the ballot throughout the South, dominated New England and Great Lakes states while Buchanan capture nearly all the rest.

After the Loss

Fremont may have lost the election, despite his fame and national respect, but he remained active in the military, receiving another commission as a Union general in its first command in the Western United States. He jumped the gun on abolitionism, however, issuing an order not approved by President Lincoln to free slaves in his territory. That moral error in judgment resulted in him losing his post.

Lincoln fell out of favor among some in the party. Included was Fremont, who joined the Radical Republican, a splinter group of extreme abolitionists who did not believe the president was taking enough of a hardline antislavery stand during the war and felt bitterness of reconciliation with Southern states after it. The fly-by-night party nominated Fremont for president in 1864, but the campaign went nowhere. He withdrew his candidacy more than a month before the election.

Fremont bought what became known as the Southwest Pacific Railroad in 1866 but defaulted on the loan a year later and experienced worse financial trouble during the Panic of 1873, forcing him to move to New York City. He was appointed governor of the Arizona Territory by President Hayes in 1878 but felt little affinity for that job and spent little time in the area, motiving his resignation. His struggling family was forced to live on his wife's earnings as a writer.

Fremont spent his waning years on Staten Island until he died on July 13, 1890.

Coming From Fremont

"If I am elected to the high office for which your partiality has nominated me, I will endeavor to administer the Government according to the true spirit of the Constitution, as it was understood by the great men who framed and adopted it, and in such a way as to preserve both Liberty and the Union."[1]

Did You Know?

Since his father and mother both worked during John's youth, he was primarily raised by a house slave named Hannah.

16

John C. Breckinridge

Party: Southern Democratic
Birth state: Kentucky
Represented: Kentucky
Year of defeat: 1860
Running mate: Joseph Lane
Winner: Abraham Lincoln
Campaign slogan: "The Union Must and Shall Be Preserved!" (Lincoln)
Other Notable candidate: John Bell (Constitutional Union); Stephen Douglas (Democratic)

Hon. John C. Breckinridge. Courtesy of the Library of Congress, Popular Graphic Arts Collection, LC-DIG-pga-09111

All About Breckinridge

Breckinridge had politics in his blood when he was born on January 16, 1821, in Lexington, Kentucky. His grandfather was a US senator and served in the Jefferson administration as attorney general. His father was involved in state politics. Both men died young, however, and John was raised in his mother and grandmother.

Like so many of his political contemporaries and many that followed, Breckinridge studied law after attending Centre College in Danville. He left his home state to further his law education in prestigious Princeton University before returning to study law at Transylvania University and under Judge William Owsley in Lexington. He was admitted the bar in 1841.

Breckinridge was not long for Kentucky. He became part of western expansion by moving to Iowa to launch his practice and earn a sterling reputation as an orator. His stirring address at a funeral for Kentucky soldiers killed in the Mexican-American War gained great acclaim. He had earned the rank of major during that conflict before returning. Breckinridge soon returned to his home state to establish his law practice.

Soon he was dabbling in politics. He was elected into the Kentucky state legislature and then US House of Representatives through 1855. His antislavery stance coupled with a firm belief in states' rights was deemed contradictory by many. As a Democrat he even supported the colonization movement that advocated the freeing of slaves and their return to Africa. He was unafraid to back controversial legislation, including the Kansas–Nebraska Act, which repealed the Missouri Compromise and allowed territories to choose whether to allow or ban slavery. Though he felt it would soften the debate, it had an opposite effect, intensifying the rhetoric on both sides that led to the Civil War.

His star continued to rise. Despite refusing to run for reelection in the House and returning to Kentucky to resume his law practice, the Democrats thought highly enough of his appeal to place him as its vice-presidential candidate alongside James Buchanan in 1856. But his time in that position proved uneventful. Buchanan gave him little responsibility, though he was commended for presiding over the Senate during one of its most contentious periods ever.

The division among Democrats finally boiled over in 1860 when representatives from Southern states walked out of the convention in a prelude to secession. The Northern flank nominated Stephen Douglas while the Southern delegates chose Breckinridge. That split doomed both to defeat to Lincoln in a nation by that time with more abolitionist than proslavery voters.

Issues of the Day

The issue of slavery that would inspire southern states to secede from the union immediately after Lincoln was elected and result in the Civil War was of course front and center. The Republicans were united behind abolition and the Democrats were divided by region, leading to the formation of the Southern Democrats from which Breckinridge emerged.

Though slavery dominated the conversation in 1860 other issues played a role in the outcome, Included were a national tariff and a debate over the Homestead Act, which accelerated the settlement of the West by granting adult heads of families 160 acres of surveyed public land for a small fee and five years of residence. It was passed in 1862.

The 1860 Campaign

Lincoln traveled the country for more than a year making campaign speeches not only for himself but for other Republican candidates who would eventually feel indebted to him after he earned the nomination. Voters gravitated toward his logical oratory in support of abolitionism rather than the flowery, moralistic rhetoric to which they had grown accustomed.

Having never served in office, Lincoln boasted a nomination advantage over William Seward of New York, who was roundly criticized for his unyielding views against slavery that included strong opposition to the Compromise of 1850. It was feared that he could not work in a bipartisan manner to save the union from a civil war. And his controversial support for Irish immigrants who made up most of New York's voting bloc turned off former members of the antiimmigrant American Party, which were required to win Pennsylvania and the Great Lakes states.

Seward, however, appeared set to land the nomination until a movement to stop him on the first ballot gained traction. Lincoln finally convinced delegates to nominate him on the third ballot. The Republicans presented a moderate antislavery platform that opposed its extension westward and would eventually eliminate the practice throughout the country. It also attracted voters by endorsing a protection tariff, transcontinental railroad and the Homestead Act that promised free land to settlers.

Republican unity sharply contrasted Democratic dissent. It became obvious that Douglas could receive no support in the South. The convention walkout of Southern Democrats, spurred by the defeat of a proposed flank that would codify slavery into law, and nomination of both Douglas and Breckinridge all but handed the election to Lincoln. The Democrats even held a second convention in June to iron out their differences but to no avail.

That chaos and a perceived radicalism in the Republican platform inspired political leaders from 21 states, mostly aging Southern Whigs, to form the Constitutional Union Party and nominate veteran senator and Secretary of War John Bell of Tennessee, who supported slavery but not its expansion.

The campaign featured just one speech from Breckinridge and none from Lincoln or Bell. Only Douglas was on the public stump in his futile attempt to gain popularity. He disappointed Southern voters by stating that Lincoln should be embraced by Americans if he won and that secession should be rejected as an option.

Activists campaigned zealously for the other candidates. Bell supporters provided bells to ring at rallies. But Lincoln inspired the most enthusiasm. Thousands of young men engaged in "Wide Awake" torchlight parades, barbecues, picnics, rail-splitter battalions, and marches to show their support. They praised "Honest Abe" and encouraged voters to "Vote Yourself a Farm," in extolling Lincoln's backing of the Homestead Act.[1]

Lincoln opponents battled back, citing Breckinridge's inexperience in politic, questioning his intellect, and even claiming his presidency would embarrass. The *Charleston Mercury* ridiculed that it perceived as his facial ugliness while political cartoonists showed him dancing with Black women and championing race mixing. One particularly popular cartoon showed Lincoln steering a ship with a horribly stereotypical black man seen hutting a young white girl.

Those depictions certainly scared away many, but slavery supporters would not have voted for Lincoln anyway. He was not even on the ballot in Southern states. But the vast number of abolitionists voted for him in droves. Lincoln carried every state throughout New England and most of the Midwest and West, including California. His vote total nearly exceeded those of Bell and Breckinridge combined.

After the Loss

Before leaving his post as vice-president, Breckinridge was appointed to the US Senate by the Kentucky legislature. He hoped that as a Southern senator who did not support secession he could help negotiate a solution that would prevent war. But his political peers in the South were adamant. One after the other during a four-month period, starting a month after Lincoln assumed the presidency, they seceded and launched the Confederacy. Breckinridge worked tirelessly to influence Kentucky leaders to remain neutral. Pro-Union forces chose to align the state with the North.

Breckinridge, whose allegiances to the South overwhelmed any moral beliefs about slavery, fled to Virginia to join the Confederate Army, first as a brigadier general before his promotion to major general. He commanded troops into battle at Shiloh, Chickamauga, Chattanooga, and Cold Harbor. He even led a raid on Washington in 1864 that threatened the nation's capital, reaching Maryland before being repelled. That defeat stemmed the tide and the Union never lost its momentum. Confederate president Jefferson Davis appointed Breckinridge secretary of war headed in 1865 but his goals proved fruitless. The South was forced to surrender at Appomattox in April.

Fearful of retribution, Breckinridge left the country. He traveled by Cuba, then England, other parts of Europe and finally Canada. He did not return until President Johnson announced amnesty for Confederate as a Christmas Day present in 1868.

Breckinridge was done with politics. He relaunched his law practice and dabbled in the growing railroad industry before his death on May 17, 1875.

Coming From Breckinridge

I would prefer to see these States all reunited upon true constitutional principles. . . . But I infinitely prefer to see a peaceful separation of these States, than to see endless, aimless, devastating war, at the end of which I see the grave of public liberty and of personal freedom.[2]

Did You Know?

Breckinridge was elected vice-president at the age of 36. This was only one year older than the required minimum for the office as stated in the Constitution. He has the distinction of being the youngest vice-president in American history.

17

George B. McClellan

Major General George B. McClellan. Courtesy of the Library of Congress, Popular Graphic Arts Collection, LC-DIG-pga-09400

Party: Democratic
Birth state: Pennsylvania
Represented: New Jersey
Year of defeat: 1864
Running mate: George Pendleton
Winner: Abraham Lincoln (National Union)
Campaign Slogans: "An Honorable, Permanent, Happy Peace (McClellan); "Don't Change Horses Midstream" (Lincoln)
Confederate President: Jefferson Davis

All About McClellan

McClellan was born in Philadelphia on December 3, 1826, to his namesake father, a notable surgeon and founder of Jefferson Medical college. The boy's parents were of British and Dutch heritage. His great-grandfather was a brigadier general in the Revolutionary War.

The brilliant boy began attending the University of Pennsylvania at age 14. His original intent was to follow his father into the medical field, but the expense of such an endeavor for his parents forced him to study law instead. Two years later he dedicated himself to military service. The US Military Academy accepted him at age 15, waiving its minimum age requirement of 16. He befriended southerners at West Point and gained an appreciation of their thoughts and feelings that would remain with him for decades and lead to his policy ideas during the Civil War. McClellan graduated second in his class in 1846 and was soon commissioned a second lieutenant in the US Army Corps of Engineers.

It was in that job he fought in the Mexican-American War and earned a promotion to captain. He returned to West Point after the victory that expanded US territory 500,000 square miles westward and continued to work as an engineer for three years. McClellan was then transferred to the western frontier, where his talents drew the attention of future Confederate president Jefferson Davis, who was then US Secretary of War. Davis sent him to Europe to study military strategies being used in the Crimean War.

McClellan resigned from the military in 1858 to accept work as lead engineer of the just-constructed Illinois Central Railroad. Three years later, he had gained the presidency of the Ohio and Mississippi River Railroad in Cincinnati. But soon, the Civil War came calling. He opposed the abolition of slavery but yearned for the preservation of the United States. That was his motivation as he assumed command of a Union volunteer army in Ohio. His skill in whipping that outfit into shape and winning several battles in western Virginia earned him the nickname "Young Napoleon" and earned him a promotion to major general."[1]

So enamored was the US Army with his talents that after a distressing Union defeat in the First Battle of Bull Run, he was called in to replace Brigadier General Irvin McDowell and ordered to lead forces he organized into the legendary Army of the Potomac. He had assembled 168,000 troops by November to protect Washington, DC, further impressing his superiors, leading to yet another promotion to general-in-chief of the Union Army. McClellan warned that the Confederate Army, which many in the North felt would be defeated easily, was far stronger than intelligence had led them to believe. He added that a massive offensive would be the wrong tactic.

That led to a period of idleness that irked President Lincoln and Secretary of War Edwin Stanton. They ordered the Army of the Potomac to swing south into Confederate territory and removed McClellan from his post as general-in-chief in the notion that he focus entirely on the attack in what became known as the Peninsula Campaign.

Lincoln and McClellan disagreed on strategy. The president called for an overland campaign toward Richmond while McClellan suggested an amphibious maneuver that would send troops to the Virginia Peninsula avoiding the rebels under General George Johnston. His plan was adopted and began in March 1862. He landed over 120,000 men on the coast and moved east toward Richmond, the capital of the Confederacy, pushing the enemy back. His forces nearly reached Richmond but feared being outnumbered.

Iconic Confederate General Robert E. Lee took over the defense of Richmond and launched a series of offensives that climaxed in the Seven Day Battles. McClellan asked Lincoln for reinforcements that were refused, forcing him to retreat. The president had grown disenchanted with McClellan. But he continued to utilize him after the Confederate victory at the Second Battle of Bull Run. Lincoln returned McClellan to the defense of Washington. What the president perceived as a lack of gumption in fighting for the Union would soon motivate his ouster.

That arrived in September 1862 when Lee's forces attacked McClellan's men in Maryland, leading to the bloody Battle of Antietam. Union troops pierced the Confederate lines but again stalled. He kept one-third of his army in reserve, giving Lee a chance to retreat into Virginia. And though Antietam went down in history as a Union win, it did nothing to secure victory in the war. That Lee's army was allowed to remain intact angered Lincoln, who removed McClellan from command in November 1862.

A firm commitment to save the Union inspired McClellan to run for president in 1864 as a Democratic nominee. But the party was irreparably split along pro- and antiwar lines. With the Confederacy established and of course southerners who would have appreciated his position not voting, McClellan was beaten badly by the incumbent Lincoln.

Issues of the Day

It has been contended that 1864 was the most important election in American history. McClellan had been picked by Lincoln to command all Union forces early in the war. But the result was defeat after defeat. McClellan offered excuses for each rather than resolve and was removed by Lincoln in late 1862.

McClellan had never expressed respect for Lincoln, once calling him a "well-meaning baboon." He criticized the president's war policies in regard to slavery and the rights of slaveowners, so his choice as the Democratic nominee came as little surprise. Both he and running mate George Pendleton even supported making peace with the Confederates. They were not alone. Divisions grew over Lincoln's handling of the war and his release of the Emancipation Proclamation a year and a half earlier that dug both sides in for a long conflict. War weariness ran rampant in the North.

Lincoln believed that the McClellan plan would have nullified all the Union efforts, as well as the death and destruction in the bloody war, by allowing Southern states to rejoin the union and maintain slavery. Union soldiers and their families could not have disagreed more with McClellan. They did not want all those killed to die in vain. And after Northern forces quickly turned the tide and General Sherman captured Atlanta in September 1864, the result was never questioned.

The 1864 Campaign

That the 1864 campaign occurred at all is considered amazing. Historically, during civil wars, nations have been unable to following through with the election process, but Lincoln's popularity and the division among Democrats made the process easier and the outcome predictable.

Not that the incumbent expected a calm ride back to the White House. He feared defeat, greatly because radical Republicans who questioned his commitment to political equality for former slaves and opposed his lukewarm approach to Reconstruction. Oppositional Republicans passed the Wade–Davis bill that established a more severe Reconstruction model that required a loyalty oath from 50 percent of voters in the South. Lincoln vetoed the bill, motivating strong criticism from party members. It didn't matter. He was nominated on the first ballot at the convention in Cleveland. The radicals then staged their own convention, but never successfully launched the campaign of nominee John C. Fremont. Soon, all Republicans lined up to back Lincoln.

Not everyone did-. Harper's magazine listed all the abusive terms that had been applied to Lincoln in recent months, including despot, liar, thief, braggart, buffoon, fiend and butcher. The Democrats were confident that a war-weary nation would reject him. Many Americans hated the draft—Lincoln even had to send troops to quell a draft riot in New York City.

Democrats also excused him of censoring criticism in the press. But their party was doomed by its split into factions, one that favored McClellan and the other that backed Stephen Douglas. The party tried to claim Union efforts in the war a failure and demanded its end through negotiation but after the conflict began to swing decidedly in the North's favor, the outcome was never in doubt.

Lincoln, however, remained fearful that he was spending his last days in the White House. He even authored a short memo that he asked several members of his cabinet to sign without reading it. They did. It read:

> *This morning, as for some days past, it seems exceedingly probable that this Administration will not be re-elected. Then it will be my duty to so co-operate with the President elect, as to save the Union between the election and the inauguration; as he will have secured his election on such ground that he cannot possibly save it afterwards.*[2]

His worries were unwarranted. Lincoln won the election in a landslide, taking 55 percent of the popular vote and all but Delaware, Kentucky, and New Jersey.

After the Loss

McClellan did not fade into obscurity, but his days as a military and political bigwig were certainly over. McClellan resigned from the army and spent several years in Europe before returning to take over as president of the Atlantic and Great Western Railroad in 1872. From 1878 to 1881, he served one term as governor of New Jersey and later authored his memoirs, which were published after he died unexpectedly of a heart attack in 1885 at age 58.

Coming From McClellan

Conscious of my own weakness, I can only seek fervently the guidance of the Ruler of the Universe, and, relying on His all-powerful aid, do my best to restore Union and peace to a suffering people, and to establish and guard their liberties and rights.[3]

Did You Know?

McClellan was so disdainful of Lincoln that he once made the president wait a half hour to see him, and then had someone inform him that he had gone to bed.

18

Horatio Seymour

Party: Democratic

Birth state: New York

Represented: New York

Year of defeat: 1868

Running mate: Francis Preston Blair Jr.

Winner: Ulysses S. Grant

Campaign Slogan: "Let Us Have Peace" (Grant)

Horatio Seymour (with Frank P. Blair). Courtesy of the Library of Congress, Popular Graphic Arts Collection, LC-DIG-ds-00683

All About Seymour

Seymour was born to wealthy landowners in Pompey Hill, New York, on May 31, 1810. Schooled at the finest local academies, he studied law in Utica and passed the bar in 1832. But he felt no need to open a practice after inheriting his parents' estate.

That freedom from the daily grind of an attorney freed him to pursue a career in politics. So did his lack of children to raise after he married Mary Bleecker in 1835. He had by that time moved to Albany, where he joined the staff of Governor William Marcy. Within a decade, he had been elected to the New York state legislature, and then as mayor of Utica in 1842. Seymour returned to state politics a year later and earned praise for helping broker compromise between Democratic factions on issues and policy. He was soon elected speaker of the assembly.

Among his motivations was improvements to the Erie Canal. Seymour was a member of the "Hunker" wing in New York politics that favored state government backing for such internal projects and in general backed the work of President Polk. But Seymour had yet to dabble in national politics. His wealth allowed him to remain only involved in the statewide arena. He even retired for a while as the US–Mexican War raged and federal policies and efforts expanded slavery to more areas of the country.

Seymour tossed his hat back in the ring in 1850 but lost a campaign for governor that year. He tried again and won two years later and served from 1853 to 1855. He began to establish stronger views on national affairs. Seymour drove enactment of penal reform, opposed the growing prohibition movement, and nativism, which was the protection of native-born Americans against immigrants.

He wasn't long for the job. Seymour lost reelection in a four-way battle in 1854 that included candidates from the emerging Republican Party. A widening split among Democrats, particularly over slavery, during that time forced Seymour to choose sides. Though he retired to his farm, he toiled behind the scenes to keep the party united. But his support of Stephen Douglas for the presidency in 1860 certainly did not have the desired results. The fractious Democrats split regionally and Douglas not only lost badly to Abraham Lincoln but managed to win only Missouri. The Douglas policy backed by Seymour called for voters in Western territories to decide for themselves on the question of slavery. It was not a popular policy nationwide.

Seymour continued to work in vain for compromise. He opposed the secession of southern states after Lincoln won the White House, then strongly supported the Union during the Civil War. Motivated to make a difference, he ran and won the governorship of New York in 1862. Seymour toiled endlessly to meet military quotas despite criticizing Lincoln for his tendencies toward the centralization of power in the national government, declared emancipation of the slaves during wartime, the controversial draft, and a perceived suppression of individual liberties.

The draft was a particularly divisive issue in New York. Seymour tried to delay its employment, then limit its scope but could not stem the tide. Its implementation in 1863 sparked violent riots in New York City (as well as elsewhere throughout the North). Seymour traveled to the most populous city in America to speak to a furious mob and addressed them as "My friends" in an attempt to end the violence. Those two words inspired Republicans to forever claim him to be sympathetic to unpatriotic rabble rousers.[1]

The result was a lost reelection as governor in 1864. But Seymour was not done with politics. He continued to influence Democratic policy after the war, supporting a more lenient approach to Reconstruction and opposing the more vengeful and harsh viewpoints of radical Republicans. So enamored were some in his party that after a long deadlock he attracted enough delegates to win the Democratic nomination for president in 1868. Defeat seemed inevitable, and it certainly was despite his vigorous campaign that included an extensive speaking tour.

Issues of the Day

The first national election after the Civil War focused on debates over Reconstruction in the South and suffrage for the newly freed slaves.

Arguments about Reconstruction policy had resulted in the impeachment of President Andrew Johnson and military occupation of former Confederate states earlier that year as Republicans supported civil rights for all Americans while Democrats embraced the notion of states' rights in such political issues, which would have allowed Southern states to keep Black people away from the ballot box. That thinking eventually led to the Jim Crow era, which lasted a century in the South.

The 1868 Campaign

While the Johnson impeachment trial captured the most attention from Americans, the Republicans held their national convention in May and unanimously nominated Union military leader Ulysses S. Grant as their candidate. An era in which war heroes gained favor as presidential nominees continued.

The Democrats were far less united. They considered former Republican Samuel Chase, who had become an outcast from his party over its Reconstruction policies.

They also eyed George Pendleton, whose popularity stemmed from his advocacy of using paper money to pay down the national debt. But they settled on Seymour, who was deemed a "Copperhead" for his antiwar stance. The Republicans gained support throughout the nation for claiming Seymour was unpatriotic. Grant called for peace to a war-weary nation. It worked.

Seymour was doomed when a letter written by his running mate Francis Blair was published. It stated that Reconstruction should be voided and Southern states should be allowed to form new governments with their own rules that it was feared might include the inability of Black males to vote. Republicans associated Seymour with growing incidence of violence against freed slaves in the South and complicity in the draft riots in New York.

Seymour never recovered, though he fought hard. He only lost by 300,000 votes—it has been speculated that newly enfranchised black voters might have made the difference. The electoral voting proved more lopsided. The Grant victory established voting rights for all until Jim Crow laws adopted by Southern states destroyed that right for nearly a century.

After the Loss

His White House dreams dashed, Seymour mentored younger Democrats such as Samuel Tilden and future president Grover Alexander, both of whom served as New York governors. He lived long enough to see Alexander win the presidency before dying in 1886 in Utica.

Coming From Seymour

All virtue, patriotism, and intelligence seem to have fled from our National Capitol; it has been well likened to a conflagration of an asylum for madmen— some look on with idiotic imbecility, some in sullen silence, and some scatter the firebrands which consume the fabric above them and bring upon all a common destruction.[2]

Did You Know?

President Lincoln penned a letter to Seymour in 1863 basically asking him for a meeting and for more support for his war efforts as head of the "greatest State of the nation." Seymour never replied.[3]

19

Horace Greeley

Horace Greeley. Courtesy of the Library of Congress, Popular Graphic Arts Collection, LC-DIG-pga-11424

Party: Liberal Republican/Democratic
Birth state: New Hampshire
Represented: New York
Year of defeat: 1872
Running mate: Benjamin Gratz Brown
Winner: Ulysses S. Grant
Campaign Slogans: "Grant Us Another Term" (Grant)' "Throw the Rascals Out" (Greeley)

All About Greeley

Ask even the most historically inclined Americans about Horace Greeley and the first remembrance from their learning would be that as a newspaper editor in 1865, he once famously wrote, "Go west, young man." It was a call for Western expansionism and a reflection of his philosophy on Manifest Destiny. But his impact extended far beyond those four words.

Greeley did not enjoy the benefits of wealth into which so many presidential candidates in the past and among his contemporaries fell. He was born to a poor farming family near Amherst, New Hampshire, on February 3, 1811. But his curiosity and passion for reading served him well. He even sought an apprenticeship at a print shop at age 11 before landing a job in that field three years later in Vermont. He sent most of his earnings home to help feed his family.

He returned to farm like in his later teens before heading out to seek his fortune. Greeley soon became known as what would in later years be considered a Horatio Algier, rags-to-riches success story. He claimed to have arrived in New York City with twenty-five dollars in his pocket. Though critics charged that was merely a story to build his myth, he did thrive, first as a type-setter than as a journalist. Greeley wrote his first article in the *New Yorker* in the early spring of 1834, then became editor and publisher of that publication.

The wealth that followed allowed Greeley to launch the *New York Tribune*, which at the time was perceived among intellectuals as embracing the highest journalistic standards. He also gained fame as an orator through speaking engagements and eventually even authored several books, including notably *The American Conflict*, a history of the Civil War published before its conclusion.

Greeley began to form his worldviews decades earlier. He embraced associationism, a series of beliefs espoused by French intellectual Charles Fourier that predicted the inevitability of communal associations of people who worked and lived together. Greeley strongly supported equal rights (though his later attraction to the philosophy of Manifest Destiny indicated a belief in white superiority) and railed against economic monopolies and class dominance.

Despite his calls for equality, Greeley has been criticized historically for failing to take a strong stand against slavery as the country hurtled irretrievably toward civil war. His writings about the issue and the war itself became standards of political record but his views vacillated, which led to a decline in his popularity during the conflict.

The result was an unmerciful attack on his character after he decided to run for president in 1871 and landed the nomination from the splinter Liberal Republicans and despite support from the flailing Democrats.

Issues of the Day

The issues in 1872 extended beyond policy and into personal character, particularly that of Grant. Most did not question his honesty but did assert his administration was fraught with nepotism and corruption. Grant indeed appointed friends and relatives into his Cabinet and other high positions. And many proved to be inept and disturbingly crooked. Offered Iowa Senator James Grimes: "Like all parties that have an undisturbed power for a long time, it has become corrupt, and I believe that it is today the [most] corrupt and debauched political party that has ever existed."[1]

Debates continued to rage in the midst of the Reconstruction Era. Despite the furor targeting Grant he was renominated by the Republicans, who called for federal protection of Black rights. The birth of the Ku Klux Klan, which at first simply harassed freed slaves but had grown more violent, motivated such policies that included a continued occupation of former Confederate states. That angered a faction of the party known as Liberal Republicans who supported an end to federal control in that region and nominated Greeley, who was nevertheless also backed by the Democrats.

Women's rights and power also became an issue for the first time in national politics in 1872. Victoria Woodhull, picked by the Equal Rights Party, became the first woman to run for president. Her quite notable running mate was former slammed and legendary abolitionist Frederick Douglas.

The 1872 Campaign

By 1870, many Republicans had grown disenchanted with Grant and sought another candidate to replace him and his policies, including the continued occupation of the defeated South by federal troops and high tariffs that had remained since the war.

That led to the birth of the Liberal Republicans driven by such luminaries as Greeley, Missouri Senator Carl Schurz and Chief Justice of the Supreme Court Salmon P. Chase. Schurz hosted a meeting in January 1872 that called for an end to the spoils system employed by Grant. They also scheduled its own convention for May 1 in Cincinnati, where the enthusiastic splinter group showed its wide appeal. Wrote *Louisville Courier-Journal* editor Henry Watterson:

A livelier and more variegated omnium gatherum was never assembled. There were longhaired and spectacled doctrinaires from New England, spiced by stumpy and short-haired emissaries from New York.... There were brisk Westerners from Chicago and St. Louis.... There were a few rather overdressed persons from New Orleans ... and a motley array of Southerners of every sort.[2]

Schurz constructed a platform that denounced Grant as corrupt, sought an end to military reconstruction and called for equality and justice for all. Their first choice to run for president were Adams and Chase but neither gained enough delegates. The voting continued until suddenly a huge swing landed Greeley the nomination. That send shock waves through the nation. Greeley was considered by most intelligent, learned and idealistic, but he was certainly erratic in his behavior and never deemed politically competent. He was an easy target for Grant backers in the press. The *New York Times* even offered that if "any one man could send a great nation to the dogs, that man is Mr. Greeley."[3]

A few weeks after the upstarts met the regular Republicans met in Baltimore and renominated Grant with little fanfare. Their platform also stressed equal rights for all citizens. The Democrats were so determined to defeat Grant that they through caution to the wind and in just a six-hour meeting controversially voted to accept Greeley as their candidate despite his constant bad-mouthing of the party over the years.

The mudslinging began. Supporters on both sides unleashed malicious and often untrue charges against the other. Cartoonist Thomas Nast derided Greeley, depicting him as a dishonest, near-blinded, pumpkin-headed clown who knew nothing about the issues. Nast even depicted Greeley shaking hands with a rebel who had just shot a Union soldier, handing over a defenseless black man to the Ku Klux Klan and reaching his hand out to John Wilkes Booth across Lincoln's grave.

Greeley fought back. In an era in which it was still frowned-upon for presidential candidates to hit the stump he gave a series of well-received speeches condemning Republicans for their contentious rather than conciliatory policies in attempting to bring the nation together. Meanwhile, his supporters claimed Grant to be a drunken dictator and con man.

It wasn't nearly enough. The backing of Northern businessmen and bankers and traditional Republicans overwhelmed Greeley. He carried all but six states and snagged 286 of the 349 electoral votes, leading Greeley to write ruefully about his ruin and die soon thereafter.

After the Loss

His defeat left Greeley hurt and frustrated. So did the death of his wife shortly before the election. Greeley considered himself "the worst beaten man who ever ran for high office" and even spoke to a friend about contemplating suicide.[4]

More heartache followed. He returned to the *Tribune* in 1872 to resume his position as editor but was never accepted back. It was the final blow emotionally. He died three weeks later in a hospital for mental patients a broken man.

Coming From Greeley

Fame is a vapor, popularity is an accident, riches take wings, those who cheer today may curse tomorrow and only one thing endures—character.[5]

Did You Know?

Greeley worked hard to campaign for Whig candidate William Henry Harrison in 1840, publishing a supportive political journal titled *The Log Cabin* and even writing several campaign songs for the man nicknamed "Tippecanoe."

20

Samuel J. Tilden

Samuel J. Tilden. Courtesy of the Library of Congress, Popular Graphic Arts Collection, LC-DIG-ppmsca-46596

Party: Democrat
Birth state: New York
Represented: New York
Year of defeat: 1876
Running mate: Thomas A. Hendricks
Winner: Rutherford B. Hayes
Other notable candidate: Peter Cooper (Greenback)
Campaign slogans: "Hayes the True and Wheeler Too" (Hayes); "Tilden or Blood" (Tilden)

All About Tilden

Born on February 9, 1814, in New Lebanon, New York, Tilden was raised in modest circumstances by mother Polly and his father Elam, a farmer-turned-storekeeper who joined other family members to patent medicines such as Tilden's Extract, which was derived from cannabis and gained popularity during the nineteenth century and beyond. The boy was also descended from Nathaniel Tilden, an early English writer who arrived in North America in 1634.

A staunch democrat, Elam cultivated relationships with notable members of that party in the state, including future president Martin Van Buren, whom young Samuel idolized and helped inspire to pursue a political career. He studied politics constantly and read oriented works such as *The Wealth of Nations* to gain knowledge of national and international issues.

Continued physical struggles forced Tilden to drop out of the Williams Academy after three months, then Yale College following just one term at age 20. He finally entered law school at the University of the City of New York and graduated in 1841 before opening his own practice in that metropolis. Elam's connections with Democratic leaders proved quite beneficial. His son began writing campaign blurbs for party members. He also became rich as an attorney for railroad corporations.

Tilden eventually did more than dabble in politics. He served briefly in the state legislature, but his early work was mostly behind the scenes as a party organizer and strategist. His antislavery views mirrored those of Van Buren as he developed strong opinions on other issues of the day, including an opposition to the expansionist policies of President Polk. Tilden was so tied to Van Buren that he even left the Democratic Party in 1848 to support his hero's hopeless run for the presidency on the Free Soil ticket before rejoining the party a few years later. He gained interest in running for political office, but the growing divide among Democrats before the Civil War prevented him from even being nominated aside from an unsuccessful campaign for state attorney general in 1855.

The war did not motivate strong loyalties. Tilden supported the Union military effort and refused to back Democrats who wanted to end it and make peace. But he also criticized Radical Republicans and even Lincoln's Emancipation Proclamation that sought to free the slaves while the fighting continued. Tilden also opposed the draft, which precipitated riots in New York City and in other areas of the country. After the war he expressed favor with a less vengeful Reconstruction plan than what the Republicans in power produced.

Soon Tilden was serving as chair of the New York Democratic Committee, a post he maintained from 1866 to 1874. His influence on American politics grew as the national manager for Horatio Seymour presidential campaign in 1868. He earned acclaim for exposing the infamous, corrupt Tweed Ring political machine in New York City.

Tilden's stock was rising. His reputation as an honest reformer earned him election to the state legislature in 1872 and governorship two years later. His destruction of the Canal Ring, a group of contractors who had defrauded the state by overcharging for projects, increased his popularity.

That popularity in a huge electoral state motivated the Democrats to nominate him for president in 1876. His defeat after a highly contentious campaign and controversial election did not cause bitterness. Though unhappy with the final result, he accepted it.

Issues of the Day

A banking crisis that resulted in a spate of bank failures in the northeast and Midwest radically weakened American trust in President Grant, caused the Panic of 1873 and resulted in a severe depression that remained a huge issue throughout the campaign and into election day. Hayes and Tilden battled for the confidence of voters on economic issues. And when a series of scandals weakened Grant's popularity and Secretary of War William Belknap was impeached after having received kickbacks from a military trading post in Oklahoma, Hayes found a steeper hill to climb toward the presidency.

Meanwhile, criticism over federal policy on Reconstruction grew in intensity. Constitutional amendments granting citizenship to Black Americans spurred violence against them in the South but northerners became increasingly disinterested, particularly as their own lives had been negatively impacted by economic distress. Legislation supported by Grant, including the Ku Klux Klan Act of 1871, sought to halt such attacks and protect civil rights. But they only achieved fleeting success. In fact, the Justice Department curbed prosecutions against violators of the Enforcement Acts during Grant's second term. And the Supreme Court tossed out convictions, including one in 1873 in which 150 armed White men murdered about 150 Black militia that had seized control of a courthouse in Colfax, Louisiana. Those killed had even surrendered.

Radical Republicans who had controlled national policy after the Civil War were becoming increasingly unpopular. Hayes tried to soothe voters who had become weary of Reconstruction and what many considered harsh and vengeful actions against the South. He penned a letter accepting the Republican nomination that suggested reconciliation and a new way forward giving more power to state and local governments. It would lead the way to Jim Crow laws in the South that separated the races and discriminated against African-Americans for nearly a century. It read:

> *The moral and material prosperity of the Southern States can be most effectually advanced by a hearty and generous recognition of the rights of all, by a recognition without reserve or exception . . . the efforts of the people of those States, to obtain for themselves the blessings of honest and capable local government. If elected, I shall consider it not only my duty, but it will be my ardent desire to labor for the attainment of this end. Let me assure my countrymen of the Southern States that if I shall be charged with the duty of organizing an Administration, it will be one which will regard and cherish their truest interests and the interests of the white, and of the colored people both, and equally; and which will put forth its best efforts in behalf of a civil policy, which will wipe our forever the distinction between the North and South in our common country.*[1]

His words were meant not only to sway southern voters but those in the north as well who believed it was time for military intervention in the former Confederacy states to end. Though Hayes did gain favor from some he also ruffled many feathers. Tilden was destined to run a viable campaign that nearly swept him into the White House.

The 1876 Campaign

Ku Klux Klan terrorism against Black men and their families worsened in the South in 1876, especially in South Carolina. Many were murdered and their homes destroyed. The suppression of Black voting would continue for nearly 90 years.

But it was not the campaign itself that grabbed the headlines. It was the election. Skullduggery ruled the day. It appeared on election night that Hayes had lost. The New York Times even dispatched a telegram to Hayes informing him of his defeat.

That was far from sufficient for Hayes. A bit of math confirmed that if he maintained his victories in the North and carried more southern states he could beat Tilden by one electoral vote. When Republican election boards in South Carolina, Florida and Louisiana all declared Hayes the winner in their states, Democrats contested those tallies, causing rival state governments in South Carolina and Louisiana to form and send competing results. Meanwhile, Hayes won Oregon but a question of one elector's eligibility caused another dispute.

The entire system seemed out of whack. Tilden won the popular vote by 200,000, but when the dust settled, he had lost the electoral college, 185–184. The outcome remained in question throughout the winter as both sides claimed victory and threatened violence, even an insurrection. The rallying cry "Tilden or War" was uttered emphatically by some Democratic voters and in Congress.

The rhetoric from Tilden supporters did not sway either candidate. Neither plotted to seize power or question Congressional power to decide the winner. Congress created an independent election commission favored by Democrats as their candidate had lost the electoral count that was being disputed. But enough Republicans backed the idea to make it a reality. Yet, Tilden asserted the commission to be unconstitutional.

It moved forward with five House of Representatives members, five senators and five Supreme Court justices. That led to further controversy regarding its political makeup. One example was Associate Justice David Davis, who was believed to be an independent but Tilden supporters considered an ally who would tilt the commission voting in their direction. Republicans feared the same and worked to disqualify Davis, who surprised everyone by resigning from the Supreme Court and forfeiting his spot on the commission.

A series of 8–7 votes in favor of Hayes seemed to have decided the issue. But Tilden backers introduced measures to stall the final electoral college vote count in the House. Many thought there would be no president to legally inaugurate on March 4. But Hayes was officially declared the winner two days earlier.

Even that did not end the controversy. President Grant feared violence or even a coup on inauguration day. He pushed it back to Monday, March 5, and insisted that Hayes take the Oath of Office at the White House before the official ceremony.

That moment marked the end of Reconstruction and federal military presence in the South. It in turn led to the further disenfranchisement and harassment of Black voters. Hayes withdrew his troops in South Carolina and Louisiana within two months of taking office. Soon the Jim Crow years would begin.

After the Loss

The loss ended Tilden's political career. He declined to run again in 1880 despite widespread support among Democrats. Declining health made the same decision for him in 1884. He retired to his estate near Yonkers and lived as a recluse as a bachelor until his death on August 4, 1886.

Coming From Tilden

I was never a Republican, because those gentlemen, distinguished as they are, have only one real interest, and that is the making of special laws in order to protect their fortunes. I also know they have no compassion for the masses of the people in this country who are without money and who are, many of them, without food or houses. I have always thought that only as a Democrat, reflecting Jefferson and Jackson, could justice ever be done the people because, at this moment in history, ours is the only party which is even faintly responsive to the force of ideas.[2]

Did You Know?

Tilden was the first New York governor to live in the Executive Mansion in Albany, which remains the residence for those in that office today.

21

Winfield Scott Hancock

THE BIRD TO BET ON!

The bird to bet on: Winfield Scott Hancock. Courtesy of the Library of Congress, Popular Graphic Arts Collection, LC-DIG-ds-00857

Party: Democrat
Birth state: Pennsylvania
Represented: Pennsylvania
Year of defeat: 1880
Running mate: William H. English
Winner: James A. Garfield
Other notable candidate: James B. Weaver (Greenback)
Campaign slogan: "Cutting a Swath to the White House" (Garfield)

All About Hancock

Named after War of 1812 commander Winfield Scott, Hancock was born on February 14, 1824, in Montgomery Square, Pennsylvania. His father Benjamin Franklin Hancock boasted an even more famous namesake. The family moved Winfield and twin brother Hilary to nearby Norristown when they were three years old. That is where Benjamin, a schoolteacher aspiring attorney, passed his bar and mother Elizabeth opened a millinery shop. Soon, a third brother joined the family.

Young Winfield attended a local academy before transferring to a public school. His interest in military affairs became pronounced. Perhaps inspired by the soldier after whom he was named, he enrolled at West Point at age 16. Among his classmates and military school contemporaries were future war heroes and one president—Alexander Hays, Ambrose Burnside and Ulysses S. Grant. Scott graduated in 1844 and earned the rank of second lieutenant assigned to Fort Towson, an Army outpost in the Indian Territory of modern-day Oklahoma. He spent two years with the sixth infantry there before the Mexican–American War began.

Hancock was disappointed at not being sent to battle. He was ordered to Kentucky to train troops, failing time and again to convince his superiors to allow him to fight. Finally, and coincidentally, his namesake General Winfield Scott requested that he join him in his Mexico City campaign. Hancock was soon leading a small regiment into the Battle of Churubusco, which eventually led to the capture of Mexico City and where he was slightly wounded. That earned him a promotion to first lieutenant.

Hancock became a military nomad. Promoted to captain in 1855, he later fought against the Seminole Indians and saw combat in battles between pro- and antislavery forces in the Kansas Territory. Then, he was dispatched to work as a quartermaster in Los Angeles until after the Civil War began. He embraced the Democratic platform of the time that favored states' rights and amounted to the continuation of slavery in the South. But though he made many friends from the south and disagreed with President Lincoln, he was loyal to the Union cause as a means to preserve the United States of America.

Hancock was sent to Washington DC to work as a quartermaster as the war intensified in 1861. He was then promoted to brigadier general of the Volunteer Corps and commanded a brigade in the Army of the Potomac and earned praise from Union commander George McClellan for his leadership in the Battle of Williamsburg in May 1862. He headed a division in the bloody Battle of Antietam four months later. That led to yet another promotion to Major General.

Wounded several times, Hancock continued to help the North achieve victory. He even led his Second Corps into the notorious three-day Battle of Gettysburg and a showdown against iconic Confederate general Robert E. Lee. He commanded on horseback, inspiring his soldiers. Hancock remained steadfast after a battle punctured his inner right thigh. Hancock refused to leave his men alone on the battlefield. The result was a Union victory that is still considered historically the turning point of the war.

He also distinguished himself at the Battles of Wilderness and Spotsylvania Courthouse but defeats and poor strategy decisions followed. His troops were routed at Reams' Station in late August 1864, which forced his resignation and work as a mere recruiter.

Though his army commands had helped Union forces win the war, he was not in charge militarily when the victory was accomplished. And Grant was not enamored with him after the guns fell silent. Hancock was far too sympathetic toward the South in the president's mind. That led to Hancock's dismissal from the Volunteer Corps in 1866.

Strangely, however, on that same day, he was promoted to major general of the Regular Army. He assumed command of the Department of the East in 1877, but had by that time also dabbled in politics. Hancock was even considered a Democratic presidential contender in 1868, well before landing the nomination in 1880 and losing a taut battle to Garfield.

Issues of the Day

By 1880, the spotlight on racism targeting Blacks and Native Americans had shifted to Chinese immigrants, particularly in the ever-expanding West. Violence against the group that had been coming to America since 1849 to mine gold and work the railroads—mostly boys and young men—was increasing despite their earnings of just pennies on the hour as cheap labor.

Income did not matter to those who feared that Chinese immigrants would take their jobs. Their anger was inflamed two days before the 1880 election by a letter purported to have been written by Republican candidate James Garfield and posted on store windows throughout the West. That enflamed hostilities. So did newspaper editorials that claimed Chinese immigration to be no less than an invasion.

The problem was particularly acute in Denver, where a Halloween riot began when an unprovoked white man slugged a Chinese man. Soon, thousands gathered in Chinatown to scream angry anti-Chinese epithets and rail against Garfield. Violence ensued. Chinese homes were looted, laundromats destroyed. Chinese men were attacked. Denver firefighters used water hoses to quell the riot but were hit by bricks. Even prostitutes got into the act, protecting Chinese men by brandishing stove pokers, champagne bottles and a shotgun at the mob. When it was over nearly every Chinese home and business was demolished and one Chinese man had been hanged.

Garfield had not only referred to Chinese immigration in his letter. He called for equal protection for White and Black Americans, financial support for schools and maintenance of the gold standard. And his message was far from an invitation for unlimited Chinese immigration. He asserted the need for negotiations with China to limit the influx. And though the issue was not the deciding factor in the election, it mattered to many voters in the West. They sided with the Democrats, who called for a ban on Chinese immigrants.

Among the other prominent issues weighed by the parties and voters was tariffs. Republicans supported strong tariff protection to limit foreign competition while the Democrats favored a milder tariff policy. Both sides also pitched civil service reform but the Democrats sought to leverage it into a bigger issue, accusing Garfield and vice presidentialVP candidate Chester Arthur of political corruption.

The 1880 Campaign

Garfield was among the first presidential candidates to break the mold in an era when it was still considered bad form to campaign actively. He hosted reporters and voters from the front porch of his home in Mentor, Ohio, giving speeches and answering questions. But he slipped up in October during one of those events when he claimed tariffs to be only a local issue. That turned off voters elsewhere who believed themselves to be personally affected.

Hancock continued to call for greater autonomy for former Confederate states, which resulted in a sweep of the South, as well as bordering states such as Missouri, Kentucky, Maryland, West Virginia, and even Delaware. He even won Nevada and California. He fell just 10,000 popular votes short of Garfield but was defeated badly in the rest of the country, and even lost some votes to the Greenback Party, which advocated an expanded currency as well as government regulation of labor and industry. The electoral college vote more decidedly favored Garfield.

After the Loss

Still in charge of his department on Governor's Island in New York, and despite his previous clashes with Grant, he oversaw the funeral arrangements of the former president in 1885. Hancock organized the nine-mile procession in New York City and directed a moment of silence and respect to those attending. He would soon join Grant in the great beyond, passing away at age 61 early the following year.

Coming From Hancock

My politics are of a practical kind—the integrity of the country, the supremacy of the Federal government, an honorable peace, or none at all.[1]

Did You Know?

Hancock's strong leadership at the Battle of Williamsburg in 1862 was described by Major General George McClellan as "superb." Supporters took those words and ran with them, nicknaming Hancock forever thereafter as "Hancock the Superb."[2]

22

James G. Blaine

James G. Blaine. Courtesy of the Library of Congress, Popular Graphic Arts Collection, LC-DIG-pga-08098

Party: Republican6
Birth state: Pennsylvania
Represented: Maine
Year of defeat: 1884
Running mate: John Logan
Winner: Grover Cleveland (Democrat)
Other notable candidates: John St. John (Prohibition); Benjamin Butler (Greenback/Anti-Monopoly)
Campaign slogan: "Blaine, Blaine, James G. Blaine! The continental liar from the state of Maine!" (Cleveland)

All About Blaine

Blaine was born into wealth on the last day of January 1830 at Indian Hill Farm near West Brownsville, Pennsylvania. Parents Ephraim and Maria were among the largest landowners in the state. He proved himself in the classroom at an early age, earning enrollment at Washington and Jefferson College in Western Pennsylvania at 13 and graduating near the top of his class four years later.

Work as a teacher at Western Military Institute in Kentucky followed, but soon thereafter, he moved to Philadelphia for work at the Pennsylvania Institute for the Blind. He began studying law in his spare time. In 1854, he and wife Harriet moved to her hometown of Augusta, Maine, where he served as editor of two local newspapers, helped form the state Republican Party and launched himself into politics.

Blaine was elected to the state legislature, serving from 1859 to 1862, quickly establishing himself as house speaker. Soon, he earned a reputation as a political leaderm setting his sights as a candidate at the national level. He was elected to the US House of Representatives in 1863 and remained there through three elections, Blaine was even elected three times as Speaker of the House.

By that time, he had gained a reputation as a supporter of Radical Reconstruction after having backed the impeachment of President Andrew Johnson. But he embraced a more moderate position on such timely economic issues as tariffs. The centrist wing of his Republican Party was known as the "Half Breeds" who opposed both President Grant's conservatism and the liberal faction led by Senator Carl Schurz.

By the mid-1870s, Blaine was cited as a leading presidential candidate. He was the favorite to land the Republican nomination in 1876, but his opportunity was hampered by the unveiling of the "Mulligan Letters" that alleged he was involved in graft involving railroad companies. Despite the charge, he led on the first six ballots before anti-Blaine Republicans successfully pushed instead for Rutherford B. Hayes.

Blaine, however, emerged from the event still a force within the party. He was praised for his legislative talents and patriotism, as well as his desire to preserve in Congress the freedoms for all for which Union soldiers died in the Civil War. Blaine resigned from Congress soon after the 1876 convention to replace the retired Lot Morrill as a Maine junior senator, then won an election for that seat five years later. His reputation earned him positions as chairman of the Committee on Rules and the Committee on Civil Service and Retrenchment.

His name continued to arise as a presidential candidate, first as a threat to Grant in 1880 along with Senator John Sherman of Ohio. But another convention deadlock doomed both as James Garfield emerged as the winner on the 34th ballot. Blaine did not respond with bitterness. He fought hard to get Garfield elected and was rewarded with an appointment as Secretary of State. Among his achievements was setting in motion negotiations that eventually resulted in the construction of the Panama Canal.

The assassination of Garfield changed everything for Blaine. He remained at his post for a brief time in the Chester Arthur administration before resigning in 1881 to begin writing his memoirs. But another chance at the Republican nomination occurred three years later. Popular Civil War general William Tecumseh Sherman was considered a threat but he never threw his hat into the ring. Blaine won the nomination and battled Democrat Grover Cleveland for the presidency. Cleveland was supported by independent Republicans called the "Mugwumps" who railed against Blaine's alleged corruption and opposition to civil service reform. That split hurt Blaine, who lost a close race to Cleveland.

Issues of the Day

Though Blaine made his strong support of tariff protection a spotlight issue in his campaign, charges of immorality on both sides grabbed the headlines away from policy from the start. Cleveland preached the need for honesty in claiming his opponent to be a crook who as Speaker of the House had schemed to blackmail the railroad industry. The result was demonstrations on Wall Street in New York against perceived money interests driving Blaine's presidential motivations. Cleveland seized upon public sentiment by casting the entire Republican Party as corrupt and beholden only to the rich.

Blaine and the Democrats countered with charges that Cleveland fathered an illegitimate child with a woman whom he then sent to an insane asylum. The Democrat did not deny it, motivating the Republican press to pounce and portray Cleveland as morally unfit for office. That party offered that the choice between Blaine and Cleveland was one between "the brothel and the family, between indecency and decency, between lust and law." And one popular Republican cartoon caption mocked Cleveland by reading, "Ma, Ma, Where's my Pa?"[1]

Only the last vestiges of Reconstruction remained by 1884. Many of its goals had failed in the South, where the push for equal rights and protection under the law had fallen victim to the growing violence against African-Americans that limited their societal influence and would eventually make them second-class citizens. That led to further division in the country. Southern voters continued to often cast ballots in favor of candidates that would further the cause of segregation. The result was the rejection of Republican candidates in favor of Democrats, whose states' rights platforms proved more popular in that region.

The conceivability of prohibition and perceived worsening drunkenness among Americans also swelled as an issue in 1884. A Republican campaign slogan asserting the Democrats to be the party of "Rum, Romanism and Rebellion" spoke volumes about how the Grand Old Party (GOP) wanted to paint its opponents.

The 1884 Campaign

Cleveland could not deny fathering an illegitimate child, an admission that forced him to stop making speeches and handing the campaigning over to his surrogates. They were told to defend him by admitting his guilt, but claiming such a transgression only happened once. Voters were told that while Cleveland fell to temptation in his private life, Blaine was corrupt as a politician.

Blaine made a fatal mistake late in the campaign as he fought for votes from the growing Catholic population. Reared as a Presbyterian, he proposed a constitutional amendment that would restrict all federal funds from going to religiously affiliated schools. It passed in the House but failed in the Senate. Its failure haunted the Blaine camp. Democrats contended he was anti-Catholic. Then, as the campaign wound down, he visited a group of Protestant ministers in New York. Welcoming speaker Rev. Dr. Samuel Burchard criticized Republicans as the party of "Rum, Romanism, and Rebellion." Those words were picked up by the Democratic National Committee, who used them to further undermine Blaine.

Those issues likely turned a Blaine victory into a close defeat. He lost by less than 58,000 popular votes and 37 votes in the electoral college. He dominated much of the Midwest and Western states and even won Massachusetts but Cleveland took New York, Texas, and the entire South.

After the Loss

Blaine continued to plug away. After finishing a second volume of his memoirs and a tour of Europe, when he met many heads of states, he tried again for the Republican nomination in 1888. He was even considered the frontrunner, but his ambitions were overtaken by his loyalty to the party. Blaine declined to enter the race in the fear that it would cause more division among Republicans and toiled tirelessly to nominate Benjamin Harrison, who won the election and placed him back to his position of Secretary of State. He chaired the first Pan-American Conference and fought for a reciprocal tariff agreement between Latin America and the United States.

Blaine resigned from the cabinet in 1892 to try yet again for the Republican nomination, this time against the incumbent Harrison, who was chosen on the first ballot with Blaine and William McKinley nearly tied and far behind. Blaine would not have served even if he won. He died on January 27, 1893.

Coming From Blaine

The United States is the only country with a known birthday. All the rest began, they know not when, and grew into power, they know not how. If there had been no Independence Day, England and America combined would not be so great as each actually is. There is no "Republican," no "Democrat," on the Fourth of July— all are Americans. All feel that their country is greater than party.[2]

Did You Know?

Robert Ingersoll, a noted author, lawyer and orator who placed Blaine into nomination at the 1876 Republican Convention, certainly held him in high esteem. He referred to Blaine as an "armed warrior" and a "Plumed Knight."[3]

23

Grover Cleveland

Grover Cleveland. Courtesy of the Library of Congress, Popular Graphic Arts Collection, LC-DIG-ppmsca-46707

Party: Democratic
Birth state: New Jersey
Represented: New York
Year of defeat: 1888
Running mate: Allen G. Thurman
Winner: Benjamin Harrison (Republican)
Other notable candidates: Clinton B. Fisk (Prohibition); Alson Streeter (Union/Labor)
Campaign slogans: "Rejuvenated Republicanism" (Harrison); "Unnecessary Taxation Oppresses Industry" (Cleveland)

All About Cleveland

Few babies in America would have seemed less likely to become president than Grover Cleveland when he was born the son of Reverend Richard Cleveland on March 18, 1837, in Caldwell, New Jersey. His father was a Yale-educated Presbyterian minister but had little money to provide for his family. Young Grover grew up in the central New York towns of Fayetteville and Clinton, where his father served in the church until he died when his son was 16.

His father's death forced Cleveland to sacrifice his desire to attend college in favor of work to support the family, first as a clerk then as a part-time law student in Buffalo, despite never receiving a college education. He was admitted to the bar in 1858 at age 22.

Cleveland spent the Civil War as an assistant district attorney in Erie County. He avoided the controversial draft in New York and military service by hiring a replacement as a solder for $300. That would come back to haunt him during his political career as opponents deemed him a coward and a slacker. But he gained a positive reputation for his strong work ethic and effectiveness as a lawyer that superseded such negative accusations. Particularly impressive was his ability to memorize arguments before judges and juries. He would eventually deliver his inaugural address as president without the benefits of notes—a first in American history.

After three years as Erie County sheriff, Cleveland returned to his law practice and enjoyed a wide range of simple activities, frequenting restaurants and saloons, hunting and fishing with friends, and attending poker parties. But he was far from a cultural sort, rarely listening to music, reading fiction or poetry, or even traveling.

He did dabble in Democratic organizing but avoided partisan politics. So he was stunned when he was chosen to run for mayor of Buffalo. He accepted the challenge as an underdog, however, and shocked everyone by winning. His effectiveness uncovering graft and corruption and efficiently saving taxpayer money further ingratiated him to the party. Soon, Cleveland was nominated to run for governor of New York. His reputation and girth grew (he weighed 280 pounds and was nicknamed Uncle Jumbo) as he was again elected and served from 1882 to 1884. Using the same strategies that earned him favor in Buffalo, he vetoed big-spending projects and challenged the significantly corrupt Tammany Hall political machine based in New York City. His work ethic inspired fellow Democrats to tout him as a potential presidential candidate.

That was not the only attraction for supporters. Cleveland was rightly considered a reformer who would crack down on business fraud. This earned him the backing not only of Democrats but Republicans known as "Mugwumps" for their opposition of traditional party hopefuls. Cleveland was also seen as a down-to-earth alternative. He felt uncomfortable with the trappings of the presidency after winning in 1884, particularly the environment in the White House. He once penned a letter to a friend that expressed his unease. "I must go to dinner," he wrote, "but I wish it was to eat a pickled herring, a Swiss cheese and a chop at Louis' instead of the French stuff I shall find."[1]

Cleveland, the only bachelor president, finally tied the knot in June 1886, marrying 21-year-old Frances Folsom. But more importantly and often controversially, he worked to maintain a policy to deny favors to any economic group. That would sometimes bring criticism—he even vetoed a bill to provide $10,000 worth of seed grain to drought-stricken farmers in Texas and another to make pension payments to Civil War veterans he suspected to be fraudulent. Cleveland enraged railroad bigwigs by ordering an investigation of western lands they held by government grant, then forcing them to return 81 million acres.

His administration continued to work in what he perceived to be an ethical manner despite making enemies of many voters and colleagues in government. Among his projects was to force Congress to lower protective tariffs.

Cleveland remained popular enough to earn more votes than Harrison in 1888 but he lost the electoral count.

Issues of the Day

Tariffs were thrust center stage in 1888 by President Cleveland when he devoted his entire message to Congress on the controversial issue in December 1887. He understood that Republicans could run hard on tariffs that millions of Americans believed protected businesses from foreign competition. But he emphasized his plan to lower tariffs and the morality of standing up for what he believed in.

The tariff debate leaked into both party conventions. The Democrats renominated Cleveland by acclamation and provided aging-but-loyal tariff revisionist senator Allen Thurman as his running mate. They sought to drastically reduce tariffs on foreign goods. The Republicans selected prime protectionist Benjamin Harrison and like-minded Levi Morton, a wealthy New York banker, to run for vice-president. Their policy was driven by a desire for consumers to buy domestically produced goods.

Cleveland also took a stance against Civil War pensions and inflated currency, which deflated the purchasing power of money and weakened the chance of inflation. That made him unpopular with Civil War veterans and farmers despite his overall support in Southern states. Another problem for Cleveland arose when he was endorsed by British Ambassador Lord Lionel Sackville under the pseudonym Charles Murchison, thereby growing anti-British sentiment and tying the incumbent to foreign interests. Harrison was not immune to scandal either. He was linked to Republican National Convention treasurer W.W. Dudley, who penned a letter to surrogates instructing them how to bribe voters in Indiana.

The 1888 Campaign

Harrison vowed to keep his campaign clean and principled, nipping negative rhetoric in the bud and focusing on convincing voters only of his positive attributes rather than get personal about his opponent. Then, his fellow Republicans broke that promise, calling Cleveland the "Beast of Buffalo" and claiming he had beaten his new bride in a drunken rage, prompting a fierce denial from the Frist Lady, who added that her husband was kind and considerate.[2]

The Democrats did not respond with personal attacks against Harrison. But they implied he was weak and blasted his perceived anti-union stand. They called him a religious bigot who supported Chinese immigration to keep wages low in America. Both candidates spoke fanatically about the contentious issue of tariffs.

Harrison was backed by a Republican party with more funds and organization than the Democrats. He was far more active in personally imploring voters to cast their ballots for him with "front porch" campaigning from Indianapolis for reporters. Thousands attended his speeches in his hometown to hear him rail on about tariffs and other issues, then reported them in newspapers throughout the country. Using money from industrialists who backed Harrison policies, the Republicans circulated millions of pamphlets, flyers, and handbills, and dispatched surrogates such as James Blaine to stump for Harrison. Manufacturers even warned their workers of layoffs if they voted Democratic.

Meanwhile, Cleveland declined to campaign for himself. He embraced the traditional strategy that voters were turned off by such direct soliciting of support. He even refused to allow Cabinet members to stump for him. That left the dirty work to 75-year-old running mate Allen Thurman, who traveled the nation to inform the public that Cleveland favored moderate reductions of tariff duties.

What Thurman did not tell anyone was about his own physical limitations. He even collapsed on the platform on one occasion.

The Democrats were overwhelmed financially and organizationally. But not at the ballot box. They dominated the South and won 90,000 more popular votes than Harrison. But the Republican captured the biggest electoral college prizes of New York and throughout the Midwest to take his party back to the White House.

After the Loss

Cleveland returned to the White House with a victory in 1892. His second tenure was highlighted by dealing directly with the Treasury, trying to get to the root of the problem that was resulting in business failures, farm foreclosures, and unemployment ravaging the American people. When Cleveland sent federal troops to enforce an injunction against striking railroad workers, he declared that post cards would get through come hell or high water.

Though many folks agreed with his harsh treatment of striking railroad workers, most railed against his policies during a period of economic crisis. The result was the rejection of his own party and the nomination of William Jennings Bryan in 1896. That forced Cleveland into retirement. He spent his last years in Princeton, New Jersey, and died in 1908.

Coming From Cleveland

What is the use of being elected or re-elected unless you stand for something?[3]

Did You Know?

Cleveland was a distant relative of Moses Cleaveland, who founded the Northeast Ohio city. But Grover Cleveland never lived in Ohio.

24

Benjamin Harrison

Benjamin Harrison. Courtesy of the Library of Congress, LC-DIG-ppmsca-55341

Party: Republican
Birth state: Ohio
Represented: Indiana
Year of defeat: 1892
Running mate: Whitelaw Reid
Winner: Grover Cleveland (Democrat)
Other notable candidate: James B. Weaver (Populist)
Campaign slogans: "Protection-Reciprocity-Honest Money" (Harrison); "Our Choice: Cleve and Steve" (Cleveland); "Equal Rights to All, Special Privileges to None," (Weaver)

All About Harrison

Harrison had politics in his blood from the moment he was born on August 20, 1833, in the cozy rural town of North Bend, Ohio. He was the great grandson of Colonel Benjamin Harrison, who signed the Declaration of Independence, and grandson of President William Henry Harrison. Even his father John Scott Harrison served as a congressman.

Young Benjamin was raised comfortably. He spent his youth hunting, fishing, and tending to livestock on the family farm. His parents could afford private tutors, allowing him to stay close to home. That sense of order gave him confidence that remained with him throughout his life, though others perceived it as inflated self-importance. His personality featured a rather stiff formality—Harrison was never described as down-to-earth. Despite growing up with seven siblings, he was a bit of a loner. He often escaped to the library on the family estate to spend hours reading. His parents gave him love but little affection.

Harrison attended Cincinnati prep school, Farmers' College, for two years before enrolling at nearby Miami University, from which he graduated near the top of his class in 1852. He married high school sweetheart Caroline Lavinia Scott a year later at the tender age of 20. He then studied law in the Cincinnati office of Storer and Gwynne, passing his bar exam in 1854 and opening up his own practice in Indianapolis.

That endeavor lasted just years. Harrison threw himself into politics and the fledgling Republican Party, even campaigning for its first presidential candidate John C. Fremont in 1856. Soon, he was voted into office as Indianapolis city attorney and continued to rise through the ranks as secretary of the Republican State Central Committee. His support helped Abraham Lincoln become the first Republican president in 1860.

The Civil War did little to alter his political trajectory. Harrison joined an Indiana infantry regiment as second lieutenant in 1862 and survived the war as a brigadier general. He even served under General Sherman as the Union forces destroyed Atlanta and the Confederacy. But he found no glory in war.

Harrison returned to his law practice and also toiled as a court reporter after the war but did more than dabble in politics. He lost a bid for Republican nomination for governor in 1872, but then won it four years later before losing a close race. His tireless and enthusiastic campaigning for presidential election winner Rutherford B. Hayes in 1876 motivated his appointment to the Mississippi River Commission in 1879. By 1880, Harrison was chairing the Indiana delegation to the Republican National Convention.

His stock continued to rise. Harrison helped James A. Garfield win the presidency in 1880 and served as a US senator from 1881 to 1887. His policies became well-established. Included were pensions for Civil War veterans, statehood for Dakota (then one territory), high tariffs, a modernized Navy, and wilderness conservation. But he made no pretense about his disagreement with mainstream Republicans over the Chinese Exclusion Act, when all immigration was barred from China.

Appealing to big business in the big electoral-haul of New York by pledging to raise tariffs, Harrison won both the Republican nomination and presidency in 1888. His administration was hit with a crisis early when the Johnstown Flood killed 2,209 in Pennsylvania. He won over veterans, many of them aging after fighting in the Civil War, by expanding pensions for them or their widows. Harrison also signed the Sherman Anti-Trust Act that sought to protect trade and commerce from illegal restraints and monopolies.

Harrison was not always successful. His push for the Sherman Silver Purchase act that forced government to use silver in its coinage depleted reserves during the Panic of 1893. The Act had to be repealed. His support of the McKinley Tariff of 1890 favored by corporations resulted in inflation and lower wages. Its failures played a significant role in the Republicans losing nearly half of its House seats in the midterm election and Harrison falling to Cleveland in 1892. The tariff was eliminated two years later.

He also suffered personally during his term. His wife died in the White House from tuberculosis two months before Christmas in 1892.

Issues of the Day

The rematch was a grudge match between the two 1888 presidential candidates and featured the same most prominent issue of tariffs.

Some voters, particularly farmers and citizens in the West, did not perceive a distinct policy difference between the Democratic and Republican candidates and looked to the new Populist Party for an answer. They combined with labor and reform groups to back the Populists, who favored women's suffrage. Their popularity was pronounced in Wyoming, which for the first time in American history, allowed women to vote in 1892. So unpopular had Cleveland become in that area of the country that he did not even appear on the ballot in Wyoming, Nevada, Colorado, Idaho, and Kansas.

Cleveland again supported reducing tariffs on foreign goods to keep them affordable. Harrison stepped up his backing of strong tariffs to grow and protect businesses. The Republicans during the Harrison administration in 1890 passed the Tariff Act, which proved greatly unpopular. That helped the Democrats rout their opponents in the midterm elections that year.

The 1892 Campaign

Cleveland had a powerful ally during an era of growing newspaper influence in *New York World* publisher and St. Louis Post-Dispatch owner Joseph Pulitzer, a staunch Democrat. He ran stories asserting the Harrison administration was corrupt in negotiating deals with the railroads. The Pulitzer campaign within the campaign proved quite effective down the stretch as the Republicans for the first time blamed the liberal media for their first presidential defeat in decades.

Yet despite such charges, the campaign was comparatively calm. This was unexpected from a battle between the 1888 combatants. Harrison, front and center in his campaigning four years earlier, stayed out of the spotlight as he remained close to his seriously ill wife. Cleveland failed to take advantage of his opponent's inactivity, staying steadfast in the traditional belief that surrogates and not candidates should be fighting directly for votes.

Cleveland and Democratic vice-presidential candidate Adlai Stevenson certainly made headlines when they departed on a steamer from Buzzard's Bay, Massachusetts, to accept the nomination in front of 20,000 supporters at Madison Square Garden in New York City. Both understood the need to unify the party behind traditional populist viewpoints on tariffs, countering the contention that Republicans wanted high tariffs to line the pockets only of elite Wall Street capitalists. Cleveland delivered a popular message to his delegates. "No plan of tariff legislation shall be tolerated ," he said, "which has for its object and purpose a forced contribution from the earnings and incomes of the mass of our citizens to swell directly the accumulation of a favored few."[1]

Cleveland pitched himself as the candidate for the common man. He promoted an us-against-them policy that would protect ordinary Americans against the tariff-pushing Republicans and their big-money interests. He painted the other party as power hungry and greedy. Cleveland only gave two major speeches—four days apart. But Stevenson campaigned throughout the South to keep that area of the country strongly Democratic and away from the upstart Populists. Stevenson tried to appeal to white Southern voters by opposing the Federal Elections Bill of 1890 that intended to protect voting rights for African Americans by allowing the federal government to monitor and state and local elections. The Democrats also sought votes from labor after violent strikes in silver mines and steel works had been motivated by wage cuts for workers. It was used by the party as evidence that the high tariffs promoted by Harrison and the Republicans were not working.

Harrison did not campaign at all as he tended to his ailing wife. Reid worked particularly hard in New York. So did their surrogates, particularly Ohio governor and future president William McKinley. But it was not enough. The economic malaise in America cost Harrison the election. Cleveland only won the popular vote by less than 400,000 but nearly doubled his opponent's electoral count. It was the most lopsided electoral victory in two decades. The Populist Weaver won several states west of the Mississippi but the party failed to earn widespread popularity.

After the Loss

After losing to Cleveland, Harrison returned to Indianapolis as an American statesman and died in 1901.

Coming From Harrison

"Have you not learned that not stocks or bonds or stately homes, or products of mill or field are our country? It is the splendid thought that is in our minds."[2]

Did You Know?

Harrison owned a pet goat, Old Whiskers, that lived in the White House.

25

William Jennings Bryan

William Jennings Bryan. Courtesy of the Library of Congress, Bain Collection, LC-DIG-ggbain-06257

Party: Democratic
Birth state: Illinois
Represented: Nebraska
Years of defeat: 1896, 1900, 1908
Running mates: Arthur Sewall (1896); Adlai Stevenson (1900); John W. Kern (1908)
Winners: William McKinley (1896, 1900); Wiliam Howard Taft (1908)
Other notable candidate: Eugene V. Debs (Socialist) 1908
Campaign slogans: 1896: "Patriotism, Protection and Prosperity (McKinley); No Cross of Gold, No Crown of Thorns (Bryan); 1900: "Four More Years of the Full Dinner Pail (McKinley); 1908: "A Square Deal for All (Taft); "Vote For Taft Now, You Can Vote for Bryan Any Time (Taft); "Shall the People Rule (Bryan)

All About Bryan

Bryan was born on March 19, 1860, a year before the launch of the Civil War, to fervently religious parents, in Salem, Illinois. Attorney father Silas Bryan was a staunch Jacksonian Democrat who supported such political heavyweights as Andrew Jackson and Stephen Douglas. He eventually passed his political beliefs on to his son. Silas was elected as a state circuit judge when William was just six years old. The family then moved into a spacious farm house north of Salem.

Tragedy struck the Bryans when all three of William's older siblings died as babies. William was home schooled until the age of 10 and displayed an amazing gift for public speaking. He even showed off that talent as early as four years old. Though his father was a Baptist and his mother, Mariah, a Methodist, they allowed their son to choose his own church. His passion for religion became more pronounced after experiencing a conversion at a revival at age 14. He would later claim that to be the most important day of his life.

Bryan was soon shipped off to the Whipple Academy, a private school in Jacksonville, Illinois. By that time, he had become quite politically involved. He joined the temperance movement by signing a pledge to abstain from alcohol. After high school, he attended law school in Chicago and worked in the office of the Abraham Lincoln cohort and US senator Lyman Trumbull. Soon thereafter, Bryan opened his own practice.

His beloved Nebraska awaited. He visited a law school friend in Lincoln after inspecting land in Iowa owned by his father-in-law. Bryan perceived the state as a land of opportunity, so he moved to Lincoln and launched a new practice there.

As for many throughout American history, that profession became a stepping stone to politics. He ran for Congress as a Democrat in 1890. His odds of victory were slim—Nebraska was a breeding ground for Republicans. But Bryan was a populist. His inspiring oratory won over voters during a time of economic desperation. He borrowed ideas coming from the growing Populist Party and won the election that year and again in 1892 before losing a Senate bid two years later.

His brief political inactivity led to work as editor of the Democratic-leaning Omaha World Herald. Bryan was no longer in office, but his writing and lecturing kept his name in the public sphere. He emerged as one of the staunchest advocates of the "free silver" movement that grew in popularity as the depression of the 1890s worsened. It was an idea embraced by Populists and liberal Democrats. The proposed policy stemmed from the issuance of paper money during the Lincoln Administration and Civil War. It was easier to print than to mine or buy gold and it helped pay for the war but it resulted in inflation. Republicans tried to ensure that every paper dollar was backed with gold reserves. Then when depression hit Nebraska and other Agricultural states, borrowers struggled to pay back bank loans. Farmers and other groups believed more plentiful silver would make it easier for them to pay off debt.

Bryan spoke passionately about "free silver" during the 1896 Democratic national convention. His memorable oratory inspired cheering that lasted a half-hour. So taken were the delegates with Bryan that they nominated him as the youngest presidential candidate in American history at age 36. But his campaign was overwhelmed by the better-financed Republicans and Bryan went down to the first of his three defeats.

A healthier economy after the turn of the twentieth century doomed Bryan to two more losses. He spent part of the Spanish–American War preparing a Nebraska regiment of mostly volunteers and ran again in 1900. With the "free silver" movement no longer a viable campaign advantage he pushed for anti-imperialism, claiming that taking over the Philippines from Spain did not jive with the nation's Democratic ideals. That too failed to attract voters, many of whom embraced expansionism.

After losing to Taft in 1900, he returned to Nebraska and began publishing a progressive newspaper that was mailed to 140,000 subscribers and maintained his widespread popularity. A new Democratic platform that backed the gold standard in 1904 left Byran on the sidelines as Theodore Roosevelt won the election. Bryan then became the first three-time presidential campaign loser in 1908.

Issues of the Day (1896)

All signs pointed to a Republican victory as the term of unpopular Democrat Grover Cleveland ended in an economic depression following the Panic of 1893. It was up to the populist Bryan to convince voters he could take the country in a different and more prosperous direction. It would not be easy. The Republicans had taken control of both the House and the Senate in the 1894 midterms.

McKinley supported protectionism for American businesses and the gold standard, which defined the value of American currency by the worth of its gold reserves. Bryan challenged those beliefs in seeking to win over farmers and the working class. It marked a temporary turnabout in party philosophies as the Democrats became the party that attracted the economic elite.

The Panic of 1893 began when two massive companies—the Philadelphia and Reading Railroad and the National Cordage Company—collapsed and set off a stock market scare. Thousands of businesses closed and caused unemployment to skyrocket to over 10 percent for five years. That motivated many from rural areas to turn away philosophically from the gold standard to the Free Silver Movement since the silver reserve was far more abundant at the time. Farmers felt that approach would increase what they could charge for their crops and allow them to emerge from the financial malaise. The 1896 election was the first in which voters from rural and urban areas of the nation were distinctly separated in their views.

The 1896 Campaign

The energy of Bryan gave Democrats hope that they could defeat McKinley, particularly in rural areas of the country. He trekked over 18,000 miles and gave over 600 speeches—sometimes up to 20 a day—crisscrossing the country by train. He often attracted crowds with his mesmerizing oratory from the back of the railroad car.

He certainly wowed his fellow Democratic conventioneers with his "Cross of Gold" speech during which he railed against government favoritism toward big business and the wealthiest of Americans at the expense of farmers and the working class. His messages resonated in particular with the most religious. "We will answer their demand for a gold standard by saying to them," he thundered to the enthusiastic crowd of 20,000 at the Chicago Coliseum. "You shall not press down upon the brow of labor this crown of thorns," he cried, placing an imaginary crown on his head. "You shall not crucify mankind upon a cross of gold."[1]

McKinely, meanwhile, remained at his Canton, Ohio, home, where he addressed Republican supporters from his front porch. About 750,000 visited over the course of the campaign while surrogates stumped elsewhere. There was no shortage of funds. The Republicans spent $4 million, mostly donated from industrialists, to push his election.

It worked. Bryan simply could not broaden his appeal beyond its populist, rural base. Progressive urban voters who backed the gold standard arrived at the polls in droves to cast their ballots for McKinley, who dominated the Northeast and Midwest states with their large electoral college counts.

Issues of the Day (1900)

An end to the economic struggles of the previous decade and the popularity of the incumbent McKinley, as well as a huge campaign fund advantage for the Republicans, led to an uphill struggle for Bryan and the Democrats that they simply could not overcome. Americans also greatly supported military efforts in the Spanish-American War, which had ended in victory a year earlier.

That triumph gave Republicans something to crow about. It had centered on the independence movement in Cuba, which was seeking to overthrow Spanish control. Spain, which was brutal in its treatment of that small nation as it tried to hold on to its last major New World colony, yielded to most US demands, including termination of hostilities against the Cubans. But it would not give up Cuba, leading to a congressional declaration of war. The Spanish were defeated in battles in the Philippines, Cuba and Puerto Rico. The result was the Treaty of Paris that not only gave Cuba its independence but ceded Puerto Rico, Guam and the Philippines to the United States.

Expansionism was a popular concept for most Americans. Fresh off the victory over Spain as the campaign heated up, McKinley continued to emphasize an expansionist foreign policy. Just as the US had claimed to do in destroying Native American culture during the nineteenth century—the 1890 Wounded Knee Massacre had ended the Indian Wars—it was philosophized that the nation had a moral and obligation to "civilize and Christianize" others such as in the Philippines. That sentiment was embraced by many.

Republicans also called for the continuation of the highly protective Dingley Tariff that had been instituted by McKinley, who justified it by citing a strong economy. They also favored building what became the Panama Canal after first offering that the waterway should run through Nicaragua. The Democratic platform, meanwhile, included a rather mild criticism of efforts in the South to disenfranchise Black voters.

The 1900 Campaign

The death of vice-president Garret Hobart during McKinley's first term resulted in the selection of New York governor Theodore Roosevelt as his replacement. It was a popular choice—Roosevelt had gained fame by leading his Rough Riders in their charge up San Juan Hill during the Spanish-American War and was considered a promising future presidential candidate.

Bryan again campaigned feverishly but failed to combat expansionist sentiment. His margin of defeat to McKinley proved nearly identical to that of 1896. His dominance of the south and a few western states could not overcome the McKinley hold in the Northeast and Midwest and even most of the west. Bryan lost by nearly one million votes.

Issues of the Day (1908)

The Democrats were seemingly grasping at straws after popular Theodore Roosevelt, who had assumed the presidency after McKinley had been assassinated in 1901, announced he would not seek a third term and promoted William Taft as his successor. Republican popularity and continued campaign funding advantage placed the Democrats in an unenviable position.

They did feel a sense of optimism knowing that Bryan did not have to run against Roosevelt. They cited graft and political corruption among Republicans as a reason for voters to switch allegiances. The Democrats sought to define themselves as party of the people with equal rights for all and special privileges for none. But a thriving economy and peace on foreign soil motivated most American voters to cast their ballots for Taft.

The 1908 Campaign

The rotund Taft promised to lose 30 pounds off his 300 to energize himself for the campaign but he didn't need such an undertaking. His ace in the hole was Roosevelt, who had decided against running for a third term and instead gave speeches and advice to Taft, who spent most of the three months at a golf resort in Hot Springs, Virginia. The dichotomy proved humorous to journalists who joked that T.A.F.T. stood for "Take Advice from Theodore." Taft hated campaigning, which was explained away by supporters who offered to the public that he simply did not want to engage in negative rhetoric against his opponent.

That Taft intended to continue with Roosevelt's policies was enough for most Americans. Bryan actually lost support over his three presidential campaigns despite his best efforts. He carried just three states outside the Democratic South as Taft nearly doubled his electoral vote count.

After the Losses

Bryan's presidential aspirations were over but not his political influence. Woodrow Wilson appointed him Secretary of State in 1912. Bryan busily worked on foreign and domestic affairs, negotiating peace treaties with twenty-nine nations and pushing through "new freedom" initiatives, including tariff reductions, banking regulations, antitrust legislation and highway construction using state grants. But Bryan resigned after becoming alarmed at Wilson's foreign policy that eventually led to American involvement in the First World War.

Bryan was far from done politically. His support of prohibition on religious grounds and women's suffrage played roles in the passage of both. And in 1925 his historical reputation became cemented for his prosecution of the Scopes Monkey Trial, during which he argued against the teaching of evolution in Tennessee. Bryan died on July 26, five days after the famed trial ended.

Coming From Bryan

You come to us and tell us that the great cities are in favor of the gold standard; we reply that the great cities rest upon our broad and fertile prairies. Burn down your cities and leave our farms, and your cities will spring up again as if by magic; but destroy our farms and the grass will grow in the streets of every city in the country.[2]

Did You Know?

The specific motivation for Bryan's resignation as Secretary of State during the Woodrow Wilson administration was the president's hard line against German submarine warfare. Bryan, known as "The Great Commoner," believed that stance would lead to war. But the US remained uninvolved in the European battles until 1917, just a year before the war ended.

26

Alton B. Parker

Alton B. Parker (with Henry G. Davis). Courtesy of the Library of Congress, Popular Graphic Arts Collection, LC-DIG-ppmsca-59689

Party: Democratic
Birth state: New York
Represented: New York
Year of defeat: 1904
Running mate: Henry G. Davis
Winner: Theodore Roosevelt
Other notable candidate: Eugene V. Debs (Socialist)
Campaign slogan: "National Unity. Prosperity. Advancement." (Roosevelt)

All About Parker

Parker was born into a third-generation family of farmers on May 14, 1852, near Cortland, New York. His father barely earned enough to support the family but he and his wife passed on a love of learning and reading to their son. His mother Harriet often read Alton, sitting in his highchair, passages from the Bible. She eventually tested him on Bible verses to repeat in Sunday school.

So poor were the Parkers that he attended elementary school barefooted. He often fought with fellow students who mocked as the only redhead in the school. A seminal moment in his life arrived at age 12 when he accompanied his juror father to a court case. Fascinated by the proceedings, he decided to become a lawyer. He refused to surrender the dream when forced to go to work at age 16 to financially aid his struggling father. He accepted a teaching job that not only helped keep his family afloat but provided savings toward law school.

Upon returning to school and graduating he trained as a teacher. He proved so successful in that role, he became principal of Accord School in Ulster County, where he met his future wife Mary Louise Schoonmaker, whose distant relative employed him as a law clerk. Parker soon enrolled at the Albany Law School and returned to the family practice. By 1874, he and a classmate had opened their own firm, which lasted four years.

He remained close to his wife's family professionally. Parker directed the winning campaign when Judge Schoonmaker ran for state senator then New York Attorney General. Parker emerged as his top surrogate. He soon tossed his own hat into the political ring. He was the lone Democrat to win a county election among a slew of Republicans who won by landslides.

Parker continued to move up the ranks. His support of the Grover Cleveland presidential candidacy in 1884 allowed him to become a delegate at the Democratic National Convention. Parker gave speeches in support of Cleveland throughout the state, which strengthened their bond when the latter won the White House.

His talents as an organizer were noticed by New York gubernatorial candidate David Hill, who hired Parker to manage his 1885 campaign. In what had been mostly a red state, Parker directed masterfully. An entire Democratic state ticket was elected. He remained in demand, turning down an offer to serve as Lieutenant Governor in favor of a spot at the state Supreme Court. Parker had gained such popularity that the Republicans chose not to run anyone in opposition for the 14-year term, during which he opted not to take suggestions that he run for US senator or New York governor.

Eventually earning a chief judgeship, Parker gained a reputation as a progressive humanitarian. He sided with unions in their rights to strike and promoted legislation that benefitted social justice.

Despite his achievements few considered him a presidential candidate until 1904 when some Democrats floated his name as a possibility. It seemed like a political death wish given the popularity of incumbent Theodore Roosevelt. Parker resisted such efforts, especially since his own term as chief judge was set for another seven years. He even offered the following in defense of his position:

> "While recognizing that situations occasionally arise which makes it the duty of a judge to lay aside his office and serve in other capacities if the people desire it, I have always held firmly to the notion that he should not seek political honors, however exalted they may be; and holding such views, I should not be true to my ideals if I acted otherwise."[1]

Parker, however, eventually decided to heed the call in deference to his party and country. But his candidacy for nomination was weakened immediately by his philosophy that a sitting judge should offer no political views. Reporters accused him of cowardice and of having no opinions on issues of the day. He doubted he would be chosen not only because of his silence but because of his hatred for the policies of two-time nominee William Jennings Bryan, whom he considered a tool of big business.

Delegates at the Democratic Convention in St. Louis were split into Parker and Bryan factions. Neither received enough initial support to be nominated on the first ballot until 20 more were transferred away from Bryan. Alton Parker was officially a Democratic presidential candidate. But he didn't want it if he was forced to accept the gold standard on the platform. He was placated when the delegates simply removed it, opting for silence on any monetary standard to the furious objection of Bryan.

Defeat seemed inevitable and Parker indeed lost decisively.

Issues of the Day

Roosevelt had made waves and inspired his nickname "Trustbuster" after taking over the White House from the assassinated McKinley in September 1901. Though he claimed preference for simply regulating rather than dismantling large corporations, his justice department used the recent Sherman Antitrust Law five months later to break up the Northern Securities Company—J.P. Morgan's railroad trust. Then when 150,000 Pennsylvania coalminers went on strike in May 1902, Roosevelt threatened a government takeover unless mine owners negotiated in good faith. He soon launched the Bureau of Corporations to investigate corporate earnings and make them public.

Roosevelt continued to sway disenfranchised and commoner voters while taking moral stands. He invited Black leader Booker T. Washington to the White House, angering White Southern leaders and motivating criticism from Democrats. He condemned the spate of lynchings in the South and even appointed African-American Dr. William D. Crum as Collector of the Port of Charleston, South Carolina.

Such policies placed him in direct contrast to the Democrats after the moralistic William Jennings Bryan gave way temporarily to the conversative wing of the party, one that sought to ingratiate themselves to big business, which they believed would attract votes in the urban North. That alienated those loyal to Bryan. Though he maintained his own loyalty to the Democratic Party and even campaigned for Parker, he openly criticized its conservative leanings.

Parker supported reduced federal spending, particularly money earmarked for the military, as well as tariff reform and a thorough investigation of public corruption, as well as an eight-hour workday for federal employees. The Democrats lambasted Roosevelt for a perceived imperialism in foreign policy and unconstitutional interference in the legislative and judicial branches of the government.

The 1904 Campaign

Parker loathed the attention and refused to be photographed. He did launch his campaign with a front porch speech and continued to campaign from his home, claiming that traveling around the country would be undignified and open himself up to criticism from muckraking reporters.

His viewpoints did not strongly separate himself from Roosevelt. Parker, in fact, was an early believer in the practices of future president Franklin Roosevelt—he supported government taking an active role in protecting the health, safety and welfare of Americans in an industrialized society. He rarely even criticized his opponent until late in the campaign when he claimed that Theodore Roosevelt had accepted large donations from corporations, a charge that the incumbent vigorously denied. Three years later he admitted to Congress that he had indeed taken contributions from insurance companies and a railroad magnate.

Parker also offered views on foreign affairs, calling for greater isolationism and less military spending. But nothing helped. He lost the popular vote by more than 2.5 million and carried no states outside the South.

After the Loss

Parker returned to his law practice in New York City after his loss. He remained a friend of unions, even representing labor leader Samuel Gompers before the United States Supreme Court and House of Representatives. Parker did not give up on politics. He managed the successful gubernatorial campaign for John Dix and in 1912 was named chairman of the Democratic convention. He gave the keynote address despite Bryan's objections.

Parker was the founder and director of the American Bar Association, for which he twice served as president. He remained in New York City for the rest of his life. He suffered a heart attack and died at age 74.

Coming From Parker

I am a judge of the Court of Appeals. I shall neither embarrass the court by my opinions nor use the dignity of the court to give weight to them. I shall do nothing and say nothing to advance my candidacy. If I should receive the nomination, I shall then resign from the Bench and state my views as a citizen.[2]

Did You Know?

Parker did not promise to be a feared taskmaster as a 16-year-old teacher. He was, in fact, younger than many of his students. But when one troublemaker lit a match near a stove and ignited a small fire, Parker grabbed him by the collar and knocked him to the floor. The student caused no more problems.

27

Theodore Roosevelt

Party: Progressive
Birth state: New York
Represented: New York
Year of defeat: 1912
Running mate: Hiram Johnson
Winner: Woodrow Wilson
Other notable candidates: William Howard Taft (Republican); Eugene V. Debs (Socialist)
Campaign slogans: "It is Nothing But Fair to Leave Taft in the Chair" (Taft); "I am for Wilson and an 8-Hour Day" (Wilson)

Theodore Roosevelt. Courtesy of the Library of Congress, LC-DIG-ppmsca-35830

All About Roosevelt

Born into wealth on October 27, 1858, Roosevelt was the second of four children to a highly successful businessman and philanthropist father and mother who had been raised on a Georgia plantation.

Afflicted by asthma as a sickly child, Theodore was nurtured and loved by his parents and siblings. He dutifully worked to strengthen his body through a program of gymnastics and weightlifting, which had its desired effects. He maintained a strong workout regimen throughout his life and developed a rugged physique. He embraced such activities as hiking, horseback riding and swimming.

Homeschooled by private tutors, his well-to-do parents often sent him overseas for trips, which helped shape his worldview. He traveled through Europe and the Middle East, even staying with a host family in Germany for five months.

Roosevelt enrolled at Harvard College in 1876. He studied such subjects as natural history, zoology, forensics, and composition while adding to his physical pursuits through boxing and wrestling. He also met future wife Alice Hathaway Lee, who came from a prominent New England banking family.

Wasting little time to enter politics, Roosevelt dropped out after one year following a transfer to Columbia Law School. He was elected to the New York Assembly in 1882 and 1884. Devastated and motivated by the death of both his mother and wife two days apart in 1884, he gave his daughter to his sister to raise then moved to the Dakota Badlands to purchase two ranches and a thousand head of cattle. He hunted grizzly bears, rode horses, herded cows, and chased outlaws as a sheriff.

Roosevelt returned East to reunite with childhood sweetheart Edith Carow, whom he married in 1886. The couple moved to New York, where they raised his first child and five others. He soon began to write professionally, authoring a book about naval battles of the War of 1812 and many others. But he had not given up on his political aspirations. Roosevelt lost a bid for New York City mayor in 1886, then campaigned for successful Republican presidential nominee Benjamin Harrison two years later. The grateful president appointed him to the US Civil Service Commission, a post he maintained under Democratic president Grover Alexander in 1893. Though the combative Roosevelt clashed with party members who wanted him to use his power to help further their careers, he thrived in that post, enforcing civil service laws dutifully. He also served honorably and honestly after assuming the presidency of the New York City Police Board in 1895.

Newly elected Republican president William McKinley was impressed in 1897. Roosevelt was front and center for the explosion of the US battleship Maine in 1898, putting the Navy on full alert and instructing Commodore George Dewey to prepare for war with Spain and a possible invasion of the Philippines.

Roosevelt was not one to sit on the sidelines during wartime. He resigned his post when the conflict began and volunteered to command an elite cavalry unit that would legendarily become known as the Rough Riders. He famously led the company on foot up Kettle Hill (better known as San Juan Hill). They continued to battle through heavy casualties before returning to the United States as heroes. Roosevelt admitted that he took more pride in the bravery of the men he commanded than anything he could ever achieve as a politician.

"I would rather have led that charge and earned my colonelcy than served three terms in the United States Senate," he said. "It makes me feel as though I could now leave something to my children which will serve as an apology for my having existed."[1]

His new status as war hero inspired Republican leaders to push Roosevelt as a New York gubernatorial candidate. He agreed to run and narrowly defeated Democrat Augustus van Wyck. Roosevelt continued to strengthen his reputation as a moralistic leader who refused to be influenced by self-serving big business. His popularity in that role motivated the Republicans to run him as their vice-presidential candidate in 1900. His whirlwind travels took him more than 21,000 miles to 567 cities to promote McKinley. He made hundreds of speeches to more than three million people. His tireless efforts helped McKinley win in a landslide, and he emerged as a future presidential contender.

That candidacy was expected in 1904. But an assassin's bullet killed McKinley in September 1901 and forced the 42-year-old Roosevelt into the White House as the youngest president in American history.

Similar to his distant cousin Franklin Roosevelt during the Depression, Theodore expanded the role of government to serve the economic needs of the people. He earned his reputation as the "trust buster." He forced the dissolution of a massive railroad trust and used the Sherman Act to weaken other corporate combinations. He ensured the construction of the Panama Canal to shorten the route between the Atlantic and Pacific. The Roosevelt administration prevented the building of foreign military bases in the Caribbean and established the United States as the only country with the right to intervene in Latin American affairs. He even won a Nobel Prize for mediating the Russo-Japanese War. Roosevelt's pet issue was conservation. He oversaw huge ventures to add to Western national forests, reserved lands for public use, and fostered massive irrigation projects.

Not all of Roosevelt's policies were loved by voters nor historians. His terms were turbulent. He railed against "race suicide" after learning of falling birth rates among White Americans. He led a crusade to dishonorably discharge 167 African-American soldiers who had rioted in Brownsville, Texas, over tensions caused by their white peers. Roosevelt assumed their guilt and none of the soldiers received a trial.

A love for adventure drove Roosevelt to embark on an African safari upon the end of his terms in office in 1909 but he jumped back into the political ring as a presidential candidate on the Progressive ticket in 1912. He survived an assassination attempt but not the decision by voters to place Woodrow Wilson into office.

Issues of the Day

The United States had settled into a two-party election for decades but a temporary shift resulted in three major candidates fighting for the White House in 1912, greatly due to the division in the Republican Party from which the Progressive Party (also known as the Bull Moose Party) emerged with Roosevelt leading the way.

The chaos among Republicans led to a campaign issue in itself. That is, how should nominees be chosen? They had throughout American history been selected solely by conventional delegates. New Hampshire would become in 1920 the first state to host a primary but early primaries had little effect on the final choice. Primary elections became more impactful by 1952 and grew into the final decision-maker by 1968.

Each candidate in 1912 competed to offer a vision to Americans in a changing nation. The country had become more industrialized as many left their farms and rural communities to live in cities. Immigration, particularly from Europe, meant a growing population mostly in urban areas. The United States had also emerged as a military and economic power in foreign affairs. Meanwhile, in Europe, winds of war began blowing.

Perhaps the biggest issue argued among the candidates revolved around trusts, which were large combinations of companies in related industries that threatened to destroy competition and establish monopolies in major industries such as the railroads and steel manufacturing. Trusts lowered prices to push competitors out of the market, then raised them to earn huge profits.

The 1912 Campaign

The split among Republicans that resulted in a third-party Progressive ticket, as well as the inevitable number of votes for Socialist Eugene Debs, threatened to hand the election to Wilson and the unified Democrats.

The division was showcased from the start of the campaign. Most party officials, many of them unpledged, free to support any candidate, backed William Howard Taft for the nomination. But Roosevelt won primary elections in direct showdowns against him in Illinois, California, and even in Taft's home state of Ohio. That gave Roosevelt a majority of pledged delegates. The chasm not only resulted in a split convention that left two viable candidates to run against Wilson. It also ruined the longstanding friendship between Roosevelt and Taft.

Then it happened. October 14, 1912. Roosevelt climbed into his open-air automobile destined to whisk him to a campaign stop at the Milwaukee Auditorium when an assassin's bullet fired from a revolver just a few feet away struck him on the side. Deciding it was not fatal despite a doctor telling the driver to take him to the hospital, Roosevelt amazingly decided to give his speech anyway. "It takes more than that to kill a Bull Moose," he told the crowd upon his arrival, thereby coining the nickname for the Progressive Party. He added that the folded speech in his pocket where the bullet hit might have saved it from piercing his heart. Roosevelt spoke for about 90 minutes, periodically opening his coat to show his bloody shirt to the audience.[2]

His fearlessness in plowing ahead with a bullet lodged in his body captivated voters. But the Republican Party of that era was home to both conservatives and progressives. The former supported Roosevelt. The latter backed Taft. And even though Speaker of the House Champ Clark was initially considered the likely Democratic nominee, that party united behind Wilson after the convention.

The result was inevitable. Wilson won in a landslide, capturing 42 percent of the popular vote and all but 96 Electoral College votes. Roosevelt outperformed Taft (who won only Utah and Vermont) as the most successful third-party candidate in American history but that was meaningless.

The 1912 election was not only a victory for Wilson. It was a victory for the two-party system, especially when two candidates emerged from the same party. The election also influenced American politics for decades. It planted the seeds for primary elections rather than nominating conventions.

Roosevelt had also influenced policy. He had campaigned on greater government control of the economy, which Wilson opposed but adopted upon his arrival in the White House. Such an approach to government influence played a huge role during the Franklin Roosevelt presidency as his New Deal pulled America out of the Great Depression.

After the Loss

Roosevelt responded to the defeat by embarking on an expedition to the jungles of Brazil, where he contracted a near-fatal illness. He then spoke strongly about the allied cause in the First World War and US intervention. He became angry with Wilson when the president turned down his offer to lead a division in France in the First World War.

His political aspirations had not died. Roosevelt was considered a favorite to land the Republican nomination in 1920, but he died just short of his 60th birthday in January 1919.

Coming From Roosevelt

Speak softly and carry a big stick.

Did You Know?

Roosevelt witnessed the Abraham Lincoln funeral procession in New York City at age six. A photo of him perched in a window at his grandfather's mansion as he watched the sad event surfaced in the 1950s. Roosevelt himself would be shot, though not killed, 47 years later.

28

Charles Evans Hughes

Party: Republican
Birth state: New York
Represented: New York
Years of defeat: 1916
Running mate: Charles W. Fairbanks
Winner: Woodrow Wilson
Other notable candidate: Allen L. Benson (Socialist)
Campaign slogans: "War in Europe—Peace in America—God Bless Wilson" (Wilson); "America First and America Efficient" (Hughes)

Charles E. Hughes. Courtesy of the Library of Congress, Posters: Artist Posters Collection, LC-DIG-ppss-00462

All About Hughes

The son of a Wales immigrant father and Baptist minister, Hughes was born on April 11, 1862, in Glens Falls, New York. His early childhood was marked by a tireless work ethic, love of reading, and photographic memory.

Aside from a short period in Newark High School, the boy was homeschooled by his parents as an only child. The family moved frequently, landing in Brooklyn after spending some time in Newark, New Jersey.

Hughes was so advanced educationally that at age 14, he was accepted into Madison University (now Colgate), then Brown University, where he campaigned for Republican presidential nominee James Garfield in 1880 and eventually graduated Phi Beta Kappa a year later. He continued to excel at Columbia Law School, finishing first in his class in 1884.

Soon, he opened a legal practice in New York City that he maintained for two decades, also serving as part of a legislative council that investigated and revealed irregularities in the insurance and utility industries. Like so many in American history, he used his status as a lawyer as a stepping stone into politics. Hughes did not take gradual steps—he ran for governor of New York in 1906 and won, then earned re-election two years later. Though his terms proved comparatively uneventful, he did help establish a public service commission in that state and improve insurance and labor laws.

His life took a dramatic twist in 1910, when he was appointed to the US Supreme Court during the Taft administration. Only his close-but-unsuccessful 1916 bid for the presidency and four-year run as Secretary of State under President Warren G. Harding interrupted his notable legal career. He was chosen by President Hoover to return to the Supreme Court as chief justice in 1930.

Issues of the Day

The war in Europe clearly dominated the political conversation in 1916. The majority of Americans favored neutrality but also hoped for an Allied victory as the alliance of Britain, France, and Russia fought against the Central Powers of Germany, Augustia, and the Ottoman Empire.

Wilson and Hughes both billed themselves as peace candidates but neither expressed blind loyalty to that viewpoint. Wilson, who would eventually send US troops into battle, advocated military preparedness. Hughes claimed the incumbent had failed to ready the country for war if it became necessary.

Two other issues bubbling to the surface were overshadowed by the war. The calls for woman's suffrage had grown so intense that 1916 would be the last election in which only men could vote. And the debate about Prohibition resulted in a legally dry country when the next election rolled around.

The 1916 Campaign

Wilson believed—rightly as it turned out—that he could run successfully on his track record. He boasted about maintaining neutrality as the war raged in Europe. Wilson ran a "front porch" campaign while surrogates traveled the country to tout his accomplishments. He failed to attract African–American voters, greatly due to his endorsement of segregation after assuming the presidency. Wilson also refused to support women's suffrage.

Given that women would have to wait four more years to vote in a national election, Hayes could not contrast himself to Wilson to sway enough voters to win. He was criticized for his icy personality that did not excite Americans. His lambasting of the president on foreign affairs sometimes had the opposite effect of what he intended, especially since most in the country agreed with an isolationist policy.

Yet, despite Wilson's popularity and Hughes's failure to rouse the electorate, the election results proved closer than anticipated. A major upset was averted only by 23 electoral votes as Hughes dominated the populous Northeast and Midwest states, including New York, Pennsylvania, Michigan, and Illinois.

After the Loss

Though seen by many as icy and aloof, his social skills served him well in navigating contentious waters on the highest court in the land. Hughes also went toe-to-toe with Franklin Roosevelt as the president sought to ram through New Deal legislation in attempting to extricate the country out of the Great Depression. Hughes was progressive in matters of race and social welfare programs but also a stickler on legality when making tough decisions left to the Supreme Court. And though he often sided with the minority against the conservative "Four Horsemen" majority he irked Roosevelt by opposing his "court-packing" plan that would have added more judges sympathetic to New Deal legislation. The Court had already killed the National Industrial Recovery Act and Agricultural Adjustment Act. Roosevelt feared the conservatives would strike down other New Deal laws so he proposed the Judicial Procedures Reform Bill in 1937, claiming the Court could not handle the case load and needed more judges. Hughes worked strenuously to defeat the effort, even penning a letter to Senator Burton Wheeler contending that the Court was fully capable of dealing with anything sent its way.

Hughes retired from the bench in 1941 as the nation still divided between isolationism and involvement in what was about to become the Second World War. He lived a quiet retirement in New York City before dying on August 27, 1948, at the age of 86.

Coming From Hughes

We are under a Constitution, but the Constitution is what the judges say it is.[1]

Did You Know?

Hughes was chosen by Columbia University as a Prize Fellow, which allowed him to stay on at the law school (for 500 dollars a year) to tutor and conduct quizzes for law students. He did this from 1884 to 1887 while also maintaining a private practice.

29

James M. Cox

James M. Cox (with Franklin D. Roosevelt). Courtesy of the Library of Congress, National Photo Company Collection, LC-DIG-ppmsca-33569

Party: Democratic
Birth state: Ohio
Represented: Ohio
Years of defeat: 1920
Running mate: Franklin D. Roosevelt
Winner: Warren G. Harding
Other notable candidate: Eugene V. Debs (Socialist)
Campaign slogans: "Return to Normalcy" (Harding); "Peace, Progress, Prosperity" (Cox)

All About Cox

James Middleton Cox was the youngest of seven children born to parents Gilbert and Eliza on March 31, 1870, and raised on the family farm in the tiny town of Jacksonburg, Ohio. He worked the fields as a child. Such chores instilled in him a love for the outdoors that would remain the rest of his life. He claimed that hard work in the open air gave him healthy, agility and endurance. The boy spent much of his free evening time at Shafer's, a nearby store at which he would participate in political discussions with adult men or read a book under a kerosene lamp.

Cox was educated in the Middletown suburb of Amanda. He grew fascinated with the newspaper industry and landed a job as a printer's helper in high school. He also eventually accepted work as a tutor and janitor but his first love was journalism. By the age of 21, he was spending his summers working at the *Middletown News-Signal* and *Cincinnati Enquirer*.

A career in that field would have to wait. Cox earned his teaching certificate in 1887 and landed jobs in the Rockdale and Titus school districts. He even earned a promotion to superintendent of a Middletown nigh school. But newspaper work never strayed far from his heart and mind. On Saturdays, he delivered the entire circulation of the *Weekly Signal*, which was owned by his brother-in-law. He landed a job as a reporter for the *Enquirer* in 1892.

Cox yearned to take his career to a higher level. So in 1898, he borrowed $26,000 from friends and family to purchase the Dayton Evening News Publishing Company and renamed it the Dayton Daily News, which has remained the main newspaper in that city for well over a century. Cox was forward-thinking. He added a women's society editor and increased Associated Press coverage to include national and international news, as well as sports.

The seeds of his political career were planted as secretary of US Representative Paul Sorg for three years. Cox was then elected to Congress, where he served two terms before staging a winning campaign for governor of Ohio. He faced a major challenge immediately in that role when a major flood devastated Dayton and nearby communities. Cox toured the area and his newly appointed flood commission and during the cleanup fought for the creation of an effective flood prevention agency.

He emerged as a reformer during a progressive era in American politics. Cox promoted changes that were adopted in his first term, including reorganization of the court system, tax centralization, and the formation of a commission to ensure unified management of industrial and agricultural policies. He also helped create conservation and roads programs as well as social policies such as workers compensation, pensions for mothers, and penal system reform.

Such a reformist agenda did not sit well with some voters. The result was his defeat in seeking reelection in 1914 before he won the governorship again in 1916 and 1918. Cox had become a national political figure but many were surprised when he landed the Democrat presidential nomination in 1920. They were not surprised when he lost badly to Harding.

Issues of the Day

Many Americans were happy that the presidency of Woodrow Wilson was ending as they pondered the future of the country and which candidate would be better served to achieve their own goals. Some considered his reversal on American involvement in the First World War and his failure to involve Congress in negotiations prior to the 1919 Treaty of Versailles that ended the conflict unforgivable while others quibbled with his economic policies. Wilson was also criticized for refusing to compromise with isolationist-leaning Republicans who objected to the formation of the League of Nations.

The president was also angering progressives for his hardline stances in the intensifying labor battles of the era. He sided with management in several highly publicized strikes and even forced deportation of radical leftists inspired by the Russian Revolution.

Foreign affairs were mixed in with domestic issues in the minds of voters. Of particular interest was Prohibition, which had become a controversial law in January 1920 and would soon be tested by rumrunners, bootleggers, and speakeasies.

The 1920 Campaign

Harding had come out of nowhere to land the Republican nomination at the party convention in Chicago. He snuck in after friend and political manager Harry Daugherty began to believe that none of the frontrunners could win on the first ballot. Harding was a known figure whose policy ideas were popular among the delegates and who represented populous Ohio. He said or did little controversial, opposing neither prohibition nor women's suffrage and making no political enemies. It was also believed his good looks would attract women voting for the first time. Harding won the nomination of the tenth ballot.

The new nominee and vice-presidential candidate Calvin Coolidge, who would follow Harding to the White House, campaigned on a plank of condemnation for the Wilson administration, which had received growing criticism for sending troops into the First World War battlefields after promising neutrality, and joining the new League of Nations. The Republicans also supported higher protective tariffs and sought to stem the tide of immigration. Their vision was returning to the "good old days" before progressivism—as they spouted a "return to normalcy."[1]

The level of Republican indecision at their convention was no match for that of the Democrats, who needed 34 ballots to decide on Cox. In what would prove to be a powerhouse vice-presidential matchup, they pitted young Franklin D. Roosevelt against Coolidge. The ticket was an attempt to promote the Wilson domestic and foreign agenda to the American people.

Harding did not stray during his campaign. He spoke to reporters and visitors from his Ohio home and let them spread the message. But Cox traveled the country, trekking 22,000 miles and making over 400 speeches. He was joined on the campaign trail by popular entertainer Al Jolson, who compared Cox to Abraham Lincoln.

It didn't work. Harding won in a landslide, winning the popular vote by more than seven million and carrying every state outside the South, which had for decades been a Democratic stronghold.

After the Loss

The loss ended Cox's political career, though he continued to endorse and campaign for former running mate Franklin Roosevelt during his four runs for president while other Democrats abandoned him .

Cox returned to his passion—journalism. He eventually bought other newspapers, four radio stations and two television stations in creating what became known as Cox Enterprises. Among his acquisitions was the *Atlanta Journal* in 1939, leading to his purchase of 50,000-watt powerhouse WSB, which billed itself as the dominant radio station of the South.

Cox briefly strayed from his chosen field as vice-chairman of the US delegation to the World Monetary and Economic Conference in London 1933. He was selected as president of the Monetary Commission to reach a goal of stabilizing international currencies but his attempts failed. He then avoided all other calls to political duty, even rejecting a chance to run for the US Senate in 1946. By that time, he was 76 years old. Cox died in 1957 at age 87 after a series of strokes.

Coming From Hughes

We are under a Constitution, but the Constitution is what the judges say it is.[2]

Did You Know?

Cox's purchase of the *Atlanta Journal* in December 1919 came just one week before that city hosted the premiere of epic movie classic *Gone with the Wind*.

30

John W. Davis

Party: Democratic
Birth state: West Virginia
Represented: West Virginia
Years of defeat: 1924
Running mate: Charles W. Bryan
Winner: Calvin Coolidge
Other notable candidate: Robert La Follette (Progressive)
Campaign slogans: "Keep Cool and Keep Coolidge" (Coolidge); "Honest Days with Davis" (Davis)

John W. Davis (with Henry D. Clayton Jr.). Courtesy of the Library of Congress, Bain Collection, LC-DIG-ggbain-13070

All About Davis

The only major presidential candidate ever from West Virginia, John Davis was born in Clarksburg on April 13, 1873. His paternal ancestors were rooted in western Virginia, which later became West Virginia. Great-grandfather Caleb Davis was a clockmaker and his grandfather John owned a saddle and harness business. The legal and political ties to the family began with his father John James, who established a practice in Clarksburg before his election to the West Virginia House of Representatives.

Young Davis was homeschooled, but he impressed his Sunday school teachers with his advanced speaking ability, maturity and dignified manner. His literary knowledge came courtesy of his mother, who taught him how to read before he even learned the alphabet and often read him poetry and books from the vast home library. Davis proved himself so learned compared to his classmates that he began preparing for the state teachers examination with those much older at age ten and enrolled at Washington and Lee University six years later, majoring in Latin and graduating in 1892.

Only a lack of funds prevented Davis from starting law school immediately. He opted instead for a teaching position at the home of Major Edward McDonald in Charlestown. Among his students was 19-year-old Julia, whom he eventually married. He then served as an apprentice as his father's law practice. He finally had the money to attend the Washington & Lee law school and graduated in 1895. His speech as Law Class Orator proved his belief in the importance of his field.

"[The] lawyer has been always the sentinel of the watchtower of liberty," he said. "In all times and all countries has he stood forth in defense of his nation, her laws and liberties, not, it may be, under a shower of leaden death, but often with the frown of a revengeful and angry tyrant bent upon him. Fellow classmates of 1895, shall we . . . prove unworthy?"[1]

Davis joined his father's practice and worked briefly as an assistant professor at Washington & Lee before focusing full-time on law. He adopted many of the Southern Democratic political views embraced by his father, including opposition to women's suffrage and anti-lynching legislation and other civil rights programs. He defended the poll tax, which was used in the Jim Crow era to prevent African-Americans from voting. Davis also supported several early progressive laws limiting the power of corporations.

Politics came calling in 1898 when he became the first Democrat elected to a seat in the West Virginia House of Delegates. Voters embraced his denunciation of railroad companies he had previously legally supported. Davis then served 12 years as Harrison County party chairman. He had begun to earn national recognition within the Democratic party, even landing a spot as a delegate to the 1904 national convention, where he backed conservative presidential candidate Alton B. Parker over populist William Jennings Bryan.

Davis served West Virginia in the US House of Representatives from 1911 to 1913, then as US Solicitor General for the next five years. President Wilson appointed him ambassador to Great Britian in 1921 as that nation worked to recover from the First World War. He supported in that role the ideals of the

League of Nations based on the friendship between the two countries. He grew disenchanted with Wilson over a perceived isolationist sentiment and lack of enthusiasm for the League.

His own presidential candidacy was unexpected among Democrats. Davis gained some consideration in 1920 before landing the nod in 1924 and losing badly to Coolidge. By that time, he had established several associations, including membership in the anti-Prohibition National Advisory Council of the Crusaders, presidency of the Council on Foreign Relations. and chairmanship of the Carnegie Endowment for International Peace.

Issues of the Day

The death of Warren Harding in 1923 thrust Coolidge into presidency to clean up the mess placed upon his predecessor through a scandal—wherein Navy petroleum reserves had been secretly released by Secretary of the Interior Albert Bacon Fall to the Teapot Dome oil field in Wyoming as well as two locations in California. Coolidge and Senator Thomas Walsh spearheaded an investigation that resulted in Fall's imprisonment and the restoration of trust in the federal government.

Though Prohibition remained a hot-button issue as lawbreakers continued to provide alcohol to Americans thirsting for it, debates raged on less timely topics. The united Republicans called for reducing taxes, collecting foreign debts, raising protective tariffs, banning child labor, and establishing an eight-hour workday nationwide. Divided Democrats, who disagreed on the legality and righteousness of Prohibition, finally arrived at a platform that included a reduction in tariffs, financial relief for farmers, public works projects to reduce unemployment, and a national referendum on American participation in what would prove to be an ineffective League of Nations.

The 1924 Campaign

Little could anyone have imagined it would take more than two weeks for the Democrats to decide on a nominee after their convention began in New York.

They cast 103 ballots for former treasury secretary William McAdoo and New York governor Alfred E. Smith with neither emerging victorious.

The combatants represented both sides of the prohibition issue. McAdoo supported the ban on alcohol and was particularly popular in the West, rural South and among those in the resurgent Ku Klux Klan. Smith opposed Prohibition and was supported in the populous Eastern cities. He was backed by political heavyweights William Jennings Bryan and rising Democrat Franklin Roosevelt, who made a rousing speech in his comeback after being stricken with polio. The indecision allowed Davis to sneak in on the 103rd ballot. Meanwhile, a coalition of farmers, laborers and socialists met to nominate Republican senator Robert LaFollette of Wisconsin on the Progressive Party ticket.

Known as "Silent Cal" and a man of few words, Coolidge barely campaigned. He spoke little about controversial issues, opting instead to appeal to voters through his businesslike approach and honesty, which earned him points after the Teapot Dome Scandal. Though Smith toured the country trying to attract votes, the split among Democrats resulted in a landslide and typical voting pattern for the time. Davis dominated the South but won no other state. Coolidge won the rest aside from Wisconsin, which supported their senator LaFollette.

After the Loss

Maintaining his influence on the Democratic Party, Davis served as a New York delegate at the 1928 and 1932 conventions before campaigning for Franklin Roosevelt. But Davis never agreed with the four-term president, particularly in regard to the New Deal programs designed to lift the country out of the Great Depression, He turned on his party and supported Republicans who ran against Roosevelt over the rest of his presidency. Davis was even implicated in an alleged conspiracy to overthrow Roosevelt in 1933, though his involvement was ruled in a committee report to the House as nothing more than hearsay.

Among the noteworthy cases, Davis argued before the Supreme Court during his noteworthy legal career involved the federal takeover of steel plants during the Truman administration. He spoke on behalf of the steel industry, claiming

Truman had overstepped his bounds of power. Davis helped influence the Court to uphold an injunction against the seizure of the mills.

By that time past his eightieth birthday, Davis argued unsuccessfully in the landmark Brown v. Board of Education case in which segregation in schools was ruled unconstitutional. His legacy would be forever tarnished by his fight for states rights and against integration. He died in 1955 as communities throughout the South continued to stubbornly take steps to avoid the integration of their schools.

Coming From Davis

When will we get done with the fool idea that the way to make a party grow is to scare away everybody who has an extra dollar in his pocket? God forbid that the Democratic Party should become a mere gathering of the unsuccessful![2]

Did You Know?

Davis represented a defendant into a case revolving around the battle between allegiance to the nation and obedience to religious beliefs. That was the *United States v. Macintosh* (1931). It centered on Canadian-born Baptist minister Douglas Macintosh, who applied to a Connecticut district court to be naturalized after landing on the faculty at Yale University. He refused to promise under oath that he would bear arms for the United States in wartime, claiming religious objections. So the Court denied his naturalization. A Court of Appeals reversed that decision, leading the government to appeal to the conservative-leaning Supreme Court. Davis represented Macintosh, but the Court decided in a 5–4 ruling that loyalty to the country was not consistent with what Macintosh believed to be the will of God.

31

Al Smith

Alfred E. Smith. Courtesy of the Library of Congress, National Photo Company Collection, LC-DIG-npcc-24818

Party: Democratic
Birth state: New York
Represented: New York
Years of defeat: 1928
Running mate: Joseph Robinson
Winner: Herbert Hoover
Campaign slogans: "A Chicken in Every Pot and a Car in Every Garage" (Hoover); "All for Al and Al for All" (Smith)

All About Smith

Born five days after Christmas in 1873, to a German-born father and Irish mother, Smith was raised near the Lower East Side of Manhattan around what is now Chinatown. His neighborhood was crowded with immigrants. He identified more as Irish, particularly after his father died when he was 12 years old. His neighborhood was an enclave of European immigrants. Italians and Eastern European Jews arrived in droves to the shores of New York City.

Smith spent much of his time on the South Street waterfront, swimming in the East River and climbing onto docked ships. He ignored his mother's pleas that he avoid the sailors, saloons, and brothels that surrounded their apartment building. He recalled in later years growing up alongside the Brooklyn Bridge that was being constructed at the time. Smith seemed destined for politics. He used his friendly demeanor, charm, and wit to communicate with friends and neighbors while sporting a broad smile, smoking a cigar, and wearing a brown derby hat.

Influenced by the Tammany Hall political organization in New York City, which had been fraught with corruption through the years, Smith began to serve in city and state government, including sheriff, state assembly member, and speaker, before his election to governor. He strongly supported progressive causes popular in his day, including legislation to improve factory conditions, as well as increased funding for schools and parks. He also backed labor and tenant rights and public health initiatives.

By the time Smith ended his tenure as governor to pursue the presidency, he had improved women's and children's labor regulations and spearheaded a tunnel project between New York and New Jersey.

Issues of the Day

Prohibition was thrust front and center during the campaign as rumrunners and bootleggers continued to defy the ban on alcohol in a successful and sometimes violent battle against law enforcement. But a booming economy—at least until the Stock Market Crash in 1929—made Hoover the Republican a sure winner.

The decision by Calvin Coolidge to not seek re-election seemingly left his replacement wide open but Hoover promised continued prosperity fueled by lower taxes and protective tariff. He also pledged a "final triumph over poverty." Little could he have imagined the impending economic disaster or that his support of the then-popular Ku Klux Klan would place him in historical disgrace.[1]

His Prohibition stance stood in stark contrast to that of Smith, who tempered his viewpoint by securing "dry" running mate Joseph Robinson of Arkansas. The Democrats hoped in vain that featuring candidates on both sides of the issue would attract enough voters to defeat Hoover. They also dreamed wrongly that the combination of a Catholic (Smith) and Protestant (Robinson) would prove beneficial.

The Democratic platform highlighted support for public works projects and federal aid to farmers and schools. It also promised enforcement of Prohibition laws despite Smith's desire to repeal the Eighteenth Amendment.

Historians were eventually left to debate whether Smith's religion played a role in his lopsided defeat. No Catholic had ever been elected president due to strong anti-Catholic sentiment in many parts of the country.

The 1928 Campaign

Hoover appeared all but certain to win back the presidency in 1928 when the Republicans met for their convention in Kansas City that summer. Despite policy and personal disagreements with many in his party, he had dominated the primaries with massive support from women, progressives, isolationists, and big business. He secured the nomination on the first ballot.

Hoover took no chances. He said or did nothing risky, opting to deliver his messages to the voters through three radio speeches while never even mentioning Smith by name. His surrogates painted Hoover as efficient and a skilled administrator during a new age of advanced technology who would continue to spur economic growth and financial security for families. Republicans tied him to the previous two administrations during which the American economy thrived. Hoover was also portrayed as a humanitarian, citing his cleanup efforts after the Great Mississippi Flood the previous year.

Smith brought little ammunition to the battle. His Catholicism was lambasted by Protestant preachers and the resurgent Ku Klux Klan who suggested that Smith would take orders from the Pope and even take such steps as declaring all Protestant children illegitimate and annul all their marriages. One Smith rally in Oklahoma City was met with burning KKK crosses and jeering crowd.

His anti-Prohibition views also proved unpopular. After treading lightly on the subject he eventually called for its repeal. That inspired such organizations as the Anti-Saloon League and Women's Temperance Union to nickname him

"Al-coholic" and spread rumors about his own penchant for drinking and lack of morality. One radio preacher tied him to "card playing, cocktail drinking, poodle dogs, divorces, novels, stuffy rooms, dancing, evolution, Clarence Darrow, nude art, prize-fighting, actors, greyhound racing, and modernism."[2]

The result was predictable. Smith performed even worse than his Democratic predecessors. He even lost five Southern states that his party had previously won. Hoover won the popular vote by more than six million and the electoral college tally, 444–87. His defeat could certainly not be pinned to voter apathy—13 million more Americans cast ballots than had in 1924. Hoover simply proved himself too popular during a time of economic boom. It would last less than a year.

After the Loss

Smith became disenchanted with politics after his defeat to Hoover in 1928. He was especially disillusioned with Franklin Roosevelt, his handpicked predecessor at governor of New York. His bitterness stemmed not only from jealousy, who swept into the White House four times as perhaps the most popular president in American history, but from being passed over as an advisor candidate. Smith's gradual change to more conservative views and disagreement with Roosevelt's New Deal policies also caused friction. Their relationship eventually improved. Roosevelt nicknamed Smith "The Happy Warrior of the Political Battlefield" and credited him with sparking his support for progressive legislation that would give birth to the New Deal.

After losing badly in 1928, Smith focused on his new post as president of the Empire State Building Corporation and other business ventures. His initial support for Roosevelt in 1932 waned, motivating his backing of Republican candidates Alf Landon and Wendell Willkie during the next two campaigns despite growing incumbent popularity. Smith did not live long enough to see Roosevelt lead the country to victory in the Second World War and get elected for a fourth time. He died in October 1944, just one month before Roosevelt secured yet another term (albeit a short one before he too passed away).

Coming From Smith

The cure for the evils of democracy is more democracy.[3]

Did You Know?

Smith had earned enough respect, at least from the US Postal Service, to be pictured on a three-cent stamp in November 1945, just 13 months after his death.

32

Herbert Hoover

Herbert Hoover. Courtesy of the Library of Congress, LC-DIG-ppmsca-83250

Party: Republican
Birth state: Iowa
Represented: California
Years of defeat: 1932
Running mate: Charles Curtis
Winner: Franklin Roosevelt
Campaign Slogans: "Happy Days are Here Again" (Roosevelt); "We are Turning the Corner" (Hoover)

All About Hoover

The only native Iowan to win the presidency was born in August 10, 1874, in the small down of West Branch. He was raised by a Quaker father, who toiled as a blacksmith and farm equipment salesperson until a heart attack ended his life when Herbert was six years old. His mother died three years later, leaving her son an orphan and forcing him to move in with his uncle John Minthorn in Oregon.

Hoover seemed an unlikely presidential possibility as a painfully shy youth who had been emotionally damaged by the loss of his parents. His schoolwork suffered. He earned average grades at best in all subjects but math. But he showed the determination to continue his education at the new Stanford University in Palo Alto, California. He studied diligently to pass his entrance exam before majoring in geology and improving his social skills by serving as class treasurer and managing the school baseball and football teams. He even launched a student laundry service to help pay for tuition.

That work ethic served him well. So did his travels. He joined geological survey teams in Arkansas, California and Nevada as a student assistant as a precursor to his plans for a career as a surveyor that fell through. Hoover ended up laboring 70 hours a week pushing iron courts at a gold mine in Nevada City, California before landing an office job in San Francisco that connected him with a firm seeking an engineer to examine and assess mines for possible purchase. The result was mining engineer jobs that dispatched him to live in Australia and China and expanded his horizons. He returned in 1908 to open his own mining business and within six years had gained considerable wealth from control of Burmese silver mines and even authoring a textbook on his field.

By that time Hoover had developed a strong philosophical base. Raised a Quaker, he valued the notions of freedom, conscientiousness, charity, and the power of the individual. As an engineer, he believed that science was important to pushing human progress. He also grew quite politically aware, particularly in the opinion that unionization and corporate interests could comfortably coexist.

Soon, Hoover became interested in politics. He agreed with policies supported by the progressive wing of the Republican Party as espoused by third-party candidate Theodore Roosevelt in 1912. He was first thrust into the national spotlight when asked during the First World War to organize the evacuation of 120,000 Americans trapped in Europe and to held fund the Committee for the Relief of Belgium after the German invasion of that country. Hoover raised millions of dollars to supply food and medicine.

His work caught the attention of President Wilson, who placed Hoover in charge of the US Food Administration after American inclusion in the war. His work was praised so strongly that the rationing of household materials became known nationwide as "Hooverizing." So impressed was Wilson that he appointed Hoover to lead the European Relief and Rehabilitation Administration after the signing of the armistice treaty in November 1918. The result was 34 million tons of American food, clothing, and supplies to war-ravaged Europe.

The tragedies of war motivated Hoover to support American participation in the new and eventually failed League of Nations. By 1920, he was considered a possible presidential candidate but a Senator Hiram Johnson, a fellow Californian who disliked Hoover's support for the League, blocked his nomination. That did not stop President Harding from appointing him Secretary of Commerce, a post he maintained until his run for the White House in 1928. The department grew in stature and influence during his tenure as he supported new industries such as radio and aviation and aggressively pushed for international trade partners for American business. Hoover was credited during the economic boom of the 1920s. He worked to organize the economy to produce steadier outcomes and prevent downturns. Hoover based his economic philosophies on the principles and power of individualism. He rejected far-right capitalism and far-left socialism because he believed both hampered individual economic freedom. But he also felt the federal government needed to create conditions that could allow individuals to thrive.

It also worked well until his presidency, which he launched with his infamous proclamation that the nation was nearing its permanent defeat of poverty. The stock market crashed just eight months into his term in office. His response plan of cutting taxes and expanding public works failed when in 1931 affected European economies collapsed, causing a worldwide depression. His proposed Reconstruction Finance Corporation to help businesses, aid farmers, push banking reform, provide federal loans to feed the impoverished, and expand public works did not have the desired results. Congressional opponents whom he feared were sabotaging his plans for their own political benefits thrust the blame for the Depression squarely on his shoulders. Hoover was doomed to defeat in 1932 to the forward-thinking Roosevelt, whose optimism and plans for recovery were embraced by voters.

Issues of the Day

It seemed like nothing mattered in 1932—not even the growing call for the repeal of Prohibition—aside from the terrifying effects of the worst depression in American history. Hoover was saddled with voter images of soup lines, scores of unemployed sitting hopelessly on street curbs, dirty shacks housing the homeless now called "Hoovervilles" as a mocking reminder of the president blamed for the financial misery, and empty pockets turned inside-out by men in bread lines that became known as "Hoover flags."

The country was a shambles. Hoover's unpopularity grew when encampments of the First World War veterans demanding their bonus pay immediately were routed by General MacArthur troops.

The 1932 Campaign

The Hoover defeat came as no surprise, even to fellow Republicans, given the worsening of the depression. Yet, despite no displays of enthusiasm at their convention they plowed forward by renominating him on the first ballot in Chicago. Their platform featuring calls for a balanced budget and protective tariff, as well as repeal of Prohibition to help spur an economic revival. The latter reversed Hoover's 1928 stance but Republicans believed a change in the outlook of voters on the president might be helpful.

While a sense of doom and gloom permeated the Republican convention, one of optimism washed over the Democratic event in the same city. The depression gave them reason to believe that their party would take over the White House for the first time since Woodrow Wilson won in 1916. Roosevelt emerged with the nomination on the fourth ballot and defied tradition by flying in to make his acceptance speech directly to the delegates and prove that a body stricken with polio could survive the rigors of a campaign. The conventioneers reacted with raucous cheers and applause to his promise for a "new deal"—words that would become synonymous with his plan to pull America out of its economic morass.

Roosevelt treaded lightly thereafter. He understood Hoover's massive unpopularity and carefully avoided any verbal blunders that could cost him votes. He continued his vow to give the people a "new deal" and it resonated. promise but he provided few details at first, which resulted in criticism from some. But he delved further into his plans during a speech in San Francisco seven weeks before the election, asserting that the federal government needed to assume responsibility over the welfare of the people while assisting both business and labor in an attempt to distribute wealth fairly. His words gave Americans a sense of optimism as they would for more than a decade to come.

Hoover had no chance. He delivered nine major addresses to defense his record and attack Roosevelt. He tried to divert blame for the depression on the aftermath of the First World War, which had ended more than a decade earlier, and claimed his administration had prevented a complete economic collapse. He warned against federal government overreach in the Roosevelt plan. But his bland personality and speeches contrasted negatively against those delivered by his opponent. His fellow Republicans were rightHoover was cooked.

The voters proved it. A record of more than 40 million cast their ballots. Roosevelt won the popular count by more than seven million and won all but six states. Hoover captured none outside of the Republican Northeast stronghold. The Democrats also dominated the Congressional races to start a two-decade domination of presidential elections that would not end until Dwight Eisenhower won in 1952.

After the Loss

Hoover responded with criticism of the president and the New Deal, which he complained gave too much power to the federal government. His hopes for another shot at the White House faded when other Republicans such as Alf Landon and Wendall Willkie tried and failed to unseat Roosevelt. He also sided with isolationists after Germany invaded Poland to launch another war and even railed against the Lend-Lease policy to aid Great Britain in 1940. Though he understood the need for American involvement after the Japanese bombing of Pearl Harbor in December 1941 he warned that the nation should not side with the Soviet Union to defeat the Axis powers.

Such disliked views simply added to his unpopularity, even among Republican politicians who discouraged him from running for president in 1944. President Truman chose Hoover to chair a commission tasked to reorganize the executive departments in 1947 and was given a similar assignment by President Eisenhower six years later. Upon retirement, he authored many articles and books before dying in New York city at age 90 in October 1964.

Coming From Hoover

Once upon a time my opponents honored me as possessing the fabulous intellectual and economic power by which I created a worldwide depression all by myself.[1]

Did You Know?

Herbert and wife Lou spoke Chinese. In fact, Lou was fluent in eight languages. The couple reportedly spoke Chinese in the White House when they wanted to talk privately.

33

Alf Landon

Alfred Landon. Courtesy of the Library of Congress, LC-USZ62-106389

Party: Republican
Birth state: Pennsylvania
Represented: Kansas
Years of defeat: 1936
Running mate: Frank Knox
Winner: Franklin Roosevelt
Campaign slogans: "Remember Hoover!" (Roosevelt); "Defeat the New Deal and Its Reckless Spending" (Landon); "Let's Make it a Landon-Slide!" (Landon)

All About Landon

Landon was born on September 9, 1887, in West Middlesex, Pennsylvania. But he spent most of his youth in Marietta, Ohio, where his father John worked as a superintendent of an oil refinery company. After Alf graduated from Marietta Academy in 1904, the family moved to the oil-boom town of Independence, Kansas. It was in that state he would make his mark. Landon received his law degree from the University of Kansas four years later.

Unlike others through American history who believed opening a law practice would plant the seeds for a political career, Landon instead began working as a bookkeeper at the Independence State Bank of Commerce, then moved across the street to the First National Bank. He followed in his father's footsteps by investing in oil-drilling projects, eventually switching fulltime to the oil industry and gaining tremendous wealth.

By that time, he had formed political views tied to the Republican progressivism of the era. His father served as a delegate to their 1912 national convention to endorse Theodore Roosevelt, who lost to William Howard Taft. Alf then joined the new Progressive Party to help get Roosevelt elected while also delving into local politics by spearheading the county campaign in support of Kansas gubernatorial candidate Arthur Capper.

The new party eventually faded, forcing Landon to return to his political roots as a progressive Republican. Landon continued to back candidates with matching views, including Capper, whom he supported in a bid for US Senate and successful gubernatorial candidate Henry Allen in 1918. Meanwhile, Landon's independent oil and gas business thrived.

Landon proved his morality in 1924, when he campaigned for independent William Allen White in a Kansas governor race after opponent Ben Paulen refused to criticize the increasingly popular Ku Klux Klan. Landon served campaign manager in 1928 for eventual winner Clyde Reed.

He was ready to throw his own hat into the ring. Landon ran successfully for Kansas governor in 1932. He felt it inappropriate during the Great Depression to throw a lavish inauguration party. There were no parades, no 17-gun salute, not even invitations to dignitaries. He accepted no new car as governor, not even new dishes for the executive mansion. In response to the growing call for government intervention to stem the tide of the Great Depression, he set the tone for his future battle against Franklin Roosevelt in his inauguration speech.

"We have grown to expect a lot for nothing," he said. "We expected government to strew our paths with roses. We wanted to keep on taking out, hardly realizing that we have to pay in as well. This condition "built castles on the sand" that crumbled. ...We are on the frontier of a new world... We have come a long way since governments were chiefly of a patriarchal nature over agricultural states."[1]

Landon toned down his progressivism in office. He worked to lower taxes, reorganized state administration, and sought relief for farmers and the unemployed while cutting salaries for state employees. His office interviewed hundreds of applicants daily to fill the scarce number of state jobs available. Kansas grew more dependent on federal programs initiated by Roosevelt with little state funds available. Meanwhile, severe droughts and Dust Bowl storms caused further hardship.

His work proved popular. Landon easily won re-election over Democrat Omar Ketchum in 1934. He emphasized again at his inauguration speech about the perceived danger of government intervention into the economic recovery and spending that ran up debt.

Landon emerged a logical choice as a Republican presidential candidate to oppose Roosevelt, whose New Deal policies had yet to end the Depression and were being scrutinized by all and criticized by many. But Landon was no match for the beloved president in one of the most lopsided defeats in American history.

Issues of the Day

The New Deal and its potential effectiveness in combatting what had for five years been referred to as the Great Depression dominated the political discourse in the United States in 1936. Roosevelt had yet to push through Congress much of his proposed initiatives but Social Security and unemployment benefits had already taken hold and been proven popular among voters, so was legislation passed to build homes and give workers the right to collective bargaining.

Big business railed against regulation of the banking industry and other financial institutions but most Americans with the Stock Market Crash still fresh in their minds approved. The "alphabet" initiatives of the New Deal such as the Public Works Administration (PWA) and Works Progress Administration (WPA) had begun to lower unemployment. The Civilian Conservation Corps alone was in the process of putting nearly three million young men to work.

The opposition railed against government overreach and runaway spending on such programs but failed in the end to convince voters of their plan to extricate the country out of the economic mess.

The 1936 Campaign

He who controlled the radio airwaves in 1936 boasted a huge advantage politically, and that was Roosevelt, who had enchanted and comforted the nation with his "fireside chats" that always began with the words "my friends" and had been described as hypnotizing.

Landon was not strongly opposed to New Deal legislation. He considered himself a practical progressive and even criticized his own party for rejecting it entirely. He did condemn business regulation and Social Security while asserting late in the campaign that Roosevelt had corruptly gained excessive executive power. Such charges were perceived as a desperate attempt to influence voters. Yet Landon stumped infrequently and dispassionately, perhaps in the knowledge that he stood little chance against his popular foe.

The legitimacy of his fears were confirmed by George Gallup, who famously used what he claimed to be scientific polling to predict an FDR victory. Such methods to forecast results would be utilized from that time forward. But it was certainly not necessary in 1936. Most knew Roosevelt would win in a landslide—and he did. He captured 11 million more votes than Landon and every state but Vermont and Maine. The Democrats also maintained control of Congress, allowing Roosevelt to continue pushing through New Deal initiatives that eventually pulled the country out of the Great Depression.

After the Loss

Landon's loss ended his career as a political candidate. He remained in Kansas, working as an independent oil developer and radio station owner. He served as a delegate to the 1940, 1944, and 1948 Republican conventions as that party continued to fail in bids to win back the presidency. He became an elder statesman, sometimes expressing preferences for particular candidates. Landon lived long enough to receive on his 95th birthday a visit from President Reagan, who spoke as part of the Landon Lecture Series at Kansas State University and visited him at his Topeka home five years later. Landon died 34 days after his 100th birthday on October 12, 1987.

Coming From Landon

America bids fair to join in the procession of nations of the world in their march toward a new social and economic philosophy... Some say this will lead to socialism, some communism, others fascism. For myself I am convinced that the ultimate goal will be a modified form of individual rights and ownership of property out of which will come a wider spread of prosperity and opportunity.[2]

Did You Know?

Landon's daughter Nancy Kassebaum served Kansas as a Republican in the US Senate from 1978 to 1997.

34

Wendell Willkie

Wendell Lewis Willkie. Courtesy of the Library of Congress, LC-USZ62-48851

Party: Republican
Birth state: Indiana
Represented: New York
Years of defeat: 1940
Running mate: Charles McNary
Winner: Franklin Roosevelt
Campaign slogans: "Better a Third Termer than a Third Rater!" (Roosevelt); "Willkie for the Millionaires, Roosevelt for the Millions" (Roosevelt); "Roosevelt for Ex-President" (Willkie); "Third Reich. Third International. Third Term" (Willkie)

All About Willkie

Eventually choosing to be known by his more alliterative middle name, Lewis Wendell Willkie was born on February 18, 1892, in the tiny farming community of Elwood, Indiana. Both his parents were lawyers—his mother Henrietta was among the first females admitted to the state bar. His abolitionist grandparents moved to Indiana after the Kansas Territory in which they had been living was opened to slavery in the mid-1850s.

Willkie's father was a Prussian immigrant who embraced progressive politics after moving to the United States. He even joined a torchlight procession in 1896 in support of Democratic presidential candidate William Jennings Bryan, who was visiting Elwood during his campaign. Little Wendell showed loyalty to his father by fighting a buy from a Republican-backed family on the sidewalk. The Willkies became such ardent supporters that Bryan stayed at their home in his 1900 campaign stop.

A lack of discipline and poor posture concerned his parents. So at 14, he was sent to the Culver Military Academy in the summer to correct both problems. He eventually thrived educationally, though he was sometimes punished for arguing with teachers. Willkie was named class president as a senior. He traveled often in the summer, taking one job in a South Dakota flophouse where he rose from dishwasher to co-owner, and another at Yellowstone National Park, where he was fired for losing control of stagecoach horses.

Willkie was greatly influenced by the political leanings of his father, who represented striking workers at a local tin plate factor. He accompanied his dad to Chicago to try to convince legendary liberal attorney Clarence Darrow to take over representation and learned that, though willing, he was far too expensive for the union to pay. Darrow explained that the compensation for which he asked was ethical for anyone advocating for a cause for which they strongly believe.

Willkie enrolled at Indiana University after his high school graduation in 1910. He emerged as a student rebel, reading the works of Karl Marx, dabbling in socialism, and even petitioning the school to offer courses on the political theory. He threw himself into campus politics but lost his bid for student office.

Soon, Willkie was earning money for law school by teaching high school history and coaching debate in Coffeyville, Kansas. He left that job to work as a lab assistant in Puerto Rico, where the worker abuse he witnessed strengthened his commitment to social justice. It was a cause he continued to further while thriving as a student at Indiana School of Law and joining his parents' law firm.

That career was placed on hold for the First World War. He volunteered for the army the day President Wilson asked Congress for a declaration of war against Germany. Willkie was commissioned as a first lieutenant and sent to artillery training but the war ended before he reached the front. He spent his next few months defending soldiers who had bolted from their units to spend time in Paris.

Upon his return, he left Elwood for a job with the Firestone Rubber Company in Akron, Ohio, before earning a partnership with a law firm in that city. He continued to rise as an attorney as general counsel for the Commonwealth and Southern, an expansive utility holding company for which he assumed the presidency after the depression resulted in near-bankruptcy. Behind Willkie's legal and financial wizardry it began turning a profit. His most notable legal battles during the Franklin Roosevelt administration were fought against New Deal legislation, including the Tennessee Valley Authority, which he asserted was competing unfairly against privately owned utility businesses.. He later founded the law firm of Willkie, Farr, and Gallagher. Willkie wrote and spoke in support of struggling businessmen.

Little could he have imagined he would be called upon to run against Roosevelt for the presidency in 1940. His strong criticism against government restraints against private businesses motivated Republicans to push him as a dark-horse presidential candidate in 1940. After his nomination on the sixth ballot at the convention, it became obvious he had no chance to defeat the wildly popular incumbent.

Issues of the Day

No legal precedence prevented Roosevelt from seeking a third term as president in 1940—that would not come until the 22nd Amendment was passed in 1951. But it was certainly a controversial decision by the incumbent that was heatedly argued before the campaign began. Some Republicans even compared Roosevelt to German dictator Adolf Hitler, who had destroyed the last vestiges of democratic government in his country.

Potential American involvement in a war that Hitler had already launched in Europe dominated conversation. The debate grew more intense in the spring when the German blitz overran France and threatened to take over England. Roosevelt was criticized by some for pushing military aid to Great Britain that would result in 1941 in the Lend-Lease program that sent food, oil and military supplies to England (and later France, China, and the Soviet Union). Isolationists railed against it, contending it was a precursor to the United States sending troops to fight and die overseas.

No domestic issues were viewed as controversial after Roosevelt spearheaded a rebound of the economy. That all but ensured his reelection to an unprecedented third term in the White House.

The 1940 Campaign

The popularity and morality of Roosevelt, who had pulled the country out of the Great Depression and kept it out of war while supporting the allies, preventing Willkie from taking a strong stand against him. Willkie voiced agreement with his policies, condemning only that New Deal legislation had been executed inefficiently and with partiality.

Willkie had come out of nowhere to secure the Republican nomination. Other candidates such as 1944 nominee Thomas Dewey (New York), Arthur Vandenberg (Michigan), and Robert Taft (Ohio) appeared more likely to run against Roosevelt but none were pushed through on the first ballot at the convention, opening up the path for Willkie, who amazingly had been a Roosevelt delegate for the Democrats in 1932. But Willkie failed to strongly campaign in favor of the Republican platform that opposed American involvement in the overseas war. His admonitions to slash federal spending and against executive branch power proved weak in convincing voters to abandon Roosevelt.

Antiwar sentiment did result in Willkie performing better on election day than Landon did in 1936, though it was still a Democratic landslide. He won ten states in various areas of the country and lost the popular vote by less than five million.

After the Loss

Though Willkie had criticized Roosevelt for some of his New Deal initiatives, he supported the president's approach and actions before and during American participation in the war. He publicly backed the Lend-Lease program, placing him at odds with the Republican establishment. Roosevelt appreciated the support. He sent Willkie to England to demonstrate American fellowship in the knowledge that a visit from the head of an opposition party would convince the British that the United States was by their side. Willkie visited bombed-out sites in London and other cities during the blitz and spoke with Prime Minister Winston Churchill.

He returned to successfully convince Congress to pass Lend–Lease and engage in a series of written debates against leading isolationist Charles Lindbergh. Willkie lambasted the famed aviator for accusing American Jews of agitating for American involvement and fought for the repeal of the Neutrality Act.

Willkie was named chairman of the board for the 20th Century-Fox Film Corporation in 1942 and authored a book based on his travel experiences that influenced many Republicans to support the war effort. But those urgings turned some away from Willkie as a potential presidential candidate, forcing him to withdraw from the race after losing the Wisconsin primary.

He would not have been able to take over the White House anyway. Always neglectful of his health and diet while smoking heavily and rarely exercising, Willkie suffered a series of heart attacks and died a month before the presidential election and seven months before the allies emerged from the war in Europe victorious.

Coming From Willkie

We are not isolationists except in so far as we seek to isolate ourselves completely from war. Yet we must avoid isolation of a selfish and narrow sort.[1]

Did You Know?

Willkie was the last major party presidential nominee with no previous government experience until Donald Trump ran for the Republicans in 2016.

35

Thomas E. Dewey

Thomas E. Dewey, waving from floor of convention hall. Courtesy of the Library of Congress, LC-DIG-ppmsca-51659

Party: Republican
Birth state: Michigan
Represented: New York
Years of defeat: 1944, 1948
Running mate: John Bricker (1944); Earl Warren (1948)
Winner: Franklin Roosevelt (1944); Harry S. Truman (1948)
Other notable candidate: Strom Thurmond (States Rights)
Campaign slogans: 1944: "Don't Swap Horses in Midstream" (Roosevelt); "Dewey or Don't We?" (Dewey); "Win the War Quicker with Dewey and Bricker" (Dewey); 1948: "I'm Just Wild About Harry" (Truman); "The Buck Stops Here" (Truman); "Dew it with Dewey" (Dewey)

All About Dewey

Dewey was born into a politically active family on March 24, 1902, in Owosso, Michigan. He was the first major presidential candidate born in the 21st century. His grandfather was believed to have been a charter member of the Republican Party and father George a newspaper publisher and Republican county chairman. His family tree reached far back into American history. Earliest ancestor Thomas Dewey settled in Massachusetts in 1634.

Young Thomas spent much of his time doing chores at his father's newspaper office and eliciting the help of friends to join him. He earned enough money in that job and working on a farm to pay his first-year tuition at the University of Michigan. Dewey graduated from that school in 1923. His experiences there extended beyond his studies. He proved himself a fine baritone, led his college glee club for two years, and even won a Michigan singing contest before placing third in a national competition. He later met his future wife Francis at a singing school.

Dewey traveled to New York to study voice and enrolled in Columbia Law School to ensure an alternative career. He became torn between singing and the legal field. Serving as a local Republican election official swayed him toward the latter. Following his graduation in 1925 he toured England and France, then decided to pursue law full-time. He accepted a junior partnership then opened a private practice. By 1931, he had been appointed chief assistant in charge of 52 other attorneys for New York's Southern District.

Soon Dewey gained a measure of fame for prosecuting beer runner Irving Wechsler for an income tax violation. Returning to private practice in December 1933 he earned a then-substantial annual salary of $75,000. Two years later, he accepted an appointment as a special prosecutor and soon became known as a "gangbuster." He attacked the underworld, convicting mobster Charles (Lucky) Luciano. He had 72 racketeers convicted, mostly in the trucking and restaurant industries. Only one target was acquitted.

Soon, Dewey was elected New York District Attorney. The convictions piled up as one racketeer after another served jail sentences. He lost a bid to become governor of that state in 193 but was reelected as district attorney in 1941 and made a successful run for the governorship the following year. His achievements in that role included increased state aid for education and the establishment of the first state commission to end employment discrimination based on religion or race.

Issues of the Day (1944)

Perhaps if Roosevelt was up for re-election two years earlier, the Republicans could have successfully separated war policies with his. But the early struggles of the American military in fighting Japan and Germany were in the distant past and the allies were on the verge of winning the Second World War with significant US aid in late 1944.

The result was little ammunition for Dewey, who criticized the administration for the federal deficit generated during the war and again for wielding excessive executive power. The Republicans sought to portray Roosevelt as an aging leader and asserted it was simply time for a change. But they could not convince the majority of voters.

The 1944 Campaign

The perceived growing threat of Dewey motivated Roosevelt to energize his campaign and deliver significant political speeches and tour big cities in New England, New York, New Jersey and Pennsylvania in an open car, even in rainstorms, despite his continued focus on bringing World War II to a successful conclusion.

Dewey considered it his patriotic duty do avoid criticism of Roosevelt's work as commander in chief. That might have proven to be political suicide anyway given that the United States was on the verge of winning the war. Dewey simply claimed it was time for a change and challenged how the federal government had been run.

Though many voters agreed, he still proved to be the fourth lopsided victim of the Roosevelt onslaught. Dewey lost by 3.6 million votes and won just 12 states.

Issues of the Day (1948)

Civil rights was thrust front and center in 1948 though the civil rights movement had yet to begin in earnest. The Republicans were still the most progressive party at the time—at least until Barry Goldwater was nominated in 1964. Among their pursuits was integration of the military and abolition of the poll tax in the South that prevented nearly all African-Americans from voting, they also sought independence for the state of Israel.

Democratic agreement on desegregation of the military and its July implementation inspired a "Dixiecrat" movement in that party resulting in Strom Thurmond running as a third-party candidate.

The 1948 Campaign

Convention chaos among Democrats did not prevent Dewey from eventually losing by just a whisker. The Mississippi delegation walked out in protest and many in the Alabama contingent followed suit when the party platform revealed backing for integration of the military. Dewey still won on the first ballot over Southern favorite Richard Russell of Georgia. Future presidential candidate Hubert Humphrey helped set the Democrats on a more liberal civil rights path with an impassioned speech.

"To those who say we are rushing this issue of civil rights, I say to them we are 172 years late," Humphrey said. "To those who say that this civil rights program is an infringement on states' rights, I say this: The time has arrived in America for the Democratic Party to get out of the shadows of states' rights and walk forthrightly into the bright sunshine of human rights."[1]

Days later, a group of "Dixiecrats" formed the States' Rights Party and nominated Thormond from South Carolina. Some liberals supported Progressive Party candidate Henry Wallace.

That splintering cost Dewey the presidency. He nearly won it—the *Chicago Daily Tribune* famously offered a headline that proclaimed Dewey the winner. He was indeed expected to win but surprisingly lost states in the Midwest and West. A lack of campaign aggression in the belief that Dewey was destined for victory played a role in his defeat. Dewey did not speak out strongly, motivating Truman to claim he was evading the issues. Passage of the anti-union Taft–Hartley Act by the Republican congress inspired labor organizations to back Truman.

It all added up to a close defeat that a united Democratic Party should have won. Thurmon stole five states and millions of votes. Dewey lost the popular vote by more than two million and the electoral college, 303–189.

After the Losses

Dewey remained governor during and after his presidential bid defeats to Roosevelt in 1944 and Harry S. Truman in 1948. He remained wildly popular in New York, winning reelection as governor in 1946 by the widest margin in state history. He finished his three successive terms in office in 1954. By the time he left office, he had reorganized many of the state departments, revised tax laws, and planned public works projects including a new hospital and highway.

After leaving the governorship, he joined a prominent New York law firm that represented many international clients, including the Turkish government. But Dewey was still considered a viable presidential candidate. Dwight D. Eisenhower suggested him as a possible successor while weighing not running for a second term in 1956, but Republican Party leaders made it clear they did not want to renominate a two-time loser. Dewey, however, remained influential. He convinced Eisenhower to keep embattled Richard Nixon as his running mate. Dewey strongly backed Nixon in his unsuccessful run for the presidency in 1960. He continued to back Republican candidates throughout the 1960s though he expressed doubts about the ultraconservative Barry Goldwater when he ran for the White House in 1964. Dewey supported the more liberal-minded Nelson Rockefeller.

Dewey declined many offers to return to government office, even turning down a spot as Chief Justice on the Supreme Court. He did not live long enough to learn the outcome of the 1972 election or see Nixon and his party dragged down by the Watergate scandal. Dewey died on March 16, 1971.

Coming From Dewey

We need not be afraid of the future, for the future will be in our own hands. We shall need courage, energy and determination, but above all, we shall need faith in ourselves, in our communities and in our country.[2]

Did You Know?

Among Dewey's first targets as a prosecutor was legendary mobster Dutch Schultz and his illegal gambling and prostitution rings. Schultz asked "Lucky" Luciano to have Dewey killed but the hit was rejected on the grounds that it would be bad for business to murder a public official. Schultz tried to have Dewey murdered anyway and was killed by Luciano. That freed up Dewey to prosecute murder-for-hire enterprise head Louis Lepke, whom Dewey convicted and was eventually executed.

36

Adlai Stevenson

Adlai Stevenson. Courtesy of the Library of Congress, LC-DIG-ppmsca-19176

Party: Democratic
Birth state: California
Represented: Illinois
Years of defeat: 1952, 1956
Running mate: John Sparkman (1952); Estes Kefauver (1956)
Winner: Dwight D. Eisenhower (1952, 1956)
Campaign slogans: 1952: "I Like Ike" (Eisenhower); "Madly for Adlai" (Stevenson); 1956: "Peace and Prosperity" (Eisenhower); "Adlai and Estes—The Bestest" (Stevenson)

All About Stevenson

Stevenson was born 36 days after the turn of the 21st century in Los Angeles. His father worked for the Hearst Newspaper Company, and his uncle served as publisher of a prominent Republican publication. The marriage of his parents in 1893 had been considered a merger of the two most influential political families in the region, though his father's side sided with the Democrats and his mother's family with Republicans.

The Stevensons were not long for Los Angeles. They moved in 1906 to Bloomington, Illinois, where Adlai attended elementary school just two blocks from his home. He was enrolled seven years later in the Thomas Metcalf

Training School on the Illinois State campus, then at University High School as a teacher trainee.

By that time, young Adlai had been forced to overcome an emotional tragedy after accidentally shooting his cousin Ruth in the head with a rifle and killing her while showing off his proficiency in the manual of arms. The coroner ruled it an accident, which cleared the boy of wrongdoing, but he grieved over the incident for the rest of his life. He kept it hidden for decades until recounting the entire story in a 1952 magazine article.

Stevenson was a disinterested student and often missed school due to illness or family travels. He was moved in 1916 to an all-male boarding school in Connecticut, where he blossomed socially, working as managing editor of its newspaper, and becoming more politically aware. His grades improved enough to land him at Princeton University, where he again earned a managing editor spot on the newspaper. Upon graduation he was accepted into the Harvard School of Law, from which he flunked out in the second year.

That educational failure motivated a move back to Bloomington and journalism. He began working at *The Pantagraph*, where his varied jobs included answering phones to writing features. But dissatisfaction led to his return to his legal studies. He graduated from Northwestern Law School in 1927 and passed the Illinois Bar before settling in Chicago and joining the prestigious firm of Cutting, Moore, and Sidely.

Despite death-bed words of warnings from his father against pursuing a political career, Stevenson seemed destined to throw his hat into a ring. He began doing legal work during the height of the Depression for the New Deal Agricultural Adjustment Administration and soon earned the presidency of the Chicago Council on Foreign Relations, which generated public interest in overseas affairs. As the Second World War approached, he joined the local Committee to Defend American by Aiding Allies. Its goal was to garner support for Great Britain and other European democracies, particularly after the German invasion of Poland in September 1939 launched the war. Stevenson worked extensively for Special Assistant to the Secretary of the Navy Frank Knox during the war. He wrote speeches and toured various areas where battles raged.

Stevenson turned his attention after the war to the formation of the United Nations. He served as part of a US delegation, organizing a conference in San Francisco and attending others in London and New York. He was then thrust into the political scandals in Chicago upon his return. The administration of Illinois Governor Dwight Green was accused of rampant corruption. Stevenson was urged to run for that office by those who believed a political outsider could attract more voters. They were right. Stevenson gave rousing speeches and was perceived as honest and clean. He defeated Green with the largest margin of victory ever received by any candidate in the state.

Using a strategy of bipartisanship—Stevenson cared more about honesty than party affiliation—he cleaned up Illinois politics. He crusaded for a new state constitution to replace the existing one, which had been written in 1870 when Illinois had a mostly rural population. He failed to overhaul the constitution but passed an amendment that made it easier to alter it and set the stage for its total replacement in 1970. Among his other achievements as governor were streamlining law enforcement agencies and expanding state jurisdiction. He finished his term having pushed 78 bills through the majority Republican legislature.

His decision to not run for reelection coincided with plans by some Democrats to push him as a presidential candidate. Though reluctant and stunned when President Truman all but ensured his nomination, for which Stevenson insisted he had not ambition, he eventually relented despite his awareness that he would be an underdog against Eisenhower. And he knew that an endorsement from the unpopular Truman would be more harmful than helpful. His lopsided defeat in 1952 surprised nobody.

Stevenson ran more aggressively and confidently against Eisenhower four years later. Unlike in 1952, he wanted the nomination and got it. But he was beaten by an even larger margin. His push for the presidency was dead.

Issues of the Day (1952)

Neither party supported immediate withdrawal of American troops fighting the Korean War, but the Republicans certainly had plenty of ammunition as they tried to win back the White House for the first time since Herbert Hoover occupied it. Democratic President Harry Truman, who was not seeking reelection though eligible for another term since he had only been elected once, received a flurry of criticism from Republicans for relieving popular General Douglas MacArthur from command of United Nations forces in Korea for insubordination. Americans debated—as they would more heatedly in the next decade with the US military bogged down in Vietnam—the righteousness and practicality of trying to save South Korea from a Communist takeover.

The Red Scare was also in the spotlight at home as Wisconsin Senator Joseph McCarthy had two years earlier claimed to own a list of Communist sympathizers working in the State Department. Freedom of political affiliation had become an issue.

Taking a back seat temporarily in the American scene was civil rights, though controversial Jim Crow laws in the South that continued to relegate African-Americans to second-class citizenship remained a topic of debate and politicians in that area of the country grew more isolated and steadfast in their stand against integration.

The 1952 Campaign

After a push in several states to support ousted general Douglas MacArthur as a presidential candidate failed, it had become apparent that Eisenhower would become the first Republican president since Herbert Hoover. He ran a vigorous campaign while his wartime heroics and engaging personality attracted voters.

It was not all smooth sailing. The New York Post revealed that VP candidate Richard Nixon had a secret "slush fund." Eisenhower insisted to Nixon that he extricate himself out of the scandal, which motivated the famous nationally televised "Checkers speech" in which he acknowledged the fund but asserted no illegality. Nixon concluded the address by admitting he accepted a cocker spaniel named Checkers as a political gift. The public responded favorably, leading Eisenhower to keep Nixon on the ticket.

Stevenson, who had accepted the Democratic nomination with great reluctance, was doomed. Eisenhower won by more than six million votes and captured all but nine states, all in the traditionally Democratic South. Soon, that region of the country would turn red. The 1952 election proved to be a strong repudiation of the Truman administration.

Issues of the Day (1956)

Two major events had placed civil rights atop the topics of discussion among many American voters in 1956. The first was the *Brown v. Board* ruling in the Supreme Court that banned school segregation and demand that Jim Crow states in the South integrate with "all deliberate speed." That less-than-forceful edict allowed for dawdling and plenty of time for debating. So did the courageous act of Black activist Rosa Parks, whose refusal to give up her bus seat to a white passenger on December 1, 1955, inspired the Montgomery Bus Boycott, the first organized well-publicized civil rights protest of the era.

Despite such events neither party emerged as a moral leader in favor of integration or a leader in promoting national legislation, which would have to wait until the mid-1960s. President Eisenhower did not take a stand until 1957, when he dispatched federal troops to help the Little Rock Nine, who were stopped in a violent show of force from integrating the high school in that city.

Other issues that had arisen involved foreign policy. Uprisings against the Soviet-controlled Communist regimes in East Germany (1953) and Hungary (1956) motivated some Americans to call for military intervention. Another troubled spot was the Middle East, where Egyptian president Gamal Nasser announced the nationalization of the Suez Canal Company, which had been owned and operated jointly by the French and British for nearly a century. Many grew suspicious over his perceived intention to weaken European influence in the region, which they believed Nasser resented. Other contentious issues overseas included continued US participation in the North Atlantic Treaty Organization (NATO) and the admission of Red China into the United Nations.

The 1956 Campaign

Stevenson entered the fray in 1956 with far greater enthusiasm and a stronger moral base. He called for a "New America" in which poverty was abolished, freedom bells rang for one and all and the threat of nuclear war was eliminated. He called for extension of New Deal programs to senior citizens, as well as the realms of health, natural resources, economics, and education.

Such lofty goals were deemed unrealistic by Eisenhower and the Republicans, who cited general prosperity as the main reason to vote for the incumbent. He had ended the Korean War with South Korea still intact, pushed successfully for the construction of a massive highway system, and extended Social Security. His first term even ended in a budget surplus.

The dye was cast. Eisenhower won in a bigger landslide than in 1952, even stealing some Southern states away from Stevenson, who lost by more than nine million votes.

After the Losses

Stevenson considered running again in 1860 but stepped aside in favor of young upstart John F. Kennedy. He hoped that Kennedy would appoint him Secretary of State but he was instead used as US Ambassador to the United Nations. Though angered at Kennedy after the Bay of Pigs fiasco in 1961, Stevenson famously confronted the Soviet delegation at a United Nations security council meeting during the Cuban Missile Crisis and presented a resolution calling for an immediate dismantling and withdrawal of the Russian weaponry. His courage helped bring the frightening event to a peaceful conclusion.

Serving three more years as UN ambassador, during which time he had gained a reputation as one of the most effective diplomats in the world, Stevenson focused on nuclear disarmament. His efforts helped create the Limited Nuclear Test Ban Treaty of 1963. But his lifestyle that included extensive traveling, drinking and smoking began to take a toll on his health. He grew disenchanted after the assassination of Kennedy with his lack of influence on the President Johnson administration and the growing conflict in Vietnam. He planned retirement after leaving his job as ambassador but died during a trip to London on July 14, 1965.

Coming From Stevenson

We travel together, passengers on a little space ship, dependent on its vulnerable reserves of air and soil; all committed for our safety to its security and peace; preserved from annihilation only by the care, the work, and I will say, the love we give our fragile craft. We cannot maintain it half fortunate, half miserable, half confident, half despairing, half slave to the ancient enemies of man half free in a liberation of resources undreamed of until this day. No craft, no crew can travel with such vast contradictions. On their resolution depends the survival of us all.[1]

Did You Know?

In 1952, Stevenson got caught up in a scandal as Illinois governor. It began with rumors that State Department of Agriculture employees had been bribed to accept horse meat as cow meat and one official was bribed to say nothing. Soon, reports claimed that restaurants had served hamburgers with 40 percent horse meat, which were jokingly called "Adlaiburgers." Stevenson wasted no time firing the perpetrators but the scandal damaged his reputation.

37

Richard Nixon

Richard M. Nixon. Courtesy of the Library of Congress, LC-DIG-ppmsca-83254

Party: Republican
Birth state: California
Represented: California
Years of defeat: 1960
Running mate: Henry Cabot Lodge
Winner: John F. Kennedy
Other notable candidate: Harry F. Byrd (Independent)
Campaign slogans: "A Time for Greatness" (Kennedy); "Peace. Experience. Prosperity" (Nixon)

All About Nixon

Richard Nixon, the only president in American history forced out of office before finishing his term, was born on January 9, 1913. He was raised the second of five brothers on a citrus farm in Yorba Linda, California. His childhood was marked by the financial struggles of his family and the untimely death of brother Arthur at age seven.

The failure of his parents as ranchers forced a move to nearby Whittier, where they opened a grocery store and gas station. The entire Nixon clan worked there to make ends meet. Richard continued to help run the business while living at home during his years at Whittier College, where he became involved in many groups and social activities including student government., drama and football.

Nixon budgeted his time well enough to thrive in his studies and earn a scholarship to the Duke University School of Law during the height of the Great Depression in 1934. He served as president of the Student Bar Association and graduated in 1937 before returning to Whittier and joining the law firm Wingert and Bewley. He soon met schoolteacher and future wife Pat, whom he married in 1940. The couple moved to Washington, DC in 1942 when Nixon joined the Office of Price Administration, then served in the US Naval Reserve. He eventually volunteered for active duty as an officer in the Pacific Fleet. Nixon in the Pacific Fleet, where he was active in air combat transport. Promoted to lieutenant in October 1943, he worked at various military offices throughout the United States and was eventually promoted to the rank of Commander in the Naval Reserve in 1953.

By that time, his reputation had reached Republican politicians in Whittier who approached him about seeking political office. He embarked on a successful run for Congress in 1946 and returned with Pat and his family to Washington. Nixon served on the Education and Labor Committee and backed enactment of the Taft-Hartley Act, which limited the power of labor unions, and traveled to Europe to help initiate the Marshall Plan, which provided aid to war-torn European nations.

Nixon gained fame during the Red Scare period when he investigated charges against former State Department official Alger Hiss, who was accused of spying for the Soviet Union before and during the Second World War. Nixon's star was rising in conservative circles. He easily defeated a Democratic candidate he deemed too liberal for a US Senate seat in 1950, then embarked on a campaign to discredit President Truman's handling of the Korean War and warn the nation about the threat of global Communism.

Two years later, he was running alongside Dwight D. Eisenhower in a winning presidential campaign. He survived a scandal with his nationally televised "Checkers speech" and was presented with such tasks as chairing the National Security Council and traveling as a goodwill ambassador to foreign countries during the Cold War. Not all were friendly visits. Nixon and wife Pat were spat upon by protesters at a Venezuelan airport in 1958, and his motorcade was later assaulted. He was later praised for his coolness in the face of such threats.

Nixon famously engaged in a verbal battle with Soviet leader Nikita Khrushchev during the opening of the American National Exhibition in Moscow in July 1959. The two stopped at a model kitchen and debated the ideological and political differences between the two nations. The debate strengthened Nixon's reputation in the United States and raised his stature as a 1960 presidential candidate.

Issues of the Day

Personal and national issues stole the spotlight in 1960. The former was both the youth and religion of Democratic candidate John F. Kennedy. Some believed the 43-year-old Catholic was too inexperienced for the job. The two far more consequential concerns were the Cold War and growing Soviet influence in the Western Hemisphere, particularly in Cuba, and the civil rights movement, which was reaching its height.

Most Southern politicians and voters had grown disenchanted with both parties for taking moral stands against segregation. The massive switch from Democratic to Republican support in that region would have to wait four more years. But African-Americans who could vote in other areas of the country backed Kennedy in huge numbers after he reached out to the governor of Georgia and other local authorities to try to secure his release from jail after joining a sit-in at an Atlanta department store.

Fears that the United States had fallen behind the Soviets technologically and militarily intensified when the artificial satellite Sputnik became the first in the world to orbit the earth in 1957. Three years later, the Soviets had placed military installations in Cuba. That scare benefitted Kennedy and hurt Nixon, who was still tied as vice-president to Eisenhower, who some asserted had let Russia overtake the United States in nuclear weaponry and other military hardware.

The 1960 Campaign

The 1960 campaign marked the first time the comparatively new medium of television greatly influenced its outcome. By that time nearly 90 percent of all

Americans had TV sets and millions tuned in to watch the four Kennedy–Nixon debates that arguably cost the latter the presidency. Viewers watched a cooler and calmer Kennedy discuss the issues against Nixon, who appeared nervous and less trustworthy. The first debate on September 26 was all many voters needed to cast their ballots for the Democrat.

Kennedy campaigned as the candidate for change and a new generation. He tied himself to the successful policies of Franklin Roosevelt and sought to win back fellow Catholics, who had deserted his party in favor of Eisenhower in 1952 and 1956. He straddled the fence on civil rights in fear of losing Southern Democrats but managed to sway Black voters to his side with his support of civil rights leader Martin Luther King. Meanwhile, Eisenhower broke away from his presidential duties to embark on a speaking tour for Nixon.

It proved to be too little too late. Kennedy won the popular vote by a mere 118,550 but took the electoral college more soundly, 303–219, to become the youngest president in American history.

After the Loss

Following his close defeat to Kennedy, he returned to his law practice in California, then ran a losing campaign for governor, after which he famously and bitterly told the gathered media that it was his last press conference and that they would not "have Nixon to kick around anymore."[1]

The Nixon family moved to New York City after his defeat. He returned to practicing law and dabbled a bit in politics, commending on the Kennedy and Lyndon Johnson administrations. He worked to help Republicans in their bids for office in the 1966 midterm elections, which gained him support for another presidential run in 1968. Chaos in the country and in the Democratic Party helped Nixon defeat Hubert Humphrey.

Nixon was dogged by the issues of the day and his own dishonesty, especially in his abbreviated second term. His "Vietnamization" policy that withdrew American military support in the most unpopular war in US history, visits to Red China and the Soviet Union that promoted peaceful relations, and a strong economy were popular enough with voters to push him to a landslide victory over antiwar Democrat George McGovern in 1972.

That popularity didn't last. The Watergate scandal that killed his presidency began with a break-in at the Democratic National Committee offices. Investigations and tape recordings Nixon was forced to turn over led to revelations of a cover-up by Nixon as well as other abuses of power and his forced resignation in 1974.

Nixon was controversially pardoned for all offenses by President Gerald Ford and remained out of the limelight for the next two decades, though during the Reagan administration he embarked on a fact-finding tour of Asian nations and met with their leaders. He died at his New Jersey home on June 22, 1993.

Coming From Nixon

"People have got to know whether or not their president is a crook. Well, I'm not a crook. I've earned everything I've got."[2]

Did You Know?

Nixon made a cameo appearance during the 1968 campaign on the immensely popular TV comedy show "Laugh-In." He uttered the phrase "Sock it to Me?" in question form before millions of viewers. Opponent Hubert Humphrey refused his opportunity to appear on the show.

38

Barry Goldwater

Barry Goldwater. Courtesy of the Library of Congress, LC-DIG-ppmsca-83251

Party: Republican
Birth state: Arizona Territory
Represented: Arizona
Years of defeat: 1964
Running mate: William Miller
Winner: Lyndon Johnson
Campaign slogans: "All the Way with LBJ" (Johnson); "In Your Heart You Know He's Right" (Goldwater); "In Your Guts You Know He's Nuts" (Johnson)

All About Goldwater

Goldwater was born in Phoenix on January 2, 1909, three years before Arizona was granted statehood. His American roots reached back to the mid-19th century when grandfather "Big Mike" Goldwasser emigrated from Poland to avoid conscription in the Russian Army, Mike and his brother struggled in the business world until they opened a store east of Yuma. The business thrived and expanded to different locations. By 1900, Goldwater's was the leading department store in Arizona Territory.

Barry was baptized in a church before learning of his father Baron's Jewish heritage. He was a disinterested student but popular and was eventually elected president of his freshman class. He enjoyed extracurricular activities but his grade suffered and he flunked out. His alarmed parents dispatched him to the Staunton Military Academy in Virginia. That is where he found his footing academically. But his education was interrupted in 1925 at the University of Arizona when his father died of a heart attack, forcing Goldwater to help run the family business. By his late twenties, he had become president of the store and had even designed unique white boxer shorts with images of red ants on them called "antsy pants" that took off nationally.

Goldwater and the store remained viable during the Depression. He began to form political viewpoints that included opposition to trade unions. He also struggled emotionally with the strain of running the growing company and suffered nervous breakdowns in 1937 and 1939. Goldwater drank heavily and failed several attempts to give up alcohol.

His marketing career halted when he join the US Army Air Corps several months before the Japanese bombing of Pearl Harbor thrust the country into the Second World War. He was assigned to organizing a military supply depot near Phoenix before serving as director of ground training at the base, as well as a huge gunnery range. He finished the war with the rank of brigadier general.

Goldwater returned to marketing after the war but the rapid population growth of Phoenix, where prostitution and gambling had become big business while the unsteady city council hired and fired 30 city managers in 35 years, turned his attention to politics. He was disturbed by allegations of bribery in the local government. So he headed a coalition of wealthy citizens and business owners to launch a new charter government. It cleaned up the mess. His group even helped end segregation in city schools in 1952. But he fell on the wrong side of history during that time by supporting McCarthyism and his virulent anti-Communist campaign.

Politics was in his blood. Goldwater managed the gubernatorial campaign of underdog Howard Pyle, who emerged with a surprising victory. He ran that same year for US Senate and won, starting a 30-year stint in that chamber.

Goldwater became a proponent of states' rights. His run for president was destroyed by a lack of progressivism on civil rights. Though he had ten years earlier hired an African-American woman as his assistant, he opposed the Civil Rights Act of 1964 and was defeated badly by Johnson in the presidential election.

By the time of his loss, Goldwater had promoted himself from president of the family business to chairman of the board. He remained in that position until the stores were sold to a New York enterprise in 1962 that eventually became known as the May Company.

Issues of the Day

The shift of the Republican Party toward ultraconservatism and Democrats as the party of civil rights resulted in a monumental shift politically in the South and to a lesser extent in other areas of the country. Jim Crowism was on its last legs as both the Voting Rights Act and Civil Rights Act that ended all vestiges of legal segregation were within two years of passage.

A keen awareness of the civil rights movement culminating in the historic March on Washington and "I Have a Dream" speech from Martin Luther King made it the most important issue in 1964, though the Cold War and threat of nuclear war following the Cuban Missile Crisis in 1962 also loomed large on the minds of voters.

The 1964 Campaign

The thrust of the Democratic message to voters about Goldwater was delivered on a television ad that ran only on Labor Day. It showed a young girl picking flowers when a nuclear explosion blasted and a mushroom cloud formed. The stark notion that Goldwater was dangerous raised fear among voters and all but cemented his defeat.

The message had merit. Goldwater's anti-Communist views as the nation had begun to be bogged down in Vietnam made Americans nervous, particularly when he admitted he would be willing to use nuclear weapons against enemy forces there. Such dangerous claims encapsulated the hesitations of his own party to make him the nominee. Many delegates believed he was taking the party down the wrong path and they were proven right.

Johnson, meanwhile, had calmed the country with his message of continuity after the tragic assassination of President Kennedy the previous November. His support of the Civil Rights Act in 1964 was largely applauded everywhere in the country outside the South. It was no wonder that Goldwater only won states in that region. He was the victim of one of the biggest landslides in American history, losing the popular vote by nearly 16 million and winning just six states, all in the South.

After the Loss

Goldwater won back his Senate seat in 1968 and became the standard bearer of American conservatism. He supported the successful White House run of Richard Nixon in 1968 and remained loyal to him nearly throughout the Watergate scandal until forced to join the forces favoring impeachment in 1974. Goldwater remained loyal to his party. His conservatism eventually triumphed with the election of Ronald Reagan in 1980 and subsequent run of Republican presidents.

By that time, he had authored two books, including an autobiography titled *No Apologies*. Goldwater died on May 29, 1998.

Coming From Goldwater

Extremism in the defense of liberty is no vice. Moderation in the pursuit of justice is no virtue![1]

Did You Know?

The chemical equation "AuH_2O" was often used as a symbol for support of Goldwater during his presidential campaign. "Au" is the Periodic table symbol for gold, and "H_2O" hydrogen (x_2) and oxygen, creating water. So "AuH_2O" translates into "gold water."

39

Hubert Humphrey

Party: Democratic
Birth state: South Dakota
Represented: Minnesota
Years of defeat: 1968
Running mate: Edmund Muskie
Winner: Richard Nixon
Other notable candidate: George Wallace (Independent)
Campaign Slogans: "This Time, Vote Like Your Whole World Depended on It" (Nixon); "Some People Talk Change, Others Cause It" (Humphrey); "Send Them a Message" (Wallace)

Hubert Humphrey. Courtesy of the Library of Congress, LC-DIG-ppmsca-71275

All About Humphrey

Humphrey was born in Wallace, South Dakota, on May 27, 1911, and raised on the flat farm country of nearby Doland. His parents owned a drug store in the tiny community. The family business instilled in Humphrey the values that would inspire his public service and carry with him throughout his political career.

Nicknamed "Pinky" in his youth, Humphrey thrived educationally and proved himself a particularly strong debater. He was imbued with a natural sense of optimism and friendliness that he showed customers on his paper route. But there was little to be happy about in Doland during his teenage years. While most of the country was thriving in the years before the depression, his community was collapsing economically under the weight of plummeting farm prices. By the end of the decade banks began to close. Then came drought and dust storms.

Among the many business victims was the Humphrey drug store. But his father, who soon moved the family to nearby Huron, showed his compassion by forgiving all pharmacy debts owed by his customers. It was a gesture his son would never forget.

Hubert attended public school in Dolan before enrolling at the University of Minnesota. The Depression forced him to return to help out at the drugstore, where he continued to work from 1931 to 1937. He pursued a career in the field, attending the Capitol College of Pharmacy in Denver and earning his license in 1933. But the notion of spending life doling out drugs proved uninspiring. Humphrey returned to the University of Minnesota and graduated with a Bachelor of Arts degree in 1939 before moving with his wife to Baton Rouge, Louisiana. He then began to fulfill his passion and earned a master's in political science. He gained practical experience as an instructor at the school.

Soon Humphrey, a staunch Democrat and avid supporter of President Franklin Roosevelt, whose New Deal initiatives had pulled the country out of the Great Depression, began working for the Works Progress Administration in war production and reemployment programs. His attempts to join the fight in the Second World War was thwarted by the Navy and Army due to color blindness and various physical ailments.

He decided to serve his country through politics. He lost a 1943 bid for Minneapolis mayor, forcing him to accept a teaching position at Macalester College in St. Paul, and played a key role in uniting the local Farmer-Labor Party with Minnesota Democrats. He offered years later that he considered that to be his greatest contribution to state politics. Humphrey also gained public notoriety with his political views as a radio commentator.

Immediately after the war Humphrey tossed his hat back in the ring and won election for a three-year run as Minneapolis mayor. He thrust himself into the national spotlight in 1948 with a stirring speech on his party's obligation to civil rights at the Democratic National Convention. Soon, he had captured a US Senate seat and a reputation as a liberal on a wide range of issues. His work on issues of equality proved instrumental in the passage of the Civil Rights Act in 1964.

That triumph helped motivate President Johnson to ask Humphrey to join the ticket for what proved to be a landslide victory. The loyal vice president became tied to Johnson's policies both popular and unpopular. He expressed doubts about US involvement in Vietnam but publicly embraced escalation. The issue forced Johnson to refuse renomination, forcing Humphrey into the race. He simply failed to separate himself from Johnson effectively enough to win.

Issues of the Day

The 1968 election campaign occurred during perhaps the most tumultuous and terrible year in the US since the Civil War. The country had been torn apart by rising death tolls in Vietnam and heated debates about still-growing American involvement, the assassinations two months apart of civil rights leader Martin Luther King and antiwar candidate Robert Kennedy, who appeared destined to win the presidency, riots in the inner cities, violent campus protests, and clashes at the Democratic National Convention, which was often described as a police riot.

The war was easily the most contentious issue on the minds of voters. By the summer of 1968, about half the country supported withdrawal from Vietnam and the rest backed the war effort. But the murder of Kennedy left neither major candidate promising an end to the conflict. Nixon billed himself as a law-and-order candidate while Humphrey scrambled to distance himself from the unpopular war policies of President Johnson.

The 1968 Campaign

Humphrey never found his footing in the campaign against Nixon until it was too late. The tumult within the Democratic Party and his own refusal to separate himself from Johnson's war policies (some believe Johnson was still pulling the strings) resulted in failure.

The success of antiwar candidates Eugene McCarthy, who attracted young voters, then Robert Kennedy, as well as the growing unpopularity of the war in Vietnam, pushed Johnson aside. Kennedy appeared destined to win the nomination until losing his life to an assassin's bullet moments after winning the California primary in early June.

One might believe the Democrats were doomed from that moment. Its convention in Chicago received more attention for the violence outside as antiwar protesters and police clashed than for anything happening inside. The defeat of the antiwar plank and nomination of Humphrey alienated many in the party.

Nixon ran as a law-and-order candidate to prevent right-wing voters from turning to Alabama governor and segregationist firebrand George Wallace, who was destined to sweep the South. It worked. Humphrey desperately and ineffectively tried to paint Nixon as anti-union and managed to close the gap—but not enough. Nixon won a razor-thin popular vote but took the electoral college, 301–191.

After the Loss

Humphrey briefly taught at the University of Minnesota and Macalester College before returning to the Senate in 1970 and winning reelection six years later. But he died of cancer while serving that term on January 13, 1978.

Coming From Humphrey

The moral test of government is how that government treats those who are in the dawn of life, the children; those who are in the twilight of life, the elderly; and those who are in shadows of life, the sick, the needy, and the handicapped.[1]

Did You Know?

Wallace chose the Second World War bombardier organizer and trainer Curtis LeMay as his running mate. The introduction of LeMay to the media and public proved disastrous when he asserted his willingness to use nuclear weapons on the enemy in Vietnam.

40

George McGovern

George McGovern (with Hubert Humphrey, left). Courtesy of the Library of Congress, LC-DIG-ppmsca-50467

Party: Democratic
Birth state: South Dakota
Represented: South Dakota
Years of defeat: 1972
Running mate: Sargent Shriver (replaced Thomas Eagleton)
Winner: Richard Nixon
Campaign slogans: "Come Home, America" (McGovern); "Nixon Now, More than Ever" (Nixon)

All About McGovern

McGovern was born on July 19, 1922, in Avon, South Dakota. He was raised by Methodist parents who instilled in him a liberal identity driven by empathy for those less fortunate. His father was a pastor at the local church. McGovern wrote in his 2011 book *What it Means to be a Democrat* that his empathy was a gift given to him by his mother and pastor father, who were Republicans. He explained that his parents believed it was their responsibility to take care of the sick, homeless, and vulnerable, as well as for those who work in mines and factories.

McGovern attended public school in Mitchell, which rests an hour north of Avon, before enrolling in Dakota Wesleyan University, where he met his wife Eleanor. He was an outstanding student with a penchant for debate that earned him a college scholarship.

His career would have to wait. McGovern volunteered for military duty immediately following the Japanese bombing of Pearl Harbor and flew 35 combat missions as a bomber pilot, earning the Distinguished Flying Cross.

McGovern developed a keen interest in politics. He returned to Dakota Wesleyan after the war to teach history and political science, work that lasted about a decade before he left to dedicate himself to the state Democratic Party. He was elected to the US Congress in 1956 as an advocate for the American farmer. He was driven by the hunger crisis throughout the world and the viewpoint that productive farmers were not paid enough for their crops. His strong opinions on the plight of farmers motivated President Kennedy to appoint him the first Director of the US Food for Peace Program. He resigned from that post to run successfully for the US Senate in 1962.

Soon another issue arose that captured his attention and passion. That was the growing American involvement in Vietnam. Like millions of others in the country he grew disenchanted the lack of progress on a peaceful solution and rising death tolls. More than 500,000 American troops were in Vietnam months when Richard Nixon took over the White House in 1969.

McGovern had not always been a dove on Vietnam. In 1963 he criticized Kennedy for a lack of commitment there. That speech did not sit well with Democrats. After the president was assassinated McGovern focused solely on food policy and helping farmers. It did not take long, however, for McGovern to oppose escalation of the war under President Johnson. McGovern believed it was undermining the anti-poverty agenda and other domestic battles that resulted in passage of the Civil Rights Act and Voting Rights Act.

Colleague urged McGovern to run for president in 1968, but he decided instead to support Robert Kennedy, whose assassination in early June after Johnson refused renomination left the Democrats with no antiwar candidate. The continuation of the war inspired McGovern to co-sponsor legislation to cut off funding for the war in 1970.

McGovern was little known outside of South Dakota when he made a surprising run for the presidency in 1972 on a promise to end the war immediately. But by that time, US troops were returning home and he had little more to offer voters.

Issues of the Day

With the Vietnam War winding down, US troops returning home, and the economy comparatively strong, McGovern had little chance to defeat the incumbent. Little had been revealed during the campaign about the illegalities leading to the Watergate scandal that would eventually bring down the Nixon presidency.

Visits to the Soviet Union and China had improved Nixon's standing on foreign policy and the nation had yet to experience the inflation and energy crisis that would result in the defeat of Nixon replacement Gerald Ford in 1976. Though troubles followed the president after the election all seemed well enough in 1972 to provide him smooth sailing back to the White House.

The 1972 Campaign

Many believe McGovern wrote his own political obituary after choosing Thomas Eagleton as his running mate, then abandoning him after reports surfaced that the Missouri senator had been hospitalized three times with depression and had undergone electroshock treatment. The campaign was perceived as disorganized and unprepared when Eagleton was shelved in favor of Sargent Shriver.

It would not have mattered. Nixon remained in control from the beginning. Even some leading Democrats supported him over McGovern. Included was John Connally, a former Lyndon Johnson ally who formed "Democrats for Nixon." The party unity that had remained intact since the Franklin Roosevelt presidency had been shattered. Just as Barry Goldwater was considered too conservative in 1964, voters believed McGovern to be too liberal in 1972. Among the views cited was amnesty for draft dodgers who had fled to Canada and the decriminalization of marijuana.

The result was one of the biggest landslides ever. Nixon won the popular vote by nearly 18 million and captured every state bit Massachusetts. McGovern even lost his home state of South Dakota handily.

After the Loss

His lopsided defeat did not end his political career. He was re-elected to the Senate in 1974 before losing another bid during a wave of conservatism n South Dakota and throughout America led by president-elect Ronald Reagan in 1980. McGovern later served as an ambassador to the United Nations Food and Agricultural Agencies in Rome and was appointed UN Global Ambassador on World Hunger in 2001. He died 11 years later at age 90.

Coming From McGovern

I opened the doors of the Democratic Party and 20 million people walked out.[1]

Did You Know?

McGovern's daughter Teresa died of exposure while intoxicated in December 1994. He later founded a non-profit alcohol research organization in her name and authored a book in which he discussed Teresa's longtime battle with alcoholism.

41

Gerald Ford

Gerald Ford. Courtesy of the Library of Congress, LC-DIG-ppmsca-72883

Party: Republican
Birth state: Nebraska
Represented: Michigan
Years of defeat: 1976
Running mate: Bob Dole
Winner: Jimmy Carter
Campaign slogans: "He's Making Us Proud Again" (Ford); "Not Just Peanuts" (Carter); "A Leader for a Change" (Carter)

All About Ford

Ford was born on July 14, 1913, in Omaha, Nebraska, but likely remembered nothing about his time there. The separation of his parents two weeks after his birth and subsequent divorce resulted in his move to Grand Rapids, Michigan at age two. His mother married paint salesman Gerald R. Ford, and soon, the boy was known by that name rather than his given name Leslie.

Young Gerald attended South High School where he blossomed into a football standout and honor student after achieving the rank of Eagle Scout at age 14. He earned money for college by working in the family paint business and at a local restaurant.

During the height of the Depression he majored in economics at the University of Michigan. He continued to work part-time and used a small scholarship from high school to finance his higher education. He continued to thrive on the gridiron, even playing center for the Wolverines on their national championship teams of

1932 and 1933, then earning team Most Valuable Player honors the following two seasons. Ford rejected offers from the NFL Detroit Lions and Greem Bay Packers to accept jobs as a boxing and assistant football coach at Yale with the intention of attending law school there. He was admitted in 1938 and earned his degree three years later. He began to dabble in politics, working on the unsuccessful Wendell Willkie presidential campaign in 1940.

Ford and fraternity brother Philip Buchen then formed a law partnership in Grand Rapids, where he forged stronger ties with the Republican Party. But soon the Second World War pushed Ford into the Naval Reserve. By 1943, he began serving on a light aircraft carrier that was involved in combat in the South Pacific. But his closest brush with death came not from enemy fire but a typhoon in the Philippine Sea in December 1944 that nearly swept him overboard.

The war changed his global outlook from isolationist to internationalist. Ford easily won the Republican nomination for a US House seat in 1948 and won election in a landslide. He was re-elected by wide margins twelve times, serving until 1973. Ford worked on the House Appropriations Committee and became ranking minority member of the Defense Appropriations Subcommittee in 1961. President Johnson also appointed him to the Warren Commission investigating the assassination of John F. Kennedy. Ford gained a reputation as a moderate on foreign policy and fiscal conservative.

Throughout his time in the House he declined offers to run for Senate or Michigan governor. He had earned enough respect to be considered a candidate for Nixon's vice-president in 1968 and 1972, but losing out on that job was not particularly frustrating. He was far more disappointed at failing to become Speaker of the House.

A higher calling awaited when charges of income tax evasion doomed Spiro Agnew's vice-presidency. Nixon appointed Ford as his replacement and he was sworn in on December 6, 1973. By that time, the Watergate scandal was in the process of pushing Nixon out of the White House and Ford into it. Nine months after being named VP he was sworn in as president.

He was thrown into the fire. Ford was confronted by a struggling economy fueled by energy shortages. He sought to curb the trend of government spending being used to solve problems but nothing worked. He vetoed several non-military appropriation bills to decrease the deficit. He declared a policy of energy independence. He famously promoted "WIN" buttons—"Whip Inflation Now." Gas prices and frustration soared, though both worsened after he was defeated by Jimmy Carter in the 1976 election. His full pardon of Nixon proved controversial.

Issues of the Day

Though Ford alienated some voters by pardoning former President Nixon, who had been forced out of office by the Watergate scandal, and the Vietnam War defeat was now only a bitter memory, a suddenly failing economy had been thrust center stage in 1976. Inflation was at nearly eight percent and gas prices were soaring. The oil crisis had risen the cost per gallon about 70 percent in the previous year.

The 1976 Campaign

Ford tried to overcome poor popularity ratings after his controversial full pardon of Nixon upon his elevation to the presidency. Despite his athletic background, the media portrayed him as clumsy and weak.

Carter smartly tied Ford to the failures of the Nixon Administration. He called for honest government and a sense of truthfulness and idealism to win back the trust of the people. Ford portrayed Carter as an inexperienced, free-spending liberal who would increase taxes.

The Democrat seemed destined to win easily. But a Carter interview with *Playboy* magazine in which he admitted that he lusted after women in his heart negatively affected his campaign. His lead in the polls disappeared. But Ford's disastrous debate claim that the Soviet Union did not dominate Eastern Europe made him look ignorant of world affairs. That slip might have cost Ford the presidency. The Georgian swept nearly the entire South as well as populous northern states such as New York and Pennsylvania to take the election.

After the Loss

Ford was considered a possible Republican nominee in 1980, but the surge of Ronald Reagan's popularity doomed his dreams to return to the White House. He was also shunned by the future president as a running mate.

Ford had spent his previous four years criticizing Carter policies and writing a book titled *A Time to Heal*. He later served on corporate boards and wrote on the issues of the day. Awarded him the Presidential Medal of Freedom in 1999. He died on December 26, 2006.

Coming From Ford

"I have not sought this enormous responsibility, but I will not shirk it… I believe that truth is the glue that holds government together, not only our Government, but civilization itself. That bond, though strained, is unbroken at home and abroad. In all my public and private acts as your President, I expect to follow my instincts of openness and candor with full confidence that honesty is always the best policy in the end. My fellow Americans, our long national nightmare is over. Our Constitution works; our great Republic is a Government of laws and not of men. Here the people rule."[1]

Did You Know?

Ford survived two assassination attempts by women two weeks apart in 1975. One was by former Charles Manson follower Lynette "Squeaky" Fromme Another was by radical activist Sara Jane Moore.

42

Jimmy Carter

Jimmy Carter. Courtesy of the Library of Congress, LC-DIG-ppmsca-56641

Party: Democratic
Birth state: Georgia
Represented: Georgia
Years of defeat: 1980
Running mate: Walter Mondale
Winner: Ronald Reagan
Other Notable Candidate: John Anderson (Independent)
Campaign slogans: "Are You Better Off Than You Were Four Years Ago?" (Reagan); "A Tested and Trustworthy Team" (Carter)

All About Carter

The first American president born in a hospital—on October 1, 1924—was raised in a home with no electricity or plumbing in the small down of Plains, Georgia. He was named after his farmer father who also ran a store and nurse mother who set a more example for his son in the segregated Deep South by counselling poor African-American women about healthcare.

Carter was a brilliant student, even graduating as valedictorian of his high school class. He enrolled in the Naval Academy during the Second World War and served as an officer under legendary captain Hyman Rickover on the branch's first experimental nuclear submarine.

The death of his father-in-law motivated Carter and wife Rosalynn to take over her family's peanut farm in Georgia. They turned it into a profitable operation. Carter also served as a deacon and Sunday school teacher in the Plains Baptist Church. His involvement in politics began on local civil boards, then two terms in the Georgia state senate. Carter showed his independence by helping appeal laws that discouraged African-Americans from voting. He also fought against wasteful government spending.

Despite his anti-segregation stand, he continued to defeat opponents with opposite and often more popular viewpoints. But he was stung by a defeat in his run for governor in 1966. There were simply too many whites among voters who preferred virulent segregationist Lester Maddox. Carter believed he needed to win them back to win in 1970 so he decreased the number his appearances before African American groups and sought endorsement from the dwindling number of segregationists in the state. Some called it hypocritical—he even declared the end of segregation in Georgia after elected.

The South had changed by the time he ran for the presidency against Ford and the susceptible Republicans in 1976. Carter swept the South and squeaked by to take the White House but overwhelming economic issues and the Iranian hostage crisis doomed him to defeat in 1980. He was also criticized for pulling the American team out of the 1980 Summer Olympics to protest the Russian invasion of Afghanistan and his recognition of Communist China. The disastrous rescue attempt of the hostages in 1980 was also roundly criticized. His lone foreign relations triumph was brokering the peace agreement between Israel and Egypt.

Issues of the Day

The Cold War and plummeting economy dominated debate in 1980. A year earlier, a group of Iranian students seized the American embassy and kidnapped diplomats working there. They remained hostages during the campaign despite diplomatic and one disastrous military effort to free them.

Meanwhile, inflation fueled by soaring gas prices angered Americans and significantly weakened Carter's popularity. The result was a surge of conservatism that carried Reagan into the White House.

The 1980 Campaign

Reagan required few clues on his own policies during the campaign. He let the issues speak for themselves while Carter tried to justify his own performance to disenchanted Americans. Double-digit inflation, rising unemployment, skyrocketing gas prices, the hostage crisis, and Cold War tensions all added up to the first incumbent defeat since Herbert Hoover lost to Franklin Roosevelt in 1932.

The Republican spoke in generalities about the need for less government spending, saying little about a solution aside from promises of tax cuts. Carter worked to paint Reagan as a right-wing extremist to no avail. The candidates met for only one debate a week before the election. Though Carter was deemed the winner on substance he failed to successfully portray Reagan as an extremist rather than a moderate.

Nothing could stop the Reagan steamroller. He won the popular vote by 8.5 million and every state west of the Mississippi.

After the Loss

Carter remained active after losing to Reagan. He served as a freelance ambassador on many international missions and an advisor on Middle East and human rights issues. His humanitarian work was lauded for decades and was considered a hero to many even after he reached his 100th birthday.

Coming From Carter

It is good to realize that if love and peace can prevail on Earth, and we can teach our children to honor nature's gifts the joys and beauties of the outdoors will be here forever.[1]

Did You Know?

Carter made a controversial move in 1977 by pardoning all those who dodged the draft during the Vietnam War, allowing those who moved to Canada to return home.

43

Walter Mondale

Walter Mondale. Courtesy of the Library of Congress, LC-DIG-ppmsca-88612

Party: Democratic
Birth state: Minnesota
Represented: Minnesota
Years of defeat: 1984
Running mate: Geraldine Ferraro
Winner: Ronald Reagan
Campaign slogans: "It's Morning Again in America" (Reagan); "America Needs New Leadership" (Mondale)

All About Mondale

Mondale was born on January 5, 1928, in Ceylon, Minnesota, a small town close to the Iowa border, before his family moved to nearby Elmore. His father was a farmer and Methodist minister and mother a musician and piano teacher.

Raised in poverty during the Great Depression, young Walter (nicknamed "Fritz") was greatly influenced by his father's religious beliefs that featured supporting civil rights. He was badly shaken when his dad died of a stroke in 1948.

Mondale attended Macalester College in St. Paul, dipping his toes in the political waters as executive secretary for Students for Democratic Action in Washington, before graduating from the University of Minnesota in 1951. Following a two-year stint in the US army, he returned to that school and graduated cum laude with a law degree in 1956. His studies were interspersed with more political work such as volunteering for Hubert Humphrey's Minneapolis mayoral campaign and organizing a liberal faction of the state's Democratic-Farmer-Labor Party. He later headed Orville Freeman's successful campaigns for Minnesota governor in 1956 and 1958.

Freeman did not forget. He appointed Mondale as state attorney general in 1960. The 38-year-old began earning a reputation as a lawyer for the people. He exposed fraud, established consumer protection reforms, and strengthened civil rights defenses.

Mondale entered national politics on the Credentials Committee at the 1964 Democratic National Convention and negotiated a controversial compromised between the segregated Mississippi delegation and the Mississippi Freedom Democratic Party, which challenged the validity of the all-white group in a state with a large Black population. Though the deal angered both sides it set rules of integration for future conventions.

Mondale replaced new vice-president Hubert Humphrey in the US Senate in 1964 and served there for twelve years. He helped pass major social and economic civil rights initiatives, including the Voting Rights Act of 1965 and Fair Housing Act of 1968, as well as the Fair Warning Act that provided greater auto safety protections. Meanwhile, his support for American involvement in Vietnam waned after a trip to that war-torn nation. His later years in the Senate were marked by membership on committees that promoted the needs of children and the elderly.

Deciding he was not schooled enough in foreign affairs, Mondale rejected calls to run for president in 1976. After Jimmy Carter ticketed him as running mate in a successful campaign for the White House, he learned more about those issues and formed opinions such as the need for more military and economic aid to Middle East allies, support of Israel and maintaining strong relationships with European allies. Mondale's role was far more than ceremonial. He outlined his potential contributions for Carter to peruse and was given an office in the West Wing unlike previous vice-presidents. Among his policy contributions was opening discussions with Israeli and Egyptian leaders that eventually led to the momentous peace accords and a trip to China that resulted in improved relations with that country. But he could not do enough to help stem the tide of an economic downturn that resulted in a Carter defeat to Reagan in 1980.

The stinging loss pushed Mondale to join a Chicago law firm as a general counsel and further study of public policy that could prepare him for a 1984 run for the presidency. But he had no chance against the immensely popular Republican.

Issues of the Day

An improved economy had Democrats scrambling for issues on which to criticize Reagan. Lower inflation and unemployment, as well as a promise to reduce taxes, spiked the incumbent's popularity. The nation had recovered from the morass of the 1970s punctuated by defeat in Vietnam and the Watergate scandal that weakened trust and confidence in the government.

The 1984 Campaign

Mondale understood he needed to do something bold to positively impact the race so he selected the first woman running mate from a major party in American history. Congresswoman Geraldine Ferraro, however, proved to be an unwise choice when tax improprieties by her husband were revealed.

It didn't matter much. Reagan was simply too popular. He ran on his record, which included a bounce-back economy. He even famously joked about his age during a debate against Mondale in which he slyly stated he would not hold his opponent's youth and inexperience against him. Even Mondale laughed as Americans drew closer to the president.

Mondale further alienated the voters by admitting he would raise taxes, arguing that he was the only candidate who would admit it. But Reagan did not admit it—even though he did indeed during his second term. The challenger sought to picture the incumbent as promoting unfairness between rich and poor and challenged his ties with fundamentalist groups but nothing stuck. Reagan portrayed himself successfully as the great communicator who had returned a sense of patriotism to the public.

The winner was a foregone conclusion. Mondale lost by 17 million votes, lost every demographic group except African Americans and won only the District of Columbia and his home state of Minnesota.

After the Loss

The 1984 campaign was not his last run for office. Mondale returned to Minnesota to join another law firm as general counsel but returned to the political world when President Clinton appointed him ambassador to Japan in 1993. Nine years later, he replaced US Senator Paul Wellstone (who had been killed in a plane crash during a reelection campaign) and lost a tight race.

Mondale continued working as a lawyer in his Asia practice. He died at age 93 in 2021.

Coming From Mondale

President Reagan likes to say Uncle Sam is a kindly old man with a spine of steel, and that he is. But I want to see Uncle Sam as well with a mind and with a heart and with a soul and a conscience.[1]

Did You Know?

Mondale would have lost all 50 states to Reagan in 1984 had Minnesota not given him a victory by fewer than 4,000 votes.

44

Michael Dukakis

Party: Democratic
Birth state: Massachusetts
Represented: Massachusetts
Years of defeat: 1988
Running mate: Lloyd Bentsen
Winner: George H. Bush
Campaign slogans: "Kinder, Gentler Nation" (Bush); "On Your Side" (Dukakis)

Michael Dukakis. Courtesy of the Library of Congress, LC-DIG-ppmsca-19607

All About Dukakis

Dukakis was born to Greek immigrants on November 3, 1933, in Brookline, Massachusetts. He attended high school there, thriving athletically and educationally. Dukakis was an honr student who played on the basketball, baseball, tennis, and cross country teams. He even ran the Boston Marathon at age 17.

Upon graduation with a Bachelor of Arts degree in political science from Swarthmore College in 1955, Dukakis opted to join the Army rather than attend Harvard Law School. He was eventually placed as a radio operator in a unit based in South Korea, where a United Nations delegation of the Military Armistice Commission had been stationed following the war.

Dukakis remained there for two years before returning home to earn his law degree from Harvard in 1960. He wasted little time with his political ambitions. Dukakis was elected as a Town Meeting member in 1960 then to the Massachusetts Legislature two years later. He served four teams in that office and proved himself so popular that he increased his margins of victory in each election. His stock continued to rise. Dukakis was the state Democratic Party nominee for lieutenant governor in 1970 but he and Boston Mayor Kevin White lost the race for governor.

The weakened reputation of the Republican Party during the Watergate scandal and his own popularity resulted in Dukakis winning the Massachusetts governorship in 1974. His term was lauded as effective in combatting record unemployment and pulling the state out of a general economic crisis. Yet job security eluded him. He lost in the 1978 Democratic primary to Edward King before avenging that defeat in 1982 and earning an unprecedented third term as governor in a landslide 1986 victory. His colleagues that year voted him as the most effective governor in the country. By that time, he was considered a promising presidential candidate. The national party certainly believed it when they sent him against George Bush in the presidential election.

Issues of the Day

The candidates themselves created the issues that decided the outcome. Dukakis alienated voters by vetoing a bill that would require students to recite the Pledge of Allegiance. His strong stand against the death penalty in an era of conservatism was spotlighted when he claimed dispassionately that he would not want the hypothetical killer of his wife put to death.

Meanwhile, folks also debated what some considered a shameless but effective Bush television ad that derided a furlough program supported by Dukakis that placed an African-American prisoner back on the streets where he raped a woman and stabbed her companion.

The 1988 Campaign

The impending departure of two-term president Ronald Reagan from the White House left an open primary but his popularity certainly provided an advantage for George H. Bush. The vice-president staved off competition from Republican heavyweight Bob Dole and—in an era of right-wing religious conservatism—the Reverend Pat Robertson.

It appeared Bush had erred by selecting young, inexperienced Dan Quayle as his running mate. The Indiana senator erred in his debate against Democratic vice-presidential candidate Lloyd Bentsen by comparing himself to former youthful president John F. Kennedy. Stating that he had been friends with Kennedy and had worked with him. Bentsen replied, "Senator, you're no Jack Kennedy." That line and other gaffes weakened public support of Quayle throughout the campaign.

Dukakis had his own problem with public perception after emerging as future Democratic presidential nominee Al Gore. After surging 17 points ahead of Bush in the polls after the convention his lead dissipated. The signature moment of his decline arrived in a photo op and campaign ad when to prove his toughness he donned a military uniform and placed himself helmet onto a tank. Most believed he looked patently ridiculous and it strengthened their feelings that he was weak after he had famously told debate-watchers that he would not seek the death penalty for his wife's hypothetical murderer.

What many predicted to be a close election earlier was a rout. Bush won 54 percent of the vote and the electoral college, 426–111. He had become the first incumbent vice-president to win an election since Martin Van Buren in 1836.

After the Loss

Dukakis decided he would not seek re-election as governor and left office in 1991. He embraced a quieter life as a visiting professor at various universities. He taught courses in political leadership and health policy and chaired forums on reforming the US health care system.

Dukakis served a five-year term as a member of the Board of Directors at Amtrak, then in 2009 at age 75 was pegged as a possible successor to the deceased Ted Kennedy for a US Senate seat. But Paul Kirk received the nod instead. Dukakis finally retired in 2024 after a long stint at Northeastern University, where he had served as a professor of political science.

Coming From Dukakis

Building bridges is always better than erecting walls.[1]

Did You Know?

His wife Kitty was named after stage and screen actress and game show *To Tell the Truth* panelist Kitty Carlisle, who was a friend of her father, conductor Harry Ellis Dickson.

45

George H. Bush

George H.W. Bush. Courtesy of the Library of Congress, LC-DIG-ppmsca-56579

Party: Republican
Birth state: Massachusetts
Represented: Texas
Years of defeat: 1992
Running mate: Dan Quayle
Winner: Bill Clinton
Other notable candidate: Ross Perot (Independent)
Campaign slogans: "For America, For the People" (Clinton); "Stand by the President (Bush); "I'm Ross, and You're the Boss!" (Perot)

All About Bush

Bush was not long for Massachusetts after his birth in Milton on June 12, 1924. His parents soon moved the family to Greenwich, Connecticut, and raised him with a sense of obligation to public service. His father Prescott was an investment banker who served as a Republican senator from 1952 to 1963.

The younger Bush left home as a teenager to attend Phillips Academy, an exclusive boarding school in Massachusetts, where he captained the baseball and soccer teams before enlisting in the Navy on graduation day during the Second World War. Having just turned 19 as the youngest pilot in that branch, Bush flew 58 missions as a torpedo bomber in the Pacific. His plane was shot down by Japanese gunners in September 1944, but he was rescued by an American submarine and earned a Distinguished Flying Cross.

After his military stint, he enrolled at Yale University to major in economics and play baseball. He graduated in 1948 and moved with his wife to Odessa, Texas, where he toiled as an equipment clerk for an oil company. By 1950, he had helped form an oil development company in Midland that three years later merged to create Zapata Petroleum. Bush was its president when he moved to Houston.

Politics eventually came calling. After cultivating relationships with Republican bigwigs for years he ran a losing campaign for Senate while fighting against a reputation as a Northern carpetbagger and the popularity of winning presidential candidate from Texas Lyndon Johnson.

That did not deter Bush. He won a House seat in 1966 and 1968 as a moderate and earned a coveted spot in the Ways and Means Committee as a mere freshman. Among the policies he supported was American involvement in Vietnam and the Civil Rights Bill of 1968 that banned housing discrimination. Bush lost another bid for the Senate in 1970, ironically to Democrat Lloyd Bentsen, who ran unsuccessfully for vice-president in 1988. But he stayed in the spotlight by becoming an ambassador to the United Nations during the Nixon administration. Bush served three years then accepted the job as chairman of the Republican National Committee during the Watergate scandal. He supported Nixon until forcing to tell the president he had lost support of the party. The result was Nixon's resignation in 1974.

Bush served briefly as director of the Central Intelligence Agency before returning to Houston when the Democrats took over the White House in 1976. He maintained his political goals and was even considered a strong presidential candidate during the primaries of 1980 before a conservative wave carried Ronald Reagan to victory. He accepted an offer to be his running mate, shielding criticism for altering his moderate views to fit the more right-wing agenda.

Bush maintained his loyalty to Reagan and his policies for eight years. He chaired several task forces and traveled often internationally. The president valued his views on foreign affairs that sometimes influenced decisions. Bush survived the Iran-Contra scandal in which he was accused of knowing about the secret sale of arms to Iran to take over the White House in 1988.

The time in office was marked by several major events. One was the collapse of Communism in Eastern Europe and the Soviet Union, as well as the reunification of Germany. Bush took advantage by signing a mutual non-aggression pact with Russia that symbolized the end of the Cold War. Another was his response to the Iraqi attack on Kuwait. His leadership as United Nations forces drove the aggressor out of that helpless nation with little loss of life earned Bush an 89 percent approval rating at its peak and seemingly a red carpet to reelection in 1992. But the recession of 1991 resulted in his one-term presidency.

Issues of the Day

During the campaign Bill Clinton surrogate James Carville coined the term "It's the economy, stupid." The frank assessment of voter priority drove Clinton to victory over Bush, whose popularity after the Gulf War soared, then plummeted when a recession struck in 1991. By the time he was renominated by the Republicans his approval rating had sunk to 29 percent.

Many Americans deemed Bush an elitist who did not identify with their financial woes. A wave of populism washed over the nation. The beneficiaries were Clinton and third-party candidate Ross Perot.

The 1992 Campaign

Bush failed in the hearts and minds of most Americans to address the economic downturn. He vetoed a bill to extend unemployment benefits with nearly eight percent out of work and was seen as an out-of-touch elitist during a visit to a Florida supermarket when he expressed wonderment about a barcode scanner. Bush famously looked at his watch when asked about the economy during a debate then rambled on about how a wealthy person could still care deeply about the plight of ordinary Americans. That served to stoke fears that he was disinterested in their plight.

The inclusion of Texas businessman Ross Perot as an independent candidate and in the nationally televised debates wrested votes away from Bush. Clinton had seemingly come out of nowhere to capture the imagination and support of voters. He lambasted the supply-side economics he claimed was ruining the country and pitched himself as the candidate for the middle class.

The result was a blowout. Clinton won the popular vote by nearly six million, dominated the Northeast and Midwest, and captured 34 of the 50 states. Perot won none but his vote count of almost 20 million certainly played a factor in the Bush defeat.

After the Loss

Bush all but left politics upon his defeat, though his namesake son served two terms as president. The elder Bush was awarded the Presidential Medal of Freedom in 2011 and died at age 94 on November 30, 2018.

Coming From Bush

We can find meaning and reward by serving some higher purpose than ourselves, a shining purpose, the illumination of a Thousand Points of Light… We all have something to give.[1]

Did You Know?

When George W. Bush was elected president in 2000, it was only the second time that a father and son had been elected president. John Adams and John Quincy Adams were the first father-son duo.

46

Bob Dole

Bob Dole. Courtesy of the Library of Congress, LC-DIG-ppmsca-85358

Party: Republican
Birth state: Kansas
Represented: Kansas
Years of defeat: 1996
Running mate: Jack Kemp
Winner: Bill Clinton
Other notable candidate: Ross Perot (Independent)
Campaign slogans: "Building a Bridge to the Twenty-First Century" (Clinton); "A Better Man for a Better America" (Dole)

All About Dole

Dole was not just raised during the Great Depression but in Kansas, where the Dust Bowl destroyed many lives. Born on July 22, 1923, in Russell, young Bob had to toil endlessly to help his family make ends meet. He held a variety of jobs such a paper boy and soda jerk at the local drug store.

He accepted his responsibilities with a strong work ethic, which he also displayed in the classroom and athletic fields. Dole attended the University of Kansas, playing basketball and football and running track while serving as vice president of his fraternity. Soon the Second World War intervened. Dole volunteered for the Army and was stationed as a second lieutenant in Italy when in 1945 he was struck in the right shoulder by German machine gun fire. He remained untreated for seven hours on the battlefield before being retrieved, then returned to the United States to heal. His military service resulted in two Purple Hearts and two Bronze Star medals. Dole still required multiple surgeries and long hospitalizations to repair the right side of his body. He never fully recovered mobility in his right arm.

Dole eventually graduated with an undergraduate and law degree from Washburn University in Kansas. By that time he had already won a two-year term as a Republican in the Kansas House of Representatives. In 1952 he became the Russell County Attorney in his hometown, then eight years later was elected to the US House of Representatives. He continued to climb the political ladder in 1968, winning a Senate seat and chairing the Republican National Committee from 1971 to 1973, by which time the Watergate scandal had begun to sink the Richard Nixon presidency.

Re-elected to the same seat every six years until his retirement in 1996, he served in many capacities, including the Agriculture and Finance committees. Dole served as Senate Majority Leader from 1985 to 1987 and 1994 to 1996 and Senate Minority Leader every year in-between.

Issues of the Day

The end of the Cold War several years earlier again focused attention on domestic issues in 1996, particularly the economy. That was a Clinton strength. Dole understood the need to separate himself from the president so he announced his intention to cut taxes 15 percent and selected tax-cut proponent Jack Kemp as his running mate. But the public saw through Dole, who had never been a supporter of tax cuts to spur the economy, which was doing well anyway. Clinton was on his way to wiping out the deficit.

Other issues such as the incumbent's mildly unpopular "Don't Ask, Don't Tell" compromise which was eventually adopted to allow gay men and lesbians to serve openly in the military were debated. Yet despite losing the House in the 1994 midterm elections for the first time since the 1950s, the Democrats felt confident that Clinton's popularity would carry him back to a second term. And they were right. Congressional Republicans were seen by many as too radical and were blamed for forcing two partial government shutdowns 2after budget squabbles.

The 1996 Campaign

While Clinton was easily renominated, Dole was no shoo-in. He received stiff primary competition from several more conservative candidates, including commentator Pat Buchanan. But he staved them off in the biggest early-March contests to ensure a battle against Clinton for the White House.

That contest was no contest. Clinton ran on his economic strength and established a double-digit lead in the polls throughout the campaign. He even became the first Democrat to win Arizona since 1948. Meanwhile, Ross Perot won less than half the number of votes he had captured in 1992. Clinton defeated Dole in the popular vote by more than eight million and the electoral college, 379–159.

After the Loss

Dole suffered two major defeats in his career. He lost the vice-presidency under Gerald Ford in 1976 and the presidency to Clinton 20 years later, then retired from politics. But not before earning a reputation as a compromiser who got legislation passed, including the Federal Food Stamp Program in 1977, rescuing of Social Security in 1983 and passage of the Americans with Disabilities Act (1990).

Upon retirement Dole worked as a special counsel for the Alston & Bird Law Firm in Washington. He also served as National Chairman of the World War II Memorial Campaign. His service was honored by President Clinton with a Presidential Medal of Freedom and a Congressional Gold Medal in 2019. Dole died on December 5, 2021.

Coming From Dole

The purpose of a tax cut is to leave more money where it belongs: in the hands of the working men and working women who earned it in the first place.[1]

Did You Know?

Wife Elizabeth Dole served on the Federal Trade Commission, as Secretary of Transportation and Secretary of Labor as the first woman US Senator from North Carolina. She ran for president in 2000.

47

Al Gore

Al Gore. Courtesy of the Library of Congress, Highsmith (Carol M.) Archive Collection, LC-DIG-highsm-15968

Party: Democratic
Birthplace: Washington, D.C.
Represented: Tennessee
Years of defeat: 2000
Running mate: Joe Lieberman
Winner: George W. Bush
Other notable candidate: Ralph Nader (Green Party)
Campaign slogans: "Leadership for the New Millennium" (Gore); "Compassionate Conservatism" (Bush)

All About Gore

Though Gore was born on March 31, 1948, in Washington, D.C., where his namesake father served in the US House of Representatives and later in the Senate, he spent much of his time on the family tobacco farm in Carthage, Tennessee. Most of his hours were in the company of adults who expected impeccable behavior from the boy. He otherwise stayed in a hotel on Embassy Row in the nation's capital. But he was lonely there and yearned for the moment he could return to his beloved Tennessee.

Gore bounced back and forth from Washington to Carthage until college. He spoke about the experience years later. "Even though I spent more time each year in Washington, Tennessee was home," he said. "Now I'm sure that part of that was me, as a kid, absorbing my parents' insistence on the political reality of their lives, that they were representing Tennessee in Washington. I'm sure I picked up a lot of that as a child. But it was more than that. "...I think I learned a great deal from the... parallactic view provided by growing up in two places because just as having two eyes gives you depth perception, having two homes allows you to see some things that stand out in relief when viewed from two different perspectives."[1]

Breaking free from his childhood routine, Gore enrolled at Harvard University and graduated in 1969 during the height of the Vietnam War. He served there as a military reporter for two years then remained in the journalism field with *The Tennessean* in Nashville until 1976. He also studied philosophy and law at nearby Vanderbilt University.

Soon his interest piqued in politics. He was election to the US House of Representatives in 1976 and proved himself popular with the populace, winning reelection three times before earning a Senate seat in 1984. His push for the presidency four years later was derailed when he failed to secure the nomination but he was reelected to the Senate in 1990 and earned favor in 1991 as one of just ten Democrats who voted to authorize American military intervention in the Persian Gulf War, an international effort that ended quickly with a victory and little loss of life.

Gore captured the attention of Democratic presidential nominee Bill Clinton, who placed him on his winning ticket in 1992. Among his achievements as vice-president was helping convince Congress to secure congressional passage of the North American Free Trade Agreement and aide Clinton in his successful push for a second term. His liberal viewpoints on women's reproductive rights, gun control and the growing climate crisis set him up as a controversial candidate for the 2000 presidential race, which he lost by a razor-thin margin to George W. Bush.

Issues of the Day

The popularity of Clinton despite the Monica Lewinsky scandal and resulting impeachment trial placed his vice-president at an advantage, though Gore sought to distance himself from it during the campaign.

With foreign affairs comparatively stable until the terrorist attacks of September 11, 2001, both Gore and Bush focused on domestic issues such as the economy, health care, tax relief after the nation had reached a budget surplus, and welfare programs such as Social Security and Medicare.

The 2000 Campaign

The selection of the first Jewish vice-presidential candidate in Joe Lieberman brought a more conservative element to the Democratic ticket. He was considered a moderate.

Bush went on the attack against the Clinton Administration as he tried to tie Gore to unpopular policies and events, such as the killing of eighteen Americans intervening in a war in Somalia. *The Republican* painted Gore as too liberal and inexperienced to work on both sides of the aisle. He also promised to restore honor and dignity to the office to a country still reeling over the Monica Lewinsky scandal. Gore avoided making public appearances with Clinton, a strategy that some believed backfired given the president's overall popularity.

It is also widely believed considering the incredible closeness of the election that the inclusion of Green Party candidate Ralph Nader cost Gore the election. Republicans even ran pro-Nader ads to split the liberal vote.

Both sides campaigned aggressively. Gore trailed in most polls. Little could anyone have imagined that the presidency would not be decided for nearly a month. The victor needed Florida, which came down to a few hundred votes. Networks declared Bush the winner in that state but the call proved too early. Decisions by both state and federal courts were required to decide the winner. A Florida Supreme Court ruled in favor of a recount but the US Supreme Court overturned it to hand Bush the presidency. Gore was forced to concede in a nationally televised speech that drew 65 million viewers.

After the Loss

Gore's loss to Bush did not remove Gore from his activism. He soon became one of the most ardent environmentalists in the world. His documentary *An Inconvenient Truth*, which won an Academy Award, strongly criticized Bush administration policies regarding climate change and its effect on the environment. Gore released a follow-up documentary titled *An Inconvenient Sequel: Truth to Power* in 2017.

Coming From Gore

Here is the truth: The Earth is round; Saddam Hussein did not attack us on 9/11; Elvis is dead; Obama was born in the United States; and the climate crisis is real.[2]

Did You Know?

Gore is friends with cartoonist and animator Matt Groening, creator of *The Simpsons*. Gore made voiceover appearances as himself on that show in its debut season of 1989 as well as *Futurama* in 1999.

48

John Kerry

Party: Democratic
Birth state: Colorado
Represented: Massachusetts
Years of defeat: 2004
Running mate: John Edwards
Winner: George W. Bush
Campaign slogans: "A Safer World and More Hopeful America" (Bush); "Let America Be America Again" (Kerry)

John Kerry. US Department of State, state.gov

All About Kerry

John Kerry was born on December 11, 1943, in Aurora, Colorado, then spent more of his early years in Massachusetts. But he likely remembered little of either location as the son of an Army officer. The family moved to Washington DC when the boy was seven. His dad had served as a pilot and diplomat during World War II. His mother Rosemary was a descendent of the first governor of Massachusetts.

Kerry was shipped off to boarding school near Zurich, Switzerland at age 11, then returned to study ats Yale University, where he majored in political science. He would eventually receive his law degree from Boston College but not before he volunteered for the Nany and spent a stint in Vietnam. Upon his return, he famously became a spokesman for the Vietnam Veterans Against the War and in

1971 appeared before the Senate Foreign Relations Committee to discuss atrocities he had witnessed in combat and proposals on the best plans for ending the conflict.

Intrigued by politics, Kerry failed in his first bid to run for Congress. So he passed his bar exam in 1976 and continued his private practice while serving as assistant attorney general for Massachusetts for five years. He won a bid for its lieutenant governor in 1982, then landed a US Senate seat two years later. There, Kerry remained for 28 years. During that time, he actively fought for campaign finance reform, investment in public education, and reduction of the federal deficit. He began his first term by helping launch hearings into the Iran–Contra affair and later helped investigate scandals in the banking industry.

Issues of the Day

The revelation one month before the election and one year after the invasion of Iraq that that country had no weapons of mass destruction had millions of Americans questioning the president's foreign policy. Kerry had voted for authorization to use force against Iraq because he deemed its leader Saddam Hussein a threat, but he and millions of others asserted that Bush had rushed into the attack without support from US allies.

The two candidates also sparred over the economy. Bush claimed it had recovered nicely from a recession he contended that he inherited while Kerry asserted he had done a poor job and proposed a substantial minimum wage hike that the president opposed. He also blasted the Bush tax that he believed favored the wealthy.

Among the other issues debated by the candidates and voters were healthcare and health insurance, including prescription drug costs, and the environment. Bush was perceived by many voters as refusing to recognize the climate crisis and take steps to reduce greenhouse gas emissions because of its perceived negative effect on the economy.

The 2004 Campaign

Among the strategies employed by President Bush to fend off the Kerry challenge was to accuse the Democrat of lying about his service in the US Navy during the

Vietnam War. Bush claimed that Kerry was on a secret mission in Cambodia rather than fighting in dangerous territory and that his three Purple Hearts were not earned honorably.

The president's popularity skyrocketed after the terrorist attacks in September 2001 and had remained relatively strong. Kerry focused during the campaign mostly on domestic issues such as reducing unemployment, increasing access to health care and ending Bush-era tax cuts for the wealthy.

It wasn't enough. Bush won a second term despite Kerry strength throughout the northeast, Great Lakes states, and West Coast. The incumbent captured the popular vote by three million.

After the Loss

The defeat to Bush in the 2004 election did not end his political influence. President Barack Obama selected Kerry as Secretary of State in 2013. He worked mostly in vain to secure peace in the Middle East by both expressing support for Israeli rights and criticizing their settlement policies and treatment of the Palestinians.

Kerry vigorously criticized the administration of President Donald Trump after the 2016 election, refusing to attend his inauguration and blasting his executive order banning immigration from seven Muslim countries. In 2021, he became the first US Presidential Envoy focusing on the climate crisis.

Coming From Kerry

Real Democrats don't abandon the middle class.[1]

Did You Know?

Kerry worked as news radio talk show host for radio station WBZ in Boston during his college years.

49

John McCain

John McCain (with wife Cindy). Courtesy of the Library of Congress, Highsmith (Carol M.) Archive Collection, LC-DIG-highsm-03810

Party: Republican
Birth state: Panama Canal Zone
Represented: Arizona
Years of defeat: 2008
Running mate: Sarah Palin
Winner: Barack Obama
Campaign slogans: "Yes We Can" (Obama); "Change We Can Believe in" (Obama); "Country First" (McCain)

All About McCain

The son and grandson of four-star Navy admirals, John McCain was born on August 29, 1936, at Coco Solo Naval Air Station in the Panama Canal Zone. The family military tradition extended back to before the Revolutionary War. Young John moved often—wherever his father was stationed. He wrote in his last memoir that he eventually lost track of all the places he resided.

Among his earliest memories was December 7, 1941, after the Japanese had bombed Pearl Harbor. He recalled his dad driving away, then seeing him only rarely until the end of the war while he served as a submarine skipper off the coast of North Africa.

The younger McCain enrolled in 1951 at Episcopal High School, a private boy's academy in Alexandria, Virginia. He thrived as a wrestler, but the fighting was not limited to physical matches on a mat. He exhibited a rebellious nature that manifested itself in occasional brawls and unpermitted off-campus excursions to visit Washington. While many of his classmates studied in anticipation of attending Ivy League schools, McCain resentfully was resigned to follow in his father's footsteps and join the Navy. He entered the Naval Academy in 1954. Among his favorite activities there was boxing.

McCain was a poor student. He engaged in classroom discussions only when motivated in the subject matter but otherwise did not even feign interest. He managed to graduate with nearly the worst grades in his class. McCain then spent two years training as a naval aviator before reporting to the Norfolk Naval Stadium for several Mediterranean deployments on the USS Intrepid. He was eventually promoted to lieutenant and was stationed in 1962 on the Enterprise, which was the first ship to arrive to enforce the blockade of Cuba during the Cuban Missile Crisis.

Four years later, he was off to fly bombers in Vietnam. McCain survived some of the most dangerous missions of the war with a squad that lost nearly one-third of its pilots. His plane was shot down over the North Vietnam capital city of Hanoi on October 26, 1967. He broke both arms, injured his knee and was captured after hitting the water. An angry crowd gathered as he was taken off on bamboo poles. They jeered him, clubbed him with a rifle butt and stabbed him with a bayonet before taking him to a prison that American soldiers referred to as the Hanoi Hilton.

McCain remained in captivity for nearly six years, surviving brutal treatment. He was released on March 14, 1973, and received two Purple Hearts and three Bronze Stars among many commendations before undergoing three operations to heal his wounds and joining his family in Orange Park, Florida.

Admiral James Holloway chose McCain in 1977 to work with the Office of Legislative Affairs, where he was exposed to many key political figures and his interest in running for office began to pique. The least known of the primary candidates, McCain threw himself into a vigorous campaign and won a tight House race in 1982. He soon earned a reputation as a Republican open to joining those across the aisle to get things accomplished. He even opposed a resolution authorizing the Reagan Administration to deploy Marines in Beirut in the belief that achieving the goals of the mission would be impossible.

McCain's interest in world affairs grew after his re-election landed him a seat on the House Foreign Relations Committee in 1985. Then, the resignation of longtime Arizona senator Barry Goldwater motivated him to run for that office. He won easily.

His stock continued to rise. He was even considered a possible running mate for George H. Bush in 1988 before Dan Quayle received the nod. McCain, however, did thrust himself into the American consciousness with a highly commended primetime speech at the Republican National Convention. He won in another landslide in 1992. Among his many second-term achievements was pushing anti-tobacco industry legislation through Congress despite the protests of those serving tobacco-growing states. McCain had grown so popularity in Arizona that he captured a third term with nearly 70 percent of the vote.

Though George W. Bush had emerged as a clear favorite for the 2000 Republican presidential nomination, McCain tossed his hat into the ring. He was open to taking all questions peppered his way in town halls and engaging in press conferences and emerged as a viable rival to Bush when he won the New Hampshire primary in a landslide. But he lacked the resources to continue throughout the campaign and defeats on Super Tuesday doomed his run.

McCain continued his productive stint in the Senate. He helped pass legislation to strengthen airport security after the 9/11 attacks and finally pushed through campaign finance reform. McCain supported the attacks on Afghanistan and Iraq but began soon after in 2003 to have second thoughts about the insurgency and its tactics. He also criticized Bush for his detainee policy that treated prisoners with cruelty and tortures such as waterboarding.

Yet another easy victory maintained his Senate seat in 2004. McCain even won the majority of Democrats. By 2007, he was considered the frontrunner for the Republican presidential nomination. It was no contest. McCain secured his spot but faced a monumental task trying to defeat Democrat Barack Obama, whose popularity had surged. His selection of folksy Alaska governor Sarah Palin, who proved woefully uninformed on the issues, doomed him to defeat.

Issues of the Day

The economy had forever been a primary issue for voters but the number of those who considered it a particularly important consideration rose in 2024. Polls in May revealed that 88 percent confirmed that the economy was critical to their decision-making, which was a 10 percent increase from 2004.

That was not the only foreign policy or domestic concern. Americans also listed health care, education, terrorism, and the war in Iraq as critical to their thinking with moral values and immigration also mentioned prominently. By 2008, certain social issues had creeped into the hearts of minds of voters, including gay marriage and the backlash against abortion rights.

The 2008 Campaign

Perhaps the highlight of one of the most respectful campaigns in recent American history arrived during a McCain rally in a Minneapolis suburb on October 10. An elderly woman expressed the racist and unproven concerns from many Republicans that Obama was not born in the United States and perhaps held Muslim beliefs. McCain shook his head and replied. "No, ma'am, he's a decent family man and citizen, who I just happen to have disagreements with on fundamental issues." McCain was booed as he explained that they had nothing to fear from an Obama presidency.

McCain had led in the polls following the Republican convention, particularly after vice-presidential nominee Sarah Palin wowed the audience with her acceptance speech. But her lack of preparedness for the job soon became readily apparent in interviews, and she became a drag on the ticket. Meanwhile, a subprime mortgage crisis that sent the stock market plunging was sinking Republican fortunes.

Americans were ready for a change and they proved it. Obama won the popular vote by nearly 10 million and captured every populous state but Texas in becoming the first AfricanAmerican president in the nation's history.

After the Loss

McCain criticized Obama policies graciously. His respectful nature helped him win two more Senate races. During his last term he became a harsh critic of President Trump's human rights agenda. McCain angered Trump when he famously gave a "thumb down" in casting the deciding vote against a Republican healthcare bill that would have repealed the Affordable Care Act without replacing it.

McCain died from complications related to brain cancer on August 25, 2018.

Coming From McCain

I've known great passions, seen amazing wonders, fought in a war, and helped make a peace. I've lived very well and I've been deprived of all comforts. I've been as lonely as a person can be and I've enjoyed the company of heroes. I've suffered the deepest despair and experienced the highest exultation. I made a small place for myself in the story of America and the history of my times.[1]

Did You Know?

McCain was investigated from 1989 to 1991 along with four other senators known as the Keating Five for allegedly interfering with regulators on behalf of Charles Keating, a financier accused of financial violations and convicted of securities fraud. McCain was cleared but the Senate Ethics Committee decided that he used poor judgment in his efforts for Keating, who was a large contributor to his campaign.

50

Mitt Romney

Mitt Romney. Massachusetts Office of the Governor, mass.gov

Party: Republican
Birth state: Michigan
Represented: Massachusetts
Years of defeat: 2012
Running mate: Paul Ryan
Winner: Barack Obama
Other notable candidate: Gary Johnson (Libertarian)
Campaign slogans: "Forward" (Obama); "America's Comeback Team" (Romney)

All About Romney

Romney was born in Detroit on March 12, 1947, the son of an automobile executive who would later serve governor of Michigan. After a precocious childhood during which he used his charm and good looks to slide through school he developed strong opinions on various subjects about which he would engage in lively dinner debates with his dad.

His parents had high hopes for Mitt but he did not reciprocate by working hard to meet those expectations. He was shipped off at age 12 to the elite Cranbrook private boarding school where the skinny boy failed much to his dismay to thrive in sports such as football, wrestling, and track. He opted instead for such activities as the Glee Club and yearbook. He also pulled pranks such as spraying shaving cream all over dorm rooms.

Despite the foolishness, he remained loyal to his Mormon faith. Romney arrived with three other missionaries to Le Havre, France, and was met with skepticism by the mostly Communist citizenry who distrusted Americans and strongly disagreement with the nation's involvement in Vietnam. Romney quickly lost belief in the mission and yearned to return to his girlfriend back home.

By that time, his father was governor of Michigan. It was also around that time he received a book in the mail about a missionary named Parley Parker Pratt that changed his life. Pratt had been a failing missionary in New York with no conversions to his name before it was claimed he saw a vision that his prayers would be heard and sacrifices accepted. Romney came to understand that his mission was about sacrifice. His new outlook helped the missionary work in France eventually gain success.

A serious car accident resulted in a return to the United States. He enrolled at Brigham Young University, from which he graduated summa cum laude, then received his law degree from Harvard in 1975. He spent most of the next two decades with various investment consulting firms and making a multimillion dollar fortune.

Politics did not come calling until nearly the age of 50 when he made an unsuccessful bid for a US Senate seat. But his work to revive the scandal-plagued 2002 Winter Olympics in Salt Lake City received national acclaim and launched him into the political spotlight. He used it in a winning Massachusetts gubernatorial campaign in 2002. During that stint as a moderate Republican, he implemented universal healthcare for the uninsured and created a scholarship for lower-income students to attend state universities.

Romney could not overcome John McCain as a presidential candidate in 2008 but rose to the top of the ticket four years later after authoring a book titled *No Apology: The Case for American Greatness*.

Issues of the Day

The economy had yet to fully recover from the recession that marked the last year of the Bush presidency and first year under Obama, leading some to criticize as wasteful government spending the stimulus package enacted in 2009 that Democrats passed with virtually no Republican support. Romney called for reduced taxes to spur job growth, though unemployment had slowed.

Another debate centered on the Affordable Care Act, also known as Obamacare. Republicans promised its repeal but its appeal to voters was coverage of pre-existing conditions. Critics who sought to dump Obamacare could never clear that hurdle with the public.

Global warming was also warming as a concern. Most Americans and both candidates agreed it was a problem but Romney called for less federal government intervention and dependence on foreign sources for oil and gas.

Also in the realm of foreign policy was Obama's fulfilled campaign promise to remove US combat troops from Iraq and plans to take them out of Afghanistan as well. The president's popularity had soared in 2011 when he announced that 9/11 mastermind Osama bin Laden had been killed.

Yet another issue was immigration. Voters debated the Obama proposal to provide legal status for immigrants residing illegally, particularly those called "Dreamers" who arrived in the United States as children. Gay marriage and abortion also remained topics of conversation.

The 2012 Campaign

Romney set aside his moderate views go appease party conservatives and land the Republican nomination. He then returned to his centrist positions to try to steal votes away from Obama in the general election.

His call to end the Affordable Care Act did not play well with many voters. Romney tried to present his experience as a governor and businessman to convince Americans that he could spur a faster recovery from the recession of 2008 and 2009.

Obama simply proved too popular in states Romney needed to win. Losses in swing states such as Florida and Ohio doomed the Republican, who lost the popular vote by five million and the electoral college, 332–206.

After the Loss

Romney may have failed to defeat the popular incumbent Obama in 2012, but he earned praise from some Americans for maintaining his moderate conservative viewpoints while the Republican Party followed Donald Trump in a different direction. Romney criticized Trump knowing it could hurt him in his 2018 run for a US Senate seat out of Utah, But his popularity won out and he was elected in November. Soon thereafter he wrote an editorial blasting Trump for a perceived failure to fulfill his duties as president. Romney was also the only Republican senator to vote for Trump's removal from office in an abuse of power and obstruction of Congress case. In early 2020, he gave a speech accusing Trump of inciting the deadly January 6 riot after the president claimed his 2020 election defeat to Joe Biden was stolen.

Coming From Romney

This is an individual [in Donald Trump] who mocked a disabled reporter, who attributed a reporter's questions to her menstrual cycle, who mocked a brilliant rival who happened to be a woman due to her appearance, who bragged about his marital affairs, and who laces his public speeches with vulgarity.[1]

Did You Know?

His father and Michigan governor George Romney ran for president in 1968, but lost the Republican nomination to Richard Nixon.

51

Hillary Clinton

Party: Democratic
Birth state: Illinois
Represented: New York
Year of defeat: 2016
Running mate: Tim Kaine
Winner: Donald Trump
Campaign slogans: "Make American Great Again!" (Trump); "Love Trumps Hate" (Clinton)

Hillary Rodham Clinton. US Department of State, state.gov

All About Clinton

The first woman to run for president from a major party was also quite obviously the first spouse of a former commander-in-chief to be nominated. The wife of Bill Clinton, she was born Hillary Diane Rodham on October 26, 1947, in the Chicago suburb of Park Ridge. A happy and disciplined childhood was filled with activities such as sports and church. She proved herself in the classroom as a National Honor Society student and class leader. Unlike some young women of her era who whose parents pushed a future of a domestic life as a wife and mother, Hillary was urged to pursue any career that inspired her.

She attended Wellesley College, where she mixed academic achievement with involvement in school government. Hillary entered Yale Law School in 1969 during the height of campus protests against the Vietnam War. She served on the Board of Editors of the *Yale Law Review and Social Action* and interned with children's advocate Marian Wright Edelman. That was when she met Bill. The two quickly meshed as a couple, working together on moot courts and political campaign. They married in 1975.

Hillary graduated during the Nixon Administration. She joined the impeachment inquiry staff in the midst of the Watergate scandal advising the Judiciary Committee of the House of Representatives. But she soon made the decision to follow Bill to his home state of Arkansas, where he had begun his political career. Far from content to toil as a homemaker, she joined the faculty of the University of Arkansas Law School and the Rose Law Firm a year later. President Carter appointed her to the board of the Legal Services Corporation in 1978, the same year her husband became governor.

Upon the birth of daughter Chelsea in 1980, she began balancing family, law, and public service as chair of the Arkansas Educational Standards Committee. Clinton also co-founded the Arkansas Advocates for Children and Families and worked on other organizations focused on the medical and legal well-being of children.

The election of Bill as president in 1992 resulted in another dramatic change to her life. She remained active as First Lady, accepting an opportunity to chair the Task Force on National Health Care Reform, for which she pushed to expand health insurance coverage. Her 1996 book titled *It Takes a Village and Other Lessons Children Teach Us* landed on bestseller lists.

Her political aspirations became apparent after her husband served two terms in the White House. Clinton became the first woman to serve New York in the US Senate upon her election in November 2000. After failing to defeat Barack Obama for the Democratic nomination, he named her as his Secretary of State in 2009.

Clinton earned a reputation for taking few risks in that role. She was criticized in the aftermath of an attack in Libya that cost the lives of a US ambassador and three others. Some have offered her unaggressive tendencies were motivated by creating as little controversy as possible as she planned a run for the White House. That run fell short in 2016.

Issues of the Day

The growing chasm between Democrats and the new Republican Party controlled by Donald Trump, as well as the right-wing and left-wing print, electronic and social media, resulted in a greater divide among the electorate on wide-ranging problems.

The economy remained the top concern but Trump, who promised he would have an impenetrable wall constructed along the southern border that Mexico and played upon public fear of terrorism, made immigration a key issue for his base, and claimed he would ban Muslims from Middle East countries from entering the country. Liberals, on the other hand, focused more on gun control and maintaining President Obama policies on healthcare and global warming.

The 2016 Campaign

The inclusion of contentious Donald Trump alone made the 2016 campaign among the most tumultuous in American history. His controversial pronouncements about immigration and terrorism, as well as what many perceived as childish insults against his political rivals, divided many Americans into two separate camps with little middle ground.

Liberal Democrats complained that their party had cast left-wing candidate Bernie Sanders aside during the primary process because they did not feel he could defeat Trump. Clinton then appeared likely to win based on polling throughout the late summer and early fall, especially after the revelation just days before the election that the Republican had spoken proudly of his sexual aggressiveness in encounters with women. But a controversy over questionable Clinton emails then hurt her cause.

The polls proved woefully inaccurate. Trump broke through the "blue wall" of Michigan, Pennsylvania, and Wisconsin to win all three states and surge to victory despite losing the popular vote.

After the Loss

The defeat to Donald Trump did not sideline her politically. In 2017, she launched Onward Together to support and fund progressive causes. She backed Joe Biden in his successful presidential campaign in 2020 and Kamala Harris before her defeat in 2024 with a speech at the Democratic National Convention and campaign stops.

Coming From Clinton

Always aim high, work hard, and care deeply about what you believe in. And, when you stumble, keep faith. And, when you're knocked down, get right back up and never listen to anyone who says you can't or shouldn't go on.[1]

Did You Know?

Hillary Clinton was a young Republican. She even campaigned for archconservative presidential candidate Barry Goldwater in 1964 before switching allegiances as a Democrat in 1968.

52

Donald Trump

Donald Trump. Courtesy of the Library of Congress, LC-DIG-ppbd-00607

Party: Republican
Birth state: New York
Represented: Florida
Year of defeat: 2020
Running mate: Mike Pence
Winner: Joe Biden
Campaign slogans: "Restore the Soul of the Nation" (Biden); "Build Back Better" (Biden); "Promises Made, Promises Kept" (Trump)

All About Trump

The most controversial president in American history was born into wealth on June 14, 1946, in the Queens borough of New York City.

His father Fred, the son of German immigrants, operated a real estate company he named after his mother and himself that developed properties for middle-class families throughout Queens, Brooklyn, and Staten Island. He employed his three sons at construction sites and offices when they got old enough to help.

Young Donald displayed behavioral issues as a child. Some who knew him accused him of bullying. His parents sent him to the New York Military Academy at age 13 before he enrolled at Fordham University, then the University of

Pennsylvania Wharton School, where he earned a bachelor's degree in economics. Trump avoided the military during the Vietnam War through college and medical deferments (a diagnosis of bone spurs).

Trump launched his business career while still in college by investing in Philadelphia real estate. He then joined his father's business in New York. The first of many scandals involving the future president centered on a 1973 US Justice Department investigation that concluded the company had discriminated against potential African–American renters.

The Trump business soon expanded its operations into Manhattan, as well as Virginia, Ohio, Nevada, and California. What was now known as the Trump Organization began building skyscrapers. The younger Trump's first big move in Manhattan was developing the Grand Hyatt Hotel.

His reputation as major player in the real estate business continued to grow in the 1980s. He build an apartment complex called Trump Plaza as well as Trump Tower on Fifth Avenue. Trump also created his own casino business in Atlantic City. His Trump Taj Mahal, built in 1990, cost nearly one billion dollars.

Such lucrative dealings did not result in a perfect financial record. He borrowed significant amounts of money to fund his projects and filed several bankruptcies along the way. A biography of Trump published in 1993 titled Lost Tycoon pained an unflattering picture of his business failures.

Such problems made nary a dent on the public perception of tremendous achievement. Offered the *New York Times* in 2004: "His name has become such a byword for success that even the most humiliating reverses barely dent his reputation. … The rules that govern others just don't apply to Trump."[1]

Aiding his reputation as a financial wizard were how-to business books authored by ghostwriters such as *Trump: The Art of the Deal* in 1987. His name was licensed to golf courses, hotel resorts and products ranging from steaks to vodka to bottled water. During a two-decade period beginning in 1996, he owned various teen and adult beauty pageants, including Miss Universe. And from 2004 to 2015, he gained his greatest fame as host of TV hits *The Apprentice* and *Celebrity Apprentice*. NBCUniversal ended his relationship with those programs after he uttered anti-immigrant rhetoric during his first presidential campaign.

Trump indeed shocked the world not only by announcing his candidacy but winning the 2016 election. His presidency was marked by controversy and comparatively low approval ratings from Americans who perceived his policies as inhumane. But his power over his base remained absolute, forcing more traditional Republican politicians to support him lest they lose their own elections.

Issues of the Day

Every other issue was swept aside during the campaign after the Covid pandemic began shutting down the nation in March 2020, eventually causing more than one million American deaths and wreaking havoc with the economy. The effectiveness of the Trump response, which began with his proclamation that the problem would simply vanish, was analyzed by voters throughout the campaign.

The 2020 Campaign

Speaking in his usual manner by touting his policies as the best ever, Trump began the campaign by boasting that he had added seven million new jobs to create the greatest economy American had ever experienced. He asserted that the military was the strongest in the world and that pride in the nation had been restored.

The Democrats countered with their typical complaint about Trump's rhetoric dividing the country, as well as his failures on health care after he'd promised to replace the Affordable Care Act with something better, as well as his tax policies that favored the wealthy.

Then came COVID-19. The pandemic that shut down the country sent unemployment soaring to nearly 15 percent. Trump never fully recovered. Though polls predicted a wider-margin Biden victory, however, the battle proved close enough for Trump to charge fraud. The huge number of write-in ballots due to the pandemic were often counted last as Trump's lead in battleground states faded away on election night and beyond. He claimed that night on national TV that he had actually won the election but that it was taken away through various shenanigans. Biden forged ahead with the victories in the "blue wall" states Trump had captured in 2016, as well as Georgia and Arizona.

After the Loss

His defeat to Biden in 2020 motivated claims that the election had been stolen. He took steps to reverse results in particular states such as Georgia, telling election officials there to "find" votes needed to turn defeat into victory. Such efforts, as well as his exhortations to supporters that resulted in rioters trying to prevent the transfer of power at the capitol on January 6, 2021, resulted in lawsuits later dropped when Trump won the 2024 election to return to the White House.

Coming From Trump

I have the support of the police, the support of the military, the support of the Bikers for Trump—I have the tough people, but they don't play it tough until they go to a certain point, and then it would be very bad, very bad.[2]

Did You Know?

When Trump appeared as himself on the sitcom *The Nanny* in 1993, it was insisted that the script that referenced him as a millionaire be changed to billionaire. Star actress joked that it should actually be changed to "zillionaire" and that is how it aired.

53

Kamala Harris

Party: Democratic
Birth state: California
Represented: California
Year of defeat: 2024
Running mate: Tim Walz
Winner: Donald Trump
Campaign slogans: "When We Fight, We Win" (Harris); "Build Back Better" (Biden); "Make America Great Again" (Trump)

Kamala D. Harris. Courtesy of the Library of Congress, LC-DIG-ppbd-01176

All About Harris

The daughter of a Jamaican-born father and Indian immigrant mother, Kamala Harris was born on October 20, 1964, in Oakland, California. Following their divorce, she was raised by her mother, who rolled her in a stroller to civil rights marches. Harris absorbed both Indian and African culture growing up in that diverse city. She even spent time visiting her grandparents in India.

Harris traveled far after high school to attend historically black college Howard University in Washington, DC. She then returned to the Bay Area to earn her degree from the University of California Hastings College of Law in San Francisco. Harris soon began her career working in the Alameda County District Attorney office. She was elected District Attorney of the City and County of San Francisco in 2003.

After serving two terms in that post, she became the first African–American and first woman to become a California attorney general. She married fellow lawyer Doug Emhoff, becoming a stepmother to his two children. Harris became a national political figure by winning a US Senate seat out of her home state in 2016. Among her tasks was serving on both the Intelligence Committee and Judiciary Committee. Her sharp inquiries during the hearings into Russian influence in the 2016 election as a former prosecutor brought her increased attention.

Harris began her first run for president against many other candidates in 2019. Considered by many as too inexperienced, she failed to win a primary but impressed eventually nominee and election winner Joe Biden enough to be named his running mate. His victory made her the first woman vice-president.

What some perceived as an ineffective term in that role, particularly in regard to stopping the flow of illegal immigrants pouring over the southwestern border, was used by opponent Donald Trump during his 2024 campaign for president.

Issues of the Day

Most Americans perceived a struggling economy when they arrived at the polls to vote in 2024 despite low unemployment and the cooling of inflation that had reached alarming rates earlier the year. That played into the hands of Trump, who blamed Biden, then his replacement Harris, for their policies.

Another issue that Trump tied to the economy was immigration. Though the number of illegal immigrants crossing the Mexican border had slowed, the former president contended that millions had arrived and many were engaging in criminal activity.

Foreign policy also played a role in voter decisions. The US military continued to spend billions on weaponry to aid Ukraine in its ongoing fight for independence after a Russian invasion. And a terrorist attack on Israel that resulted in a protracted war and thousands of civilian deaths motivated heated debates about the US role in that conflict.

The 2024 Campaign

One of the strangest twists in American presidential campaign history arrived on June 27, 2024. That was the night in Atlanta when president and Democratic candidate Joe Biden fumbled through his debate against Donald Trump, scaring supporters about his advancing age and eventually forcing him to step away from the race. Vice-President Harris replaced him and seemingly seamlessly took over, giving the campaign energy.

Polls predicted one of the tightest vote counts in American history. The two candidates remained withing two points of each other in seven battleground states. But the polls once again short-changed the Republican, who survived primary challenges from Florida governor Ron DiSantis and diplomat Nikki Haley, trials based on 28 felony convictions, a debate defeat to Harris, and two assassination attempts to win back "Blue Wall" states Pennsylvania, Michigan, and Wisconsin and the presidency.

Coming From Harris

To the children of our country, regardless of your gender, our country has sent you a clear message: Dream with ambition, lead with conviction, and see yourself in a way that others might not see you, simply because they've never seen it before.[1]

Did You Know?

Harris was the second vice-president born in California. The first was Richard Nixon, who served under President Eisenhower before losing the 1960 election to John F. Kennedy.

NOTES

Chapter 1

1. National Constitution Center. "Farewell address (1796). https://constitutioncenter.org/the-constitution/historic-document-library/detail/george-washington-farewell-address-1796

2. Library of Congress: Selected quotations from the Thomas Jefferson Papers. https://www.loc.gov/collections/thomas-jefferson-papers/articles-and-essays/selected-quotations-from-the-thomas-jefferson-papers/

Chapter 2

1. Constitutional Rights Foundation: Bill of Rights in Action. "The Troubled Elections of 1796 and 1800." https://teachdemocracy.org/images/pdf/ThetroubledElectionsof1796and1800.pdf

2. Jeremy Anderberg. "The best John Adams quotes. " July 2, 2019. https://www.artofmanliness.com/character/knowledge-of-men/the-best-john-adams-quotes/#:~:text=%E2%80%9CLiberty%20cannot%20be%20preserved%20without,and%20imperfection%20in%20this%20life.%E2%80%9D

3. Chris Robertson. "Five interesting facts about President John Adams." WVNSTV.com. May 19, 2023. https://www.wvnstv.com/history/five-interesting-facts-about-president-john-adams/

Chapter 3

1. The Avalon Project at Yale Law School. "Thomas Jefferson first inaugural address." https://avalon.law.yale.edu/19th_century/jefinau1.asp#:~:text=We%20are%20all%20Republicans%2C%20we,left%20free%20to%20combat%20it.

2. https://archive.csac.history.wisc.edu/sc_pinckney.pdf

Chapter 4

1. BooKey. "Best DeWitt Clinton quotes with image." https://www.bookey.app/quote-author/dewitt-clinton

Chapter 6

1. "The growth of political factionalism and sectionalism." Digital History. https://www.digitalhistory.uh.edu/disp_textbook.cfm?smtID=2&psid=3531#:~:text=In%201819%20a%20financial%20panic,Investment%20in%20western%20lands%20collapsed.

Chapter 7

1. Edward G. Lengel. "Adams v. Jackson: The Election of 1824." The Gilder Lehrman Institute of American History. https://www.gilderlehrman.org/history-resources/essays/adams-v-jackson-election-1824

2. Goodreads: Andrew Jackson quotes. https://www.goodreads.com/author/quotes/1376987.Andrew_Jackson

Chapter 8

1. James Klotter. "The wisdom of Henry Clay: Advice for the modern-day politician." Oxford University Press. September 27, 2018. https://blog.oup.com/2018/09/henry-clay-modern-day-politician-advice/

Chapter 9

1. Quote.org. William Crawford quotes. https://quote.org/quote/it-has-become-extremely-fashionable-to-eulogize-598840

Chapter 10

1. Hello Poetry. https://hellopoetry.com/poem/3207793/i-am-a-warrior-so-that-my-son-may-be-a-merchant-so-that-his-son-may-be-a-poet/

Chapter 11

1. William Freehling. "William Harrison: Life before the presidency." Miller Center. https://millercenter.org/president/harrison/life-before-the-presidency

2. Presidentialpower.org. https://www.presidential-power.org/quotes-by-presidents/william-harrison-quotes.htm

Chapter 12

1. Van Buren Papers. "Van Buren quotes and misquotes." https://vanburenpapers.org/van-buren/quotes-and-misquotes

Chapter 13

1. BooKey. "30 best Lewis Cass quotes with images." https://www.bookey.app/quote-author/lewis-cass
2. Willard Carl Klunder. Lewis Cass and the Politics of Moderation. Kent, OH: Kent State University Press, 1996. P. 45. https://www.google.com/books/edition/Lewis_Cass_and_the_Politics_of_Moderatio/XlQHi_dJyRUC?hl=en&gbpv=1&pg=PA47&printsec=frontcover

Chapter 14

1. American Experience. "Winfield Scott." https://www.pbs.org/wgbh/americanexperience/features/grant-scott/#:~:text=As%20a%20cadet%20at%20West,resplendent%20figure%20in%20his%20uniforms.
2. James Roselbrock. "Antietam Voices: Winfield Scott." https://jarosebrock.wordpress.com/union/winfield-scott/

Chapter 15

1. Library of Congress. https://www.loc.gov/resource/rbpe.12201000/?st=text

Chapter 16

1. Mchael Burlingame. "Abraham Lincoln: Campaigns and elections." Miller Center. https://millercenter.org/president/lincoln/campaigns-and-elections
2. United States Senate. "Expulsion case of John C. Breckinridge of Kentucky (1861). https://www.senate.gov/about/powers-procedures/expulsion/038Breckinridge_expulsion.htm

Chapter 17

1. History.com editors. "George McClellan." June 10, 2019. https://www.history.com/topics/american-civil-war/george-b-mcclellan

2. Library of Congress. "Image 1 of Abraham Lincoln papers: Series 3. General Correspondence. 1837-1897: Abraham Lincoln, Tuesday, August 23, 1864 (Memorandum on Probable Failure of Reelection; endorsed by members of cabinet)." https://www.loc.gov/resource/mal.4359700/?sp=1&st=text

3. AZ Quotes. https://www.azquotes.com/quote/898097

Chapter 18

1. Harp Week. Biographies. https://elections.harpweek.com/1868/bio-1868-Full.asp?UniqueID=4&Year=1868

2. Mr. Lincoln and New York. "Horatio Seymour." https://www.mrlincolnandnewyork.org/new-yorkers/horatio-seymour-1810-1886/

3. Ibid.

Chapter 19

1. Gilded Age Politics. "The election of 1872." https://www.sscnet.ucla.edu/history/waughj/classes/gildedage/private/gilded_age_politics/history/election_of_1872.html

2. Gilded Age Politics. "The election of 1872." https://www.sscnet.ucla.edu/history/waughj/classes/gildedage/private/gilded_age_politics/history/election_of_1872.html

3. Ibid.

4. The Vault at Pfaffs's. "Greeley, Horace." https://pfaffs.web.lehigh.edu/node/54226

5. AZ Quotes. https://www.azquotes.com/quote/353757

Chapter 20

1. Rutherford B. Hayes Presidential Libraries and Museums. "1876 acceptance speech." https://www.rbhayes.org/hayes/1876-acceptance-speech/

2. AZ Quotes. https://www.azquotes.com/quote/964269

Chapter 21

1 Brainy Quote. https://www.brainyquote.com/quotes/winfield_scott_hancock_200240

2 John Deppen. "Hancock the Superb: Winfield Scott Hancock & the Battle of Gettysburg." Warfare History Network. April 2004. https://warfarehistorynetwork.com/article/hancock-the-superb-winfield-scott-hancock-the-battle-of-gettysburg/

Chapter 22

1 Henry F. Graff. "Grover Cleveland: Campaigns and elections." Miller Center. https://millercenter.org/president/cleveland/campaigns-and-elections

2 Lib Quotes. https://libquotes.com/james-g-blaine/quote/lbh9c7z

3 Thomas Nast cartoons. "The Plumed Knight." https://thomasnast.com/cartoons/the-plumed-knight/

Chapter 23

1 The White House: Grover Cleveland. https://www.whitehouse.gov/about-the-white-house/presidents/grover-cleveland/

2 Gilded Age Politics. "The election of 1888." https://www.sscnet.ucla.edu/history/waughj/classes/gildedage/private/gilded_age_politics/history/election_of_1888.html

3 The White House: Grover Cleveland. https://www.whitehouse.gov/about-the-white-house/presidents/grover-cleveland/

Chapter 24

1 UC Press. "The Stereopticon, The Tariff Illustrated, and the 1892 Election." p. 33. https://content.ucpress.edu/chapters/13296.ch01.pdf

2 Forbes. https://www.forbes.com/quotes/1128/

Chapter 25

1 Library of Congress. Today in History: March 19. https://www.loc.gov/item/today-in-history/march-19#:~:text=%E2%80%A6we%20will%20answer%20their%20demand

,upon%20a%20cross%20of%20gold.&text=After%20serving%20two%20terms%20in,pinnacle%20of%20his%20political%20career.

2 Political Dictionary. "Grass will grow in the streets." https://politicaldictionary.com/words/grass-will-grow-in-the-streets/

Chapter 26

1 Historical Society of the New York Courts. Alton Brooks Parker. https://history.nycourts.gov/biography/alton-brooks-parker/

2 Ibid.

Chapter 27

1 Sidney Milkis. "Theodore Roosevelt: Life before the presidency." Miller Center. https://millercenter.org/president/roosevelt/life-before-the-presidency

2 Theodore Roosevelt Center. https://www.theodorerooseveltcenter.org/Research/Digital-Library/Record?libID=o308501

Chapter 28

1 Columbia 250. Charles Evans Hughes. https://c250.columbia.edu/c250_celebrates/remarkable_columbians/charles_hughes.html

Chapter 29

1 Eugene P. Trani. "Warren G. Harding: Campaigns and elections." Miller Center. https://millercenter.org/president/harding/campaigns-and-elections

2 Columbia 250. Charles Evans Hughes. https://c250.columbia.edu/c250_celebrates/remarkable_columbians/charles_hughes.html

Chapter 30

1 William Henry Harbaugh. *Lawyer's Lawyer: The Life of John W. Davis*. Oxford: Oxford University Press, 1973. P. 13.

2 Quotefancy. "Top 3 John W. Davis quotes." https://quotefancy.com/john-w-davis-quotes

Chapter 31

1. David E. Hamilton. Herbert Hoover: Campaigns and elections." Miller Center. https://millercenter.org/president/hoover/campaigns-and-elections

2. Ibid.

3. Goodreads. "Al Smith quotes." https://www.goodreads.com/author/quotes/22102.Alfred_E_Smith

Chapter 32

1. Forbes Quotes: Thoughts on the Business of Life. https://www.forbes.com/quotes/4292/

Chapter 33

1. Project Muse. Alfred Mossman Landon. https://muse.jhu.edu/pub/266/oa_monograph/chapter/2764629

2. Spartacus Educational. Alfred Landon. https://spartacus-educational.com/USAlandon.htm

Chapter 34

1. The American Presidency Project. Franklin D. Roosevelt Address at Chautauqua. https://www.presidency.ucsb.edu/documents/address-chautauqua-ny

Chapter 35

1. American Rhetoric. Hubert H. Humphrey: 1948 Democratic National Convention address." https://www.americanrhetoric.com/speeches/huberthumphey1948dnc.html

2. Forbes quotes. https://www.forbes.com/quotes/9127/

Chapter 36

1. Illinois State University Stevenson Center. https://stevensoncenter.org/about/stevenson/

Chapter 37

1 Miller Center. "Kicking Nixon around." https://millercenter.org/the-presidency/secret-white-house-tapes/kicking-nixon-around

2 NPR. All Things Considered. https://www.npr.org/2013/11/17/245830047/i-am-not-a-crook-how-a-phrase-got-a-life-of-its-own

Chapter 38

1 Will Wilkinson. "On the saying that 'Extremism in the defense of liberty is no vice." Niskanen Center. January 5, 2016. https://www.niskanencenter.org/on-the-saying-that-extremism-in-defense-of-liberty-is-no-vice/

Chapter 39

1 Pennsylvania Senate Republicans. https://pasenategop.com/browne/wp-content/uploads/sites/37/2015/05/Lightner.pdf

Chapter 40

1 Ron Elving. "George McGovern, an improbable icon of anti-war movement." NPR. October 22, 2012. https://www.npr.org/sections/itsallpolitics/2012/10/22/163355049/george-mcgovern-an-improbable-icon-of-anti-war-movement

Chapter 41

1 Gerald Ford Presidential Library and Museum. https://www.fordlibrarymuseum.gov/the-fords/gerald-r-ford/quotes

Chapter 42

1 Meghan Overdeep. "39 inspiring Jimmy Carter quotes to live by." *Southern Living*. October 1, 2024. https://www.southernliving.com/jimmy-carter-quotes-7976383

Chapter 43

1 Brainy Quote. https://www.brainyquote.com/quotes/walter_f_mondale_980345

Chapter 44

1 BooKey. "30 best Michael Dukakis quotes." https://www.bookey.app/quote-author/michael-dukakis

Chapter 45

1 Points of Light. "President George H. Bush highlights the power of volunteering." https://www.pointsoflight.org/resources/president-george-h-w-bush-highlights-the-power-of-volunteering/

Chapter 46

1 Inc. "30 inspirational quotes about taxes." https://www.inc.com/geoffrey-james/130-inspirational-quotes-about-taxes.html

Chapter 47

1 Melinda Henneberger. "A boy's life in and out of the family script." *New York Times*. May 22, 2000. https://archive.nytimes.com/www.nytimes.com/library/politics/camp/052200wh-dem-gore.html

2 Good Reads. Al Gore. https://www.goodreads.com/quotes/408086-here-is-the-truth-the-earth-is-round-saddam-hussein

Chapter 48

1 Brainy Quote. John Kerry. https://www.brainyquote.com/quotes/john_f_kerry_148012

Chapter 49

1. Politico. "'My fellow Americans': A farewell from McCain's 'The Restless Wave.'" August 25, 2018. https://www.politico.com/story/2018/08/25/john-mccain-farewell-statement-757659

Chapter 50

1. *New York Times.* "Transcript of Mitt Romney's speech on Donald Trump." March 4, 2016. https://www.nytimes.com/2016/03/04/us/politics/mitt-romney-speech.html

Chapter 51

1. Emily Canal. "25 inspirational quotes from powerful women." Forbes. https://www.forbes.com/pictures/56eb13fbe4b0c144a7f78bd9/25-inspirational-quotes-b/

Chapter 52

1. Benjamin C. Waterhouse. "Donald Trump: Life before the presidency." Miller Center. https://millercenter.org/president/trump/life-presidency
2. Isabel Fattal and Stephanie Bai. "A brief history of Trump's violent remarks." *The Atlantic.* October 31, 2024. https://www.theatlantic.com/politics/archive/2024/10/trump-violent-rhetoric-timeline/680403/

Chapter 53

1. *Washington Post.* "Read the transcript of Kamala Harris' victory speech in Wilmington. Del." November 7, 2020. https://www.washingtonpost.com/politics/2020/11/07/kamala-harris-victory-speech-transcript/

ABOUT THE AUTHOR

Martin Gitlin is the author of about 250 books, many of them educational, in the history realm. He won more than 45 awards as a newspaper journalist from 1991 to 2002, including first place for general excellence from Associated Press. That organization voted him one of the top four feature writers in Ohio in 2002. Gitlin has three grown children and lives in Connecticut.